Rust High Performance

Learn to skyrocket the performance of your Rust applications

Iban Eguia Moraza

BIRMINGHAM - MUMBAI

Rust High Performance

Commissioning Editor: Merint Mathew
Acquisition Editor: Sandeep Mishra
Content Development Editor: Akshada Iyer
Technical Editor: Abhishek Sharma
Copy Editor: Safis Editing
Project Coordinator: Prajakta Naik
Proofreader: Safis Editing
Indexer: Mariammal Chettiyar
Graphics: Jisha Chirayil
Production Coordinator: Arvindkumar Gupta

First published: March 2018

Production reference: 1270318

Published by Packt Publishing Ltd.
Livery Place
35 Livery Street
Birmingham
B3 2PB, UK.

ISBN 978-1-78839-948-7

www.packtpub.com

To my father, Manu, and to the memory of my mother, Arantza, for giving me all the opportunities I had in my life, and for being there when I most needed it.

`mapt.io`

Mapt is an online digital library that gives you full access to over 5,000 books and videos, as well as industry leading tools to help you plan your personal development and advance your career. For more information, please visit our website.

Why subscribe?

- Spend less time learning and more time coding with practical eBooks and Videos from over 4,000 industry professionals

- Improve your learning with Skill Plans built especially for you

- Get a free eBook or video every month

- Mapt is fully searchable

- Copy and paste, print, and bookmark content

PacktPub.com

Did you know that Packt offers eBook versions of every book published, with PDF and ePub files available? You can upgrade to the eBook version at `www.PacktPub.com` and as a print book customer, you are entitled to a discount on the eBook copy. Get in touch with us at `service@packtpub.com` for more details.

At `www.PacktPub.com`, you can also read a collection of free technical articles, sign up for a range of free newsletters, and receive exclusive discounts and offers on Packt books and eBooks.

Contributors

About the author

Iban Eguia Moraza is a passionate Rust developer. He has a bachelor's degree in computer engineering and a master's degree in information and communication security. He has over 10 years of experience in web development, and since 2015, he has been developing Rust applications.

Iban loves space exploration and the latest technologies. In this regard, he has developed open source software for stratospheric balloons from the ground up, and he now works at the CERN particle physics laboratory. He likes to travel to learn from the most experienced people.

> *This book would not have been possible without the moral help of my dad and coworkers. They were really motivating when I was struggling to find enough time to write the book. I also have to thank the Rust community for always being helpful in fixing all my issues and questions. Without doubt, it's the most friendly and welcoming community I have ever encountered in software development.*

About the reviewer

Daniel Durante is an avid coffee drinker/roaster, motorcyclist, archer, welder, and carpenter whenever he isn't programming. From the age of 12, he has been involved with web and embedded programming with PHP, Node.js, Golang, Rust, and C.

He has worked on text-based browser games that have reached over 1,000,000 active players, created bin-packing software for CNC machines, embedded programming with cortex-m and PIC circuits, high-frequency trading applications, and helped contribute to one of the oldest ORMs of Node.js (SequelizeJS).

He has also reviewed the following books for Packt:

- *PostgresSQL Developer's Guide*
- *PostgreSQL 9.0 High Performance*
- *Rust Programming By Example*

I would like to thank my parents, my brother, my mentors, and friends who've all put up with my insanity of sitting in front of a computer day in and day out. I would not be here today if it wasn't for their patience, guidance, and love.

Packt is searching for authors like you

If you're interested in becoming an author for Packt, please visit authors.packtpub.com and apply today. We have worked with thousands of developers and tech professionals, just like you, to help them share their insight with the global tech community. You can make a general application, apply for a specific hot topic that we are recruiting an author for, or submit your own idea.

Table of Contents

Preface

Welcome to *Rust High Performance*. In this book, you will get a gentle introduction to high-performance programming by learning how to improve the performance of your Rust code. It will show you how to translate your code from other languages properly by avoiding common bottlenecks, and it will show you how to easily increase the performance of your application using some idiomatic Rust APIs.

You will learn about the great Rust community by finding great crates that will increase the development efficiency while also improving the performance of your application, and you will write examples to use all your knowledge. You will write your own macros and custom derives, and you will learn about asynchronous and multithreaded programming.

Who this book is for

In this book, you will find everything you need to improve the performance of your Rust code; you will learn many tricks and use helpful crates and tools. Therefore, the book is written from the basis that you already have some knowledge of programming in Rust.

This book will not cover the whole world of high-performance programming since it's an incredibly wide topic. You will find a gentle introduction to most of the generic high-performance programming concepts and learn how specific patterns can be used in the Rust programming language.

What this book covers

Chapter 1, *Common Performance Pitfalls*, helps you learn why translating from languages such as C/C++ can lead to big performance decline, how to improve your algorithms using different Copy/Clone types and references, and understand how cyclomatic complexity can make compiler optimizations less effective.

Chapter 2, *Extra Performance Enhancements*, takes a step forward to understand some tips and tricks Rust gives us to improve the performance of your applications. After learning about common mistakes in the previous chapters, you will learn how to use the Rust type system to your advantage, creating complex compile-time checks and evaluations. You will also understand the difference between the common standard library collections so that you can choose the right one for your algorithm.

Chapter 3, *Memory Management in Rust*, shows you how to improve the memory footprint of your applications by taking advantage of the borrow checker. You will learn about lifetimes and how to properly use them, understand the different representation attributes that will help your data be properly structured in memory, and finally, learn how to create efficient shared pointer structures for your application using standard library types.

Chapter 4, *Lints and Clippy*, teaches you the power of lints and how to configure them to give you proper suggestions. You'll learn how to configure clippy, an incredibly powerful tool that will point out common errors and potential performance improvements. In this chapter, you will learn the most important clippy lints and use them in your development workflow.

Chapter 5, *Profiling Your Rust Application*, covers how to use profiling software so that you can easily find performance bottlenecks in your applications. You'll learn how cache misses impact your code and how to find where in the code is the application spending more time. You will learn to fix those bottlenecks and therefore improve the overall performance of the application.

Chapter 6, *Benchmarking*, discusses how to detect performance critical code and how to benchmark it in both Rust stable and nightly. You will also learn how to set up your continuous integration environment to get performance reports and track them during the development process of your project.

Chapter 7, *Built-in Macros and Configuration Items*, brings you to the world of attributes that can personalize your code so that you target specific platforms with each section of your code using all of each platform's potential. You will understand how to divide your crate so that not all the code has to be compiled for each use, and you will finally learn how to use nightly features to improve the efficiency of your code and the amount of code to write.

Chapter 8, *Must-Have Macro Crates*, introduces you to multiple metaprogramming crates—create serializable structures, deserialize data from languages such as JSON or TOML, parse log files, or create a lot of boilerplate code for your data structures. Here, you can understand how to initialize complex static structures and use a proper error handling. Finally, thanks to nightly Rust and plugins, you will be able to create a small web server with a database and even attach to it the fastest template system in existence.

Chapter 9, *Creating Your Own Macros*, covers how to write your own macros to avoid code boilerplate. You will understand how the new macros 1.1 work and create your first custom derive. Finally, you will learn how compiler plugins internally work and will create your own compiler plugin.

Chapter 10, *Multithreading*, outlines how to create multiple threads to balance the work of your application. You will understand the full power of Rust's threads and the synchronization primitives in the standard library. In addition, you will learn how to send information between threads. Finally, you will read about some useful crates that will enable you to implement work stealing algorithms, parallel iterators, and more.

Chapter 11, *Asynchronous Programming*, helps you understand how asynchronous programming works. Here, you can learn how to develop asynchronous algorithms in Rust, thanks to mio and futures, and learn the new async/await syntax. You can also create asynchronous applications using tokio and WebSockets.

To get the most out of this book

This book assumes some basic knowledge of the Rust programming language. If you are new to Rust, the first few chapters of the official Rust book are a great prelude. Nevertheless, you should have moderate to deep knowledge of at least one programming language; basic knowledge of terminal usage will also be needed.

Having basic knowledge of computer architectures is a plus, along with basic knowledge of high-performance programming in C/C++. They are not required, though, since in this book we will cover all the base theory to understand how the performance improvements work behind the scenes.

You will need a code editor or an IDE to follow the book. Rust has been heavily tested in Microsoft's Visual Studio Code, GitHub's Atom, and IntelliJ's IDEA IDE. I have personally used Atom to write the code examples, but feel free to use your favorite text editor or IDE. You will probably find plugins or extensions for your editor.

In the case of VS Code, Atom, and IntelliJ IDEA, you will find official Rust packages along with unofficial extensions. Personally, I've been using the Tokamak package for Atom.

Download the example code files

You can download the example code files for this book from your account at www.packtpub.com. If you purchased this book elsewhere, you can visit www.packtpub.com/support and register to have the files emailed directly to you.

You can download the code files by following these steps:

1. Log in or register at www.packtpub.com.
2. Select the **SUPPORT** tab.
3. Click on **Code Downloads & Errata**.
4. Enter the name of the book in the **Search** box and follow the onscreen instructions.

Once the file is downloaded, please make sure that you unzip or extract the folder using the latest version of:

- WinRAR/7-Zip for Windows
- Zipeg/iZip/UnRarX for Mac
- 7-Zip/PeaZip for Linux

The code bundle for the book is also hosted on GitHub at https://github.com/ PacktPublishing/Rust-High-Performance. In case there's an update to the code, it will be updated on the existing GitHub repository.

We also have other code bundles from our rich catalog of books and videos available at https://github.com/PacktPublishing/. Check them out!

Conventions used

There are a number of text conventions used throughout this book.

CodeInText: Indicates code words in text, database table names, folder names, filenames, file extensions, pathnames, dummy URLs, user input, and Twitter handles. Here is an example: "The iterator will not run until you call collect() method or use it in a loop. Those are the moments in which the next() method gets executed."

A block of code is set as follows:

```
for row in arr1.iter().cartesian_product(arr2.iter()) {
  print!("{:?}, ", row);
}
```

Any command-line input or output is written as follows:

```
cargo install --no-default-features --features sqlite diesel_cli
```

Bold: Indicates a new term, an important word, or words that you see onscreen.

Warnings or important notes appear like this.

Tips and tricks appear like this.

Get in touch

Feedback from our readers is always welcome.

General feedback: Email feedback@packtpub.com and mention the book title in the subject of your message. If you have questions about any aspect of this book, please email us at questions@packtpub.com.

Errata: Although we have taken every care to ensure the accuracy of our content, mistakes do happen. If you have found a mistake in this book, we would be grateful if you would report this to us. Please visit www.packtpub.com/submit-errata, selecting your book, clicking on the Errata Submission Form link, and entering the details.

Piracy: If you come across any illegal copies of our works in any form on the Internet, we would be grateful if you would provide us with the location address or website name. Please contact us at copyright@packtpub.com with a link to the material.

If you are interested in becoming an author: If there is a topic that you have expertise in and you are interested in either writing or contributing to a book, please visit authors.packtpub.com.

Reviews

Please leave a review. Once you have read and used this book, why not leave a review on the site that you purchased it from? Potential readers can then see and use your unbiased opinion to make purchase decisions, we at Packt can understand what you think about our products, and our authors can see your feedback on their book. Thank you!

For more information about Packt, please visit `packtpub.com`.

Common Performance Pitfalls

1

If you are reading this book, you are probably concerned about the performance of your Rust code. It's known that Rust can offer performance close to that of C/C++ programs, and in some cases, Rust can even win those benchmarks. The main issue, though, is that it's sometimes hard to get that efficiency, especially if you are coming from C/C++. Some concepts don't apply, and some simple efficient approaches in those languages are notably worse in Rust.

In this book, you will learn how to really take advantage of Rust to make it perform at its best while maintaining all the benefits it brings—safety, zero-cost abstractions, and great concurrency. The book can be read from start to finish, and you will probably learn new concepts in every chapter. You can go directly to the chapter that interests you, though, as each chapter contains all the required information for its completion, so that it can be used as a reference.

In this first part of the book, we will start with an introduction on how to improve the performance of your sequential code. You will learn how to avoid common performance pitfalls and how to fix direct translations from other languages. You will then learn how to get better performance from your code, and finally understand memory management in Rust.

In this chapter, we will be looking into:

- Configuration of the compilation process with profiles
- Translation pitfalls—learning how to avoid performance pitfalls with array/slice indexing and master iterators
- New iterator adaptors, both in the standard library and in external crates, and coding any complex behavior at zero cost
- How to use the borrow checker to your advantage

Most of the people that start learning Rust, myself included, tend to bring lessons learned in other languages to Rust. This is usually a great thing, as it will enable you to learn the language faster. The main issue with this approach is that some patterns used in other languages can actually be a trade-off in Rust. We will learn about the most common ones and the not-so-common ones, so that anyone trying to get better performance in Rust can learn how to do it.

Asking the Rust compiler about performance

Rust sometimes has interesting and lesser-known features that really make a difference when talking about performance enhancements. When it comes to big improvements with small changes, the first thing that you should understand is the release mode. Rust by default compiles your software in development mode, which is pretty good to check for compiling errors quickly, but if you want to run it, it will run slowly. This is due to the development mode not performing any optimizations. It will create object (machine) code directly related to the Rust code without optimizing it.

Rust makes use of the LLVM backend, which makes it easy to take advantage of its performance optimizations without having to develop all of these by themselves. They will only need to use LLVM intermediate representation. An intermediate language between Rust and assembly code that the LLVM compiler understands. While in development mode, no optimizations get performed by Rust or LLVM; enabling them is as easy as adding the `--release` flag to the cargo compilation. So, for example, if you were running your software by typing `cargo run` in the console, just by using `cargo run --release` it will compile with optimizations and run much, much faster. Usually, the gain is of more than one order of magnitude.

Optimizations

By default, Rust will perform level 3 optimizations in the code. Optimizations get divided into levels depending on how complex they are. Higher-level optimizations, in theory, improve the performance of the code greatly, but they might have bugs that could change the behavior of the program. Usually, level 1 optimizations are totally safe, and level 2 optimizations are the most-used ones in the C/C++ ecosystem. Level 3 optimizations have not been known to cause any issues, but in some critical situations, it might be better to avoid them. This can be configured, but we should first understand how the Rust compiler compiles the code to machine instructions so that we know what different options accomplish.

Rust first starts with parsing your code files. It will get the keywords and the different symbols to create a representation of the code in memory. This parsing will find common errors such as a missing semicolon or an invalid keyword. This memory representation of the code is called **High Intermediate Representation** (**HIR**). This representation of the code will be greatly simplified, removing complex flow structures and converting it into **Middle Intermediate Representation** (**MIR**).

The MIR representation is then used to check more complex flows of the software, and enables complex variable lifetime checks, along with some other improvements. This is then converted to the LLVM Intermediate Representation and gets passed to the LLVM compiler. When passing this code to LLVM, Rust adds some flags that will modify the way that LLVM optimizes the code. We have already seen that by default one of the flags it passes is the -O0 flag, or *do not optimize* flag, so it simply translates to machine code. When compiling in release mode, though, a -O3 gets passed so that level 3 optimizations get performed.

This behavior can be configured in the `Cargo.toml` file of the project and it can be configured for each profile. You can configure how to compile for tests, development, documentation, benchmarks, and release. You will probably want to keep development and documentation optimizations to a minimum, as in those profiles the main idea is to compile quickly. In the case of the development profile, you will want to check if everything compiles properly, and even test the behavior of the program a little bit, but you probably won't be concerned about the performance. When generating the documentation, the performance of the application doesn't matter at all, so the best idea is to just not optimized.

When testing, the optimization level you need will depend on how many tests you want to run and how computationally expensive they are. If it takes a really long time to run the tests, it may make sense to compile them optimized. Also, in some critical situations in which you might not be 100% sure that optimizations get performed in a completely secure way, you might want to optimize the tests the same way you optimize the release, and that way you can check if all unit and integration tests pass properly even after optimizations. If they don't, this is a compiler malfunction, and you should report it to the Rust compiler team. They will be glad to help.

Of course, benchmarks and release profiles should be the most optimized ones. In benchmarks, you will want to know the real optimized performance of the code, while in the release, you will want your users to get the best out of their hardware and your software to make things run as efficiently as possible. In these cases, you will want to optimize up to level 2 at least, and if you are not sending satellites to space or programming a pacemaker, you will probably want to optimize all the way up to level 3.

Build configuration

There is one section in the `Cargo.toml` file that enables these configurations: the profile section. In this section, you will find one subsection for each of the profiles. Each of them gets declared with the `[profile.{profile}]` format. So, for example, for the development profile, it would be `[profile.dev]`. The different profile configuration keywords are the following:

- `dev` for the development profile, used in `cargo build` or `cargo run`
- `release` for the release profile, used in `cargo build --release` or `cargo run --release`
- `test` for the testing profile, used in `cargo test`
- `bench` for the benchmarking profile, used in `cargo bench`
- `doc` for the documentation profile, used in `cargo doc`

When configuring each profile, you will have many options, and we will check all of them out here.

Optimization level

The first option is the one mentioned before, the optimization level. This configuration option can be set by using the `opt-level` key in the relevant profile section. By default, optimizations will be level 3 for benchmarking and release, and zero for the rest. For example, to only perform level 2 optimizations in the release profile, you can add this code to your `Cargo.toml` file:

```
[profile.release]
opt-level = 2
```

Debug information

The next option is the debug information. This does not directly affect performance, but it's an interesting configuration item. In this case, you can decide if the debug symbol information gets added to the final executable. This is really useful if you are developing, and especially if you are using a debugger such as GDB. Adding debug information to the executable will enable you to get the function names and even the line numbers of each instruction being executed in the processor. This will give you great insight about what is happening in the code.

In any case, debug information is not so useful in final release binaries, as final release binaries are not meant to be used in debugging. And the debug information usually adds a lot of size to the final binary. This has many times been a concern among developers, as the size of Rust binaries is usually much bigger than the ones written in C/C++. This is in part due to this configuration, and in most cases due to the panic behavior, which we will check later. Debug symbols will also show information about the original code, so it might make sense to hide it in closed-source projects.

To avoid extra debug symbols in the final binary, the debug option must be set to false. This can be done for each profile, and by default, it's true only for the development profile. If you'd like to enable it for testing also, for example, you can add this in the Cargo.toml file:

```
[profile.test]
debug = true
```

You can, of course, combine this with any other profile option:

```
[profile.test]
debug = true
opt-level = 1
```

Link-time optimizations

The next configuration option, useful for improving the performance of the application, is link-time optimizations. Usually, when a program gets built, once all the code has been optimized, it gets linked to other libraries and functions that provide the required functionality. This, however, does not always happen in the most efficient way. Sometimes, a function gets linked twice, or a piece of code gets used in many places, and in that case, the compiler might decide to duplicate some code.

The program will work perfectly, but this has two main disadvantages—first of all, duplicating code and links will make the binary bigger, which is probably something you don't want, and secondly, it will reduce the performance. You might ask why. Well, since it's the same code being accessed from different places in the program, it might make sense that if it gets executed once, it gets added to the L1/L2/L3 caches in the processor. This will enable the future reuse of these instructions without requiring the processor to get them from the RAM memory (much slower) or even the disk/SSD (extremely slow) if the memory has been swapped.

The main advantage when performing **Link-Time Optimizations**, or **LTOs** in short, is that while Rust compiles the code file by file, LTOs fit the whole, almost final, representation into a big compilation unit that can be optimized in its entirety, enabling better execution paths.

This can be performed, of course, but at a really high compilation time cost. These optimizations are very costly because they sometimes require changing the final representation, the one ready to be written to the binary. Not only that, but this requires checking lots of execution paths and code samples to find similar blocks. And remember, this is done with the object code, not the Rust code, so the compiler doesn't know about libraries or modules; it only sees instructions.

This costly optimization will improve the performance of your software and the size of your binaries, but being so costly (usually taking as much time as the rest of the compilation, or even more), it's not enabled by default in any of the profiles. And you should not enable it on any but release and maybe benchmarking profiles (you don't want to wait for an LTO every time you make a small change in a function and want to test it). The configuration item to change is the `lto` configuration item:

```
[profile.release]
lto = true
```

There is a related configuration item, which will be ignored if LTO is turned on for the given profile. I'm talking about the `codegen` units. This divides the code into multiple smaller code units and compiles each of them separately, enabling parallel compiling, which improves how fast the program compiles. This is one in the case of LTO, but can be modified for the rest. Of course, using separate compilation units avoids some optimizations that can improve the performance of the code, so it might make sense to enable faster compilation in development mode. It will be 16 by default in development mode.

This is as simple as changing the `codegen-units` configuration option in the development profile:

```
[profile.dev]
codegen-units = 32
```

An example value could be the number of processors/threads in your computer. But remember that this will make the compiled software slower, so do not use it in the release profile. It will, in any case, be ignored if you activate the link-time optimizations.

Debug assertions

The next interesting configuration item is the one that allows debug assertions to be removed. Debug assertions are like normal assertions, but by default they are only executed in the development profile. They are written in the code by prefixing the `assert!` macros with `debug_`, using for example `debug_assert!` or `debug_assert_eq!`. This enables you to fill the whole code with assertions that must be true and that take processing cycles to test, while not reducing the performance of a release application. Of course, this means that those assertions won't run in release mode. This is useful for testing internal methods, but is probably not the best for APIs, and certainly not a good idea in unsafe code wrappers.

For example, the indexing function in the standard library `Vec` object has an assertion that will check each time you get an element of the vector by index if the index is out of bounds. This is great to avoid buffer overflows, but makes the operation of getting an element of the vector slower, and if the index is out of bounds, the program will panic. We will talk about this particular example later, but in general, it shows how useful these assertions are—in this case for release mode also.

On the other hand, if you plan to create a small internal API that will input numbers between `0` and `100` and do some calculations with them, but is not exposed to the public, you could simply add a `debug_assert!(num <= 100 && num >= 0)` and, in tests and debug mode, it will panic the program if a number outside that range is received by the function, but it will not run the assertion in release mode. This can be a potential error vector, but with thorough unit testing, the odds of not getting the error in testing/development mode and an incorrect number being received in release mode are much, much lower. Of course, once again, this shouldn't be used for security-focused areas or input that would cause unsafe or undefined behavior.

By default, as explained, these assertions run in development, testing, and documentation modes. This last one is useful if you have documentation tests with debug assertions. This can be configured, in any case, easily, by changing the `debug-assertions` configuration option. For example:

```
[profile.doc]
debug-assertions = false
```

Panic behavior

The next configuration variable to check is the panic behavior. By default, Rust will unwind in a panic. This means that it will call each destructor of each variable in the stack if something goes terribly wrong and the application panics. There is another option: not calling anything and simply aborting the program (the standard C/C++ behavior).

The main advantage of the unwind is that you will be able to call the destructors, so any cleanup that should be done for your variables in the stack of the program will be done properly. The main advantage of the `abort` behavior is that it will require much less code to be compiled, since for each potential panic location a new branch gets added to the code where all the destructors are run. It also gives the code much fewer branches, which makes it easier to optimize, but the main advantage is smaller binaries. Of course, you lose the ability to run the destructors, so some complex behavior might not be properly cleaned, for example, if you need to write something to a log upon shutdown.

If you still think that in your use case, using the `abort` behavior is a good idea, you can enable it by using the `panic` keyword:

```
[profile.doc]
panic = 'abort'
```

Runtime library paths

The last configuration option is `rpath`. This configuration item accepts a Boolean and allows you to ask the Rust compiler to set loader paths when the executable looks OK for libraries at runtime. Even though, most of the time, Rust will link crates and libraries statically, you can ask a specific library to be linked dynamically. In this case, that library will be searched at runtime, not at compile time, and it will therefore use system libraries installed where the program is running.

This configuration option asks cargo to add `-C rpath` to the `rustc` compiler invocation. This will add paths to the dynamic library search paths. Nevertheless, this should not be required in most cases, and you should avoid it if it's not necessary by using `false` as the option value. If you are having issues making your application run in multiple operating systems, you might try it, since it might make the executable look for dynamic libraries in new places.

Translation issues

When translating your C/C++/Java mindset, or directly porting a project to Rust, you might find yourself writing similar code to what you wrote in your native language, but if you have tried it, you might have noticed that it performs poorly, or at least much worse than your old code. This happens, especially with C/C++, since in the case of Java the performance issue is much lower compared to the high memory and computation footprint of a Java application, with its Java Virtual Machine and its garbage collector.

But why does a direct translation hurt the performance? We will see in this section how Rust's guarantees can sometimes create unnecessary boilerplate instructions, and we will learn how to bypass them by using safe and efficient code. Of course, in some performance-critical situations, unsafe scopes might be needed, but in general, that's not the case.

Indexing degradations

Let's start with a simple example. This Rust code will perform poorly:

```
let arr = ['a', 'b', 'c', 'd', 'e', 'f'];

for i in 0..arr.len() {
  println!("{}", arr[i]);
}
```

This will, of course, work, and it's perfectly safe. We create an index that goes from 0 to the length of the array (6 in this case), but exclude the last one, so the i binding will take the values 0, 1, 2, 3, 4, and 5. For each of them, it will get the element at that index in the array and print it in a new line. There is one problem with this approach though. In C/C++, an equivalent code will simply add the size of the element to the pointer in the array and get the next element, but that sometimes causes issues. Look at this code:

```
let arr = ['a', 'b', 'c', 'd', 'e', 'f'];

for i in 0..arr.len() + 1 {
  println!("{}", arr[i]);
}
```

In this case, we are iterating until the array length + 1, and since ranges are exclusive, the last index will be 6. This means it will try to get the seventh element in the array, but there is no seventh element. In C/C++, this will create a buffer overflow and will get whatever is next in the memory. In the case that this memory is outside the program, you will get a segmentation fault, but if it's part of the program, it will print whatever was in that position, leading to leaks. Of course, that is not possible in Rust, since Rust is a memory-safe language, so what will happen?

Well, the answer is surprising—it will panic the program, unwind the stack (call all the destructors of all the variables in the stack), and exit the program safely without trying to access invalid memory. Depending on your perspective, you might think *great, I will no longer have buffer overflows*, or you might think *oh my God, the whole server will go down to prevent a buffer overflow*. Well, the second can be mitigated by stopping the panic and recovering the proper server state, already implemented in most frameworks, so it's mostly a win-win.

But is it? How does Rust know if the index is out of bounds? In this simple example, the compiler could know that the `arr` variable has only six elements, so trying to access the seventh would violate memory constraints. But what about this more complex program:

```
fn print_request(req: Request) {
  for i in 0..req.content_length {
    println!("{}", req.data[i]);
  }
}
```

Here I'm receiving an HTTP request (very naively represented) that has at least one `content_length` attribute and one `data` attribute. The first should contain the length of the data field, in a number of bytes, while the second will be a vector of bytes. Let's suppose we don't have the `len()` function in that data field, and that we trust the `content_length` attribute. What if somebody were to send us an invalid request with a bigger `content_length` than the actual length of the content? The compiler wouldn't know this in advance because the request originated at runtime from a TCP connection, but again, Rust must always be memory-safe (unless working in an unsafe scope, which is not the case).

Well, what happens is that the index operation has two parts. First, it checks the bounds of the slice, and if the index is fine, it will return the element; if not, it will panic. And yes, it does this for every indexing operation. So in this case, if the request is a valid request with a supposed 1 million bytes (1 MB), it will compare the index to the length of the vector 1 million times. That is at least 2 million extra instructions (the comparison and the branching for each, at least). That becomes much less efficient than the equivalent C/C++ code.

Using iterators

There is a way around this, though, that gives the same effect as the C/C++ code: using iterators. The previous code can be converted into the following:

```
let arr = ['a', 'b', 'c', 'd', 'e', 'f'];

for c in &arr {
  println!("{}", c);
}
```

This will compile roughly to the same machine code as the C/C++ variant since it won't check the bounds of the slice more than once, and it will then use the same pointer arithmetic. This is great when iterating through a slice, but in the case of a direct lookup, it can be an issue. Suppose we will receive thousands of 100-element slices, and we are supposed to get the last element of each and print it. In this case, iterating through all 100 elements of each array just to get the last one is a bad idea, as it would be more efficient to bounds check just the last element. There are a couple of ways of doing this.

The first one is straightforward:

```
for arr in array_of_arrays {
  let last_index = arr.len() - 1;
  println!("{}", arr[last_index]);
}
```

In this concrete case, where we want to get the last element, we can do something like this:

```
for arr in array_of_arrays {
  if let Some(elt) = arr.iter().rev().next() {
    println!("{}", elt);
  }
}
```

This will reverse the iterator with the call to `rev()` and then get the next element (the last one). If it exists, it will print it. But if we have to get a number that is not close to the end or to the beginning of the slice, the best way is to use the `get()` method:

```
for arr in array_of_arrays {
  if let Some(elt) = arr.get(125) {
    println!("{}", elt);
  }
}
```

This last one has a double bound check, though. It will first check if the index is correct to return a `Some(elt)` or a `None`, and then the last check will see if the returned element is `Some` or `None`. If we know for sure, and I mean 100% sure, that the index is always inside the slice, we can use `get_unchecked()` to get the element. This is an exact equivalent to the C/C++ indexing operation, so it will not do bounds checking, allowing for better performance, but it will be unsafe to use. So in the HTTP example before, an attacker would be able to get what was stored in that index even if it was a memory address outside the slice. You will need to use an unsafe scope, of course:

```
for arr in array_of_arrays {
    println!("{}", unsafe { arr.get_unchecked(125) });
}
```

The `get_unchecked()` function will always return something or segfault, so no need to check if it's `Some` or `None`. Remember also that upon a segfault, this will not panic, and no destructors will be called. It should only be used if a safe alternative would not meet the performance requirements and if the bounds of the slice were previously known.

In most cases, you will want to use an iterator. Iterators allow for precise iteration of elements, even filtering them, skipping some, taking a maximum amount of them, and finally, collecting them into a collection. They can even be extended or joined with other iterators to allow for any kind of solution. Everything gets managed by the `std::iter::Iterator` trait. You now understand the most-used methods of the trait, and I leave the rest to you to research in the standard library documentation.

It's important to properly use and understand iterators since they will be very useful for doing really fast loops. Iterators are cost-free abstractions that work the same way as indexing, but will not require bounds checking, making them ideal for efficiency improvements.

Iterator adaptors

Let's start with the most simple method. The basic method for the rest to work is the `next()` method. This function will return either the next element in the iteration or a `None` if the iterator has been consumed. This can be used to manually get the next element, or to create a for using a `while`, for example:

```
let arr = [10u8, 14, 5, 76, 84];
let mut iter = arr.iter();

while let Some(elm) = iter.next() {
    println!("{}", elm);
```

```
    }
```

That would be the same as this:

```
let arr = [10u8, 14, 5, 76, 84];

for elm in &arr {
    println!("{}", elm);
}
```

 Note the & before the array variable in the `for`. This is because the basic array type does not implement the `Iterator` trait, but a reference to the array is a slice, and slices implement the `IntoIterator` trait, which makes it usable as an iterator.

The next two methods you should know about are the `skip()` and the `take()` methods. These make it easy to get only the correct members of a known ordered iterator. For example, let's say we want to take from the third to the tenth element of an iterator with unknown length (at least 10 elements). In this case, the best thing would be to skip the first two and then take the next eight. We then collect them in a vector. Note that the iterator will not run until you call `collect()` method or use it in a loop. Those are the moments in which the `next()` method gets executed:

```
let arr = [10u8, 14, 5, 76, 84, 35, 23, 94, 100, 143, 23, 200, 12, 94,
72];

let collection: Vec<_> = arr.iter().cloned().skip(2).take(8).collect();

for elm in collection {
    println!("{}", elm);
}
```

This will start iterating through the array, and it will first clone each element. That's because by default an iterator will yield references to the elements, and in the case of u8 it's better to copy them than to reference them, as we will see at the end of the chapter. The `skip()` method will call `next()` twice and discard what it returns. Then, for each `next()` operation, it will return the element. Until it calls `next()` eight times, the `take()` method will return the element. It will then return `None`. The `collect()` method will create an empty vector, and will push elements to it, while the `next()` method returns `Some`, then returns the vector.

Note that the `collect()` method requires a type hint, as it can return any kind of collection—actually, any type that implements the `FromIterator` trait. We simply tell it that it will be a standard library `Vec`, and we let the compiler infer the type of element the vector will hold.

There are also a couple of functions that are a generalization of the previous ones, `skip_while()` and `take_while()`. These two will skip or take elements, respectively, while the closure they run returns `true`. Let's see an example:

```
let arr = [10u8, 14, 5, 76, 84, 35, 23, 94, 100, 143, 23, 200, 12, 94,
72];

let collection: Vec<_> = arr.iter()
    .cloned()
    .skip_while(|&elm| elm < 25)
    .take_while(|&elm| elm <= 100)
    .collect();

for elm in collection {
    println!("{}", elm);
}
```

In this case, the `skip_while()` method will run `next()` until it finds an element bigger than or equal to `25`. In this case, this is the fourth element (index 3), number `76`. The `take_while()` method starts then calling `next()` and returning all elements while they are less than or equal to `100`. When it finds `143`, it returns `None`. The `collect()` method will then include all those elements, from the `76` to the `100`, both included in a vector, and return it. Note that the `23` is also added to the final result, since even if it's lower than `25`, while the skip method stops skipping, it will never skip again.

To fine-tune the filtering of the elements in the iteration, some other very interesting methods are the `filter()` method and its companion `map()`. The first lets you filter elements of an iterator based on a closure, while the second lets you map each element to a different one. Let's explore this by using a simple iterator that yields the odd elements of an iterator and collects them into a vector:

```
let arr = [10u8, 14, 5, 76, 84, 35, 23, 94, 100, 143, 23, 200, 12, 94,
72];

let collection: Vec<_> = arr.iter()
    .enumerate()
    .filter(|&(i, _)| i % 2 != 0)
    .map(|(_, elm)| elm)
    .collect();
```

```
for elm in collection {
    println!("{}", elm);
}
```

In this case, we enumerate the iterator by calling to `enumerate()`. That will yield a tuple with the index and the element for each `next()` call. This will then be filtered by checking the index. If the index is odd, it will be returned in the `next()` call; if it's not, it will call `next()` again. This will then be mapped, as the filter will also return the tuple. The `map()` function will take only the element, discard the index, and return it.

The filter and map functions can be reduced by using the helpful `filter_map()` function, which combines the two of them:

```
let arr = [10u8, 14, 5, 76, 84, 35, 23, 94, 100, 143, 23, 200, 12, 94,
72];

let collection: Vec<_> = arr.iter()
    .enumerate()
    .filter_map(|(i, elm)| if i % 2 != 0 { Some(elm) } else { None })
    .collect();

for elm in collection {
    println!("{}", elm);
}
```

The `filter_map()` adaptor expects a closure that will return `Some(element)` when it should return the element, and `None` when it should retry and call `next()`. This will avoid some extra code. In this concrete case, you can also use the `step_by()` method, which only returns one element every *n* elements. In this case, using a two-step will have the same effect.

When trying to do calculations with iterators, instead of using a `for`, we can use the great `fold()` method. This will hold a variable between each call to `next()` that you will be able to update. That way, you can sum, multiply, and perform any other operation in the iterator. Let's, for example, perform the sum of all the elements of the iterator:

```
let arr = [10u32, 14, 5, 76, 84, 35, 23, 94, 100, 143, 23, 200, 12, 94,
72];

let sum = arr.iter().fold(0u32, |acc, elm| acc + elm);
println!("{}", sum);
```

This will print 985, without needing a loop. Of course, this will be implemented with a loop under the hood, but for the programmer, it's a zero-cost abstraction that helps a lot in terms of simplifying the code.

Real-life example

As a real-life example, here is the *VSOP87* algorithm's variable function implemented with a `fold()` method. The *VSOP87* algorithm is used to find planets and moons in the sky with really good accuracy, useful for simulators and telescope star finders, for example:

```
fn calculate_var(t: f64, var: &[(f64, f64, f64)]) -> f64 {
    var.iter()
        .fold(0_f64, |term, &(a, b, c)| term + a * (b + c * t).cos())
}
```

This is equivalent to this other code:

```
fn calculate_var(t: f64, var: &[(f64, f64, f64)]) -> f64 {
    let mut term = 0_f64;
    for &(a, b, c) in var {
        term += a * (b + c * t).cos();
    }
    term
}
```

And in C/C++, this would probably require a structure to hold the tuple. Five lines reduced to one with the same native code. As we talked about, this has no extra cost and will be compiled to the same machine code.

Specialized adaptors

In the case of a summation or a multiplication, there are specialized methods: the `sum()` and the `product()` methods. These methods will do the same as the `fold()` method that is used to add all the numbers in an iterator or to multiply all the items of the iterator. The example we saw before can be reduced to this:

```
let arr = [10u32, 14, 5, 76, 84, 35, 23, 94, 100, 143, 23, 200, 12, 94, 72];

let sum: u32 = arr.iter().sum();
println!("{}", sum);
```

Type annotations are required for now, but the code looks much simpler. You can also use the `product()` function in the same way, and it will be equivalent to this code:

```
let arr = [10u32, 14, 5, 76, 84, 35, 23, 94, 100, 143, 23, 200, 12, 94, 72];

let prod = arr.iter().fold(0u32, |acc, elm| acc * elm);
println!("{}", prod);
```

Interaction between adaptors

There are also some functions to control how the iterators interact with other iterators or even themselves. For example, the `cycle()` function will make the iterator start again from the beginning once it gets to the end of the iterator. This is useful to create an infinite loop with an iterator. There are also a couple of functions that help you deal with multiple iterators at the same time. Let's suppose that you have two slices of the same length and want to generate a new vector with that same length, but with each element being the sum of the elements with the same index in the slices:

```
let arr1 = [10u32, 14, 5, 76, 84, 35, 23, 94, 100, 143, 23, 200, 12, 94, 72];
let arr2 = [25u32, 12, 73, 2, 98, 122, 213, 22, 39, 300, 144, 163, 127, 3, 56];

let collection: Vec<_> = arr1.iter()
    .zip(arr2.iter())
    .map(|(elm1, elm2)| elm1 + elm2)
    .collect();
println!("{:?}", collection);
```

In this case, we have used the `zip()` function that will yield a tuple with each element being the next of each iterator. We can also chain them with the `chain()` function, which will generate a new iterator that, once the first starts yielding None, will start yielding elements from the second iterator. There are many more iteration functions, but we will leave the standard library here for now and focus on external crates.

Itertools

There is one external crate that can make working with iterators much easier, and gives you superpowers. Remember the idea that these iterators allow you to perform the same operations you would do in C with indexing, but with complete memory safety and zero-cost abstractions? They also make the code much easier to understand. In terms of iterator capabilities, the most important crate is the *itertools* crate. This crate provides a new trait, the Itertools trait, which gives iterators many new methods and functions that make the life of the developer much easier, while staying true to its core values of performance thanks to zero-cost abstractions. You can add it to your project by adding it to your Cargo.toml file in the [dependencies] section.

Let's explore some of its iterator adapters. We start with a simple one that helps us create batches or chunks of the given iterator, the batching() function. Let's say that we want to use an iterator over one of the previous arrays and we want to make it return elements in groups of three. It's as simple as using that method and creating a closure that directly calls the next() method and returns the required tuple:

```
// Remember
extern crate itertools;
use itertools::Itertools;

let arr = [10u32, 14, 5, 76, 84, 35, 23, 94, 100, 143, 23, 200, 12, 94,
72];

for tuple in arr.iter().batching(|it| match it.next() {
    None => None,
    Some(x) => {
        match it.next() {
            None => None,
            Some(z) => {
                match it.next() {
                    None => None,
                    Some(y) => Some((x, y, z)),
                }
            }
        }
    }
})
{
    println!("{:?}", tuple);
}
```

This will print the array in groups of three elements, in order:

```
(10, 5, 14)
(76, 35, 84)
(23, 100, 94)
(143, 200, 23)
(12, 72, 94)
```

A similar operation can be accomplished by using the `chunks()` function. We can say that the `batching()` adaptor is a generalization of the `chunks()` adaptor, since it gives you the option to create the internal logic of the function. In the case of `chunks()`, it will only receive as a parameter the number of elements in a chunk, and it will return slices to those chunks.

A really similar operation will be performed with the `tuples()` method. As you can see, the `batching()` method is a complete generalization in terms of how you create batches or chunks of an iterator. Let's see the same example we saw previously using the `tuples()` method:

```rust
// Remember
extern crate itertools;
use itertools::Itertools;

let arr = [10u32, 14, 5, 76, 84, 35, 23, 94, 100, 143, 23, 200, 12, 94,
72];

for tuple in arr.iter().tuples::<(_, _, _)>() {
    println!("{:?}", tuple);
}
```

Much less boilerplate code, right? In this case, we are required to specify the number of elements in a tuple, but if we used type inference in the `for`, we could avoid it:

```rust
// Remember
extern crate itertools;
use itertools::Itertools;

let arr = [10u32, 14, 5, 76, 84, 35, 23, 94, 100, 143, 23, 200, 12, 94,
72];

for (a, b, c) in arr.iter().tuples() {
    println!("({}, {}, {})", a, b, c);
}
```

Of course, in this case, we would be pattern-assigning the variables. There is also another interesting function that allows for creating the cartesian product of two iterators.

Unsurprisingly, the name is `cartesian_product()`. This will create a new iterator with all possible combinations of the previous two:

```
// Remember
extern crate itertools;
use itertools::Itertools;

let arr1 = [10u32, 14, 5];
let arr2 = [192u32, 73, 44];

for row in arr1.iter().cartesian_product(arr2.iter()) {
    print!("{:?}, ", row);
}
```

This will print the following:

```
(10, 192), (10, 73), (10, 44), (14, 192), (14, 73), (14, 44), (5, 192), (5,
73), (5,44),
```

There are many other methods in the `Itertools` trait, and I invite you to check the official documentation, since it's very detailed and has many examples. For now, these common methods should help you do any operation you need to perform with slices in a much more efficient way.

Borrowing degradations

Iterations are not the only place where translation degradations occur. There are also a couple of extra points where you can sometimes see that the same code performs much worse in Rust than in C/C++. One of these points is reference handling. Due to borrow checker constraints, you can do three things with variables when passing them to a function: send a reference (borrow), give the new function control of the variable (own), or copy/clone the variable to send it to a function. It seems easy to decide, right? If you do not require the variable anymore, let the function own your variable. If you require it, send the reference, and if you require it and the API only accepts ownership, clone it.

Well, it actually isn't so simple. For example, integers are faster to copy than to reference, and so are small structures. The rule of thumb is, if it's smaller than or equal to `usize`, copy, always. If it's somewhere between `usize` and 10 times that size, it's probably better to copy. If it's bigger, it's probably better to reference. If the structure has a heap allocation (such as a `Vec` or a `Box`), it's usually better to send a reference.

There are some cases, though, when you cannot decide what happens to the variable. In a macro, for example, the variable is passed as is, and the macro decides what to do with it. For example, the `println!` macro gets all elements by reference, since it does not require more. The problem is that if you are trying to print an integer, for example, a bottleneck appears. That's what happened some time ago to Robert Grosse, and he wrote an article about it.

Long story short, he had to force the copying of the integer. How did he do that? Well, it's as simple as creating a scope that will return that integer. Since integers implement `Copy`, the integer will be copied to the scope and then returned, effectively copying it to the macro:

```
let my_int = 76_u32;
println!("{}", {my_int});
```

For normal prints, this is not usually necessary, but if you need to quickly print thousands or millions of integers, you will not avoid the I/O interface, but you can at least avoid this bottleneck.

Cyclomatic complexity

Another possible bottleneck is the cyclomatic complexity of functions. While not directly related to the translation of code from other languages, it's true that Rust can sometimes increase the cyclomatic complexity of the code, since it forces you to check for optional (nullable) results, some complex iterators, functional programming, and so on. This is great for code security, but sometimes the compiler has issues properly optimizing the code we write.

The only way to avoid this is to separate the code into smaller code units that will help the compiler optimize better unit by unit. One way of doing that is by creating smaller functions, with no more than 20–25 branches each. A branch is a place where, depending on one variable, the program will run one code or another. The simplest branch is conditional, an `if`. There are many others, such as loops (especially when the loop contains returns) or the `?` operator. This will create two branches, one for each result option. One of them will return the function while the other will assign the variable.

Nested loops and conditionals make this list grow larger, and the branches can be more and more complex, so you will have to try to divide those deeply nested conditionals in new functions. It's even considered a good practice. As you will see in the *Tools* section, there are tools that will help you find these bottlenecks.

Summary

In this chapter, we learned how to avoid the most common errors new Rust programmers encounter, and we found out how Rust performs some operations so that we could take advantage of them.

We saw how to configure the build system to allow for precise compilation. You can now set up the optimization passes, the link-time optimizations, or the panic behavior, among many other things.

You have now also mastered iterators, and are now able to stop indexing slices, gaining valuable computation cycles. You also found out about the *Itertools* crate, and you can now use it to perform complex operations with iterators.

Finally, you learned a couple of tricks on cyclomatic complexity, and you learned how borrowing or copying can affect the way the program works.

From now on, we will enter the world of more complex issues, which can sometimes be difficult to understand for new developers. We will embrace the full power of the Rust programming language to create fast and safe applications.

2
Extra Performance Enhancements

Once your application avoids common performance bottlenecks, it's time to move to more complex performance improvements. Rust has many options that allow you to improve the performance of your code by using lesser-known APIs. This will give you parity with C/C++ and, in some scenarios, it can even improve the speed of most of the fastest C/C++ scripts.

In this chapter, we will be looking into the following topics:

- Compile-time checks
- Compile-time state machines
- Extra performance enhancements, such as using closures for avoiding runtime evaluation
- Unstable sorting
- Map hashing
- Standard library collections

Compile-time checks

Rust has an amazing type system. It's so powerful that it is Turing-complete by itself. This means that you can write very complex programs just by using Rust's type system. This can help your code a lot, since the type system gets evaluated at compile time, making your runtime much faster.

Starting from the basics, what do we mean by *the type system*? Well, it means all those traits, structures, generics, and enums you can use to make your code very specialized at runtime. An interesting thing to know is the following: if you create a generic function that gets used with two different types, Rust will compile two specific functions, one for each type.

This might seem like code duplication but, in reality, it is usually faster to have a specific function for the given type than to try to generalize a function over multiple ones. This also allows for the creation of specialized methods that will take into account the data they are using. Let's see this with an example. Suppose we have two structures and we want them to output a message with some of their information:

```
struct StringData {
    data: String,
}

struct NumberData {
    data: i32,
}
```

We create a trait that we will implement for them that will return something that can be displayed in the console:

```
use std::fmt::Display;

trait ShowInfo {
    type Out: Display;
    fn info(&self) -> Self::Out;
}
```

And we implement it for our structures. Note that I have decided to return a reference to the data string in the case of the `StringData` structure. This simplifies the logic but adds some lifetimes and some extra referencing to the variable. This is because the reference must be valid while `StringData` is valid. If not, it might try to print non-existent data, and Rust prevents us from doing that:

```
impl<'sd> ShowInfo for &'sd StringData {
    type Out = &'sd str;
    fn info(&self) -> Self::Out {
        self.data.as_str()
    }
}

impl ShowInfo for NumberData {
    type Out = i32;
    fn info(&self) -> Self::Out {
        self.data
```

```
        }
    }
```

As you can see, one of them returns a string and the other returns an integer, so it would be very difficult to create a function that allows both of them to work, especially in a strongly-typed language. But since Rust will create two completely different functions for them, each using their own code, this can be solved thanks to generics:

```
fn print<I: ShowInfo>(data: I) {
    println!("{}", data.info());
}
```

In this case, the `println!` macro will call to the specific methods of the `i32` and `&str` structures. We then simply create a small `main()` function to test everything, and you should see how it can print both structures perfectly:

```
fn main() {
    let str_data = StringData {
        data: "This is my data".to_owned(),
    };
    let num_data = NumberData { data: 34 };

    print(&str_data);
    print(num_data);
}
```

You might be tempted to think that this is similar to what languages such as Java do with their interfaces, and, functionally, it is. But talking about performance, our topic in this book, they are very different. Here, the generated machine code will effectively be different between both calls. One clear symptom is that the `print()` method gets ownership of the value it receives, so the caller must pass this in the registers of the CPU. Both structures are fundamentally different though. One is bigger than the other (containing the string pointer, the length, and capacity), so the way the call is done must be different.

So, great, Rust does not use the same structure for traits as Java does for interfaces. But why should you care? Well, there are a number of reasons, but there is one that will probably show you what this accomplishes. Let's create a state machine.

Sequential state machines

Let's first think about how to implement this in a C/C++ environment. You will probably have a global state and then a `while` loop that would change the state after each iteration. There are, of course, many ways of implementing a state machine but, in C, all of them require either metaprogramming or a runtime evaluation of the global state.

In Rust, we have a Turing-complete type system, so why not try and use it to create that state machine? Let's start by defining some traits that will have the power of creating the state machine. We first define a `StateMachine` trait, that will have the functionality of moving from one state to another state:

```
pub trait StateMachine {
    type Next: MainLogic;
    fn execute(self) -> Self::Next;
}
```

As you can see, I already added a new type, `MainLogic`. This will be a trait representing a structure that can perform a logic in a state. The `StateMachine` trait itself is pretty simple. It only contains a type that will be the next state and an `execute()` function that consumes itself so that nobody can execute the same state twice without going to the next state (the next state could be itself again). It simply returns a new state machine. Here we have the `MainLogic` trait:

```
pub trait MainLogic {
    fn main_logic(self);
}
```

It's just a function to execute the logic of the state. The main functionality of this state machine, that will enable it to go from one state to the next, always doing the proper logic, is defined in the default implementation of the `MainLogic` trait:

```
impl<S> MainLogic for S
where
    S: StateMachine,
{
    fn main_logic(self) {
        self.execute().main_logic();
    }
}
```

This will implement the `MainLogic` trait for any state implementing the `StateMachine` trait. It will simply execute the state and then call the main logic of the next state. If this new state is also a `StateMachine`, it will get executed and then the next state will be executed. This pattern is especially useful if you want to sequentially execute different states. The last state will be the one implementing `MainLogic` but not `StateMachine`:

```
struct FirstState;
struct LastState;

impl StateMachine for FirstState {
    type Next = LastState;

    fn execute(self) -> Self::Next {
        unimplemented!()
    }
}

impl MainLogic for LastState {
    fn main_logic(self) {
        unimplemented!()
    }
}
```

The compiler will make sure at compile time that you properly go from the first state to the second one, and it will force you to do so. But, more importantly, this will be compiled into very efficient code, as efficient as doing the sequential calls one by one, but with all the safety Rust gives you. In fact, as you can see, both `FirstState` and `Laststate` have no attributes. That is because they have no size. They will not occupy space in memory at runtime.

This is the simplest state machine though. It will only allow you to advance from one state to the next. It's helpful if that's what you want, since it will make sure your flow gets checked at compile time, but it will not perform complex patterns. If you loop over a previous state, you will endlessly continue looping. This will also be useful when each state has a defined next state and when no other possibility comes from that state.

Complex state machines

A more complex state machine, that allows you to move from one to another in your code while still using the type system to check for proper usage, can be done. Let's start by defining the state machine. We want a machine that represents the way a robot works in a car-building facility. Let's say its job is to install two doors in a car. It will first wait for the next car to come, take the door, put it in place, put the bolts in place, do the same for the second door, and then wait for the next car.

We will first define some functions that will use sensors and that we will simulate:

```
fn is_the_car_in_place() -> bool {
    unimplemented!()
}
fn is_the_bolt_in_place() -> bool {
    unimplemented!()
}
fn move_arm_to_new_door() {
    unimplemented!();
}
fn move_arm_to_car() {
    unimplemented!()
}
fn turn_bolt() {
    unimplemented!()
}
fn grip_door() {
    unimplemented!()
}
```

Of course, the real software would need to take many things into account. It should check that the environment is safe, the way it moves the door to the car should be optimal, and so on, but this simplification will do for now. We now define some states:

```
struct WaitingCar;
struct TakingDoor;
struct PlacingDoor;
```

And we then define the machine itself:

```
struct DoorMachine<S> {
    state: S,
}
```

This machine will hold an internal state that can have some information attached to it (it can be any kind of structure) or it can have a zero-sized structure, and thus have a size of zero bytes. We will then implement our first transition:

```
use std::time::Duration;
use std::thread;

impl From<DoorMachine<WaitingCar>> for DoorMachine<TakingDoor> {
    fn from(st: DoorMachine<WaitingCar>) -> DoorMachine<TakingDoor> {
        while !is_the_car_in_place() {
            thread::sleep(Duration::from_secs(1));
        }
        DoorMachine { state: TakingDoor }
    }
}
```

This will simply check every 1 second whether the car is in the proper place. Once it is, it will return the next state, the `TakingDoor` state. The function signature makes sure that you cannot return the incorrect state, even if you do a really complex logic inside the `from()` function. Moreover, at compile time, this `DoorMachine` will have zero byte size, as we saw, so it will not consume RAM regardless of how complex our state transitions are. Of course, the code for the `from()` functions will be in RAM, but the necessary checks for proper transitioning will all be done at compile time.

We will then implement the next transition:

```
use std::time::Duration;
use std::thread;

impl From<DoorMachine<TakingDoor>> for DoorMachine<PlacingDoor> {
    fn from(st: DoorMachine<TakingDoor>) -> DoorMachine<PlacingDoor> {
        move_arm_to_new_door();
        grip_door();

        DoorMachine { state: PlacingDoor }
    }
}
```

And finally, a similar thing can be done for the last state:

```
use std::time::Duration;
use std::thread;

impl From<DoorMachine<PlacingDoor>> for DoorMachine<WaitingCar> {
    fn from(st: DoorMachine<PlacingDoor>) -> DoorMachine<WaitingCar> {
        move_arm_to_car();
```

```
    while !is_the_bolt_in_place() {
        turn_bolt();
    }

    DoorMachine { state: WaitingCar }
    }
}
```

The machine can start in any given state, and moving it from one to another will be as simple as writing the following:

```
let beginning_state = DoorMachine { state: WaitingCar };
let next_state: DoorMachine<TakingDoor> = beginning_state.into();
```

You might be thinking, *why don't I simply write two functions and execute them sequentially?* The answer is not straightforward, but it's easy to explain. This makes you avoid many issues at compile time. For example, if each state has only one possible next state, you can use a generic into() function without needing to know the current state, and it will simply work.

In a more complex environment, you might find yourself doing the following pattern:

```
let beginning_state = DoorMachine { state: WaitingCar };
let next_state: DoorMachine<TakingDoor> = beginning_state.into();

// Lots of code

let last_state: DoorMachine<PlacingDoor> = next_state.into();
```

Of course, if you look at it properly, we are no longer in the first state! What will happen if the machine tries to change the state again, thinking it's still in the first state? Well, here is where Rust comes handy. The into() function takes ownership of the binding, so this will simply not compile. Rust will complain that the beginning_state no longer exists since it has been already converted to next_state.

Real-life type system check example

There is an example I love when talking about compile-time checks and high-performance computing: Philipp Oppermann wrote a type-safe paging system for a kernel with only two traits. Let's first understand the problem and then try the solution.

When a program uses the memory on a computer, it must separate virtual memory from physical memory. This is because each program running in the OS will think that the whole address space is theirs. This means that in a 64-bit machine, each program will think it has 16 **exbibytes** (**EiB**) of memory, 2^{64} bytes.

That is, of course, not the case for any computer in the world, so what the kernel does is to move memory out of RAM to the HDD/SSD, and put in RAM the required memory. For this to work properly, memory has to be managed in chunks, since it doesn't make sense to move in and out individual memory addresses. These are called pages, and they are usually 4 KiB in size for x86_64 processors (the case for most laptops and desktop computers).

For the paging to be easily manageable, a paging hierarchy gets created. Every 512 pages get added to an index called a P1 table, and every 512 P1 tables get added to a P2 table. That goes on recursively until all pages have been assigned, which will be 4 levels. That is what it's called: 4-level paging.

The idea is that a kernel should be able to ask a table for one of its pages, and if it's a P4 table, it should be able to ask for a P3, then for a P2, then for a P1, and finally load the page referenced by that P1. This address gets passed in a 64-bit registry, so all the data is there. The problem is that it could be easy to end up with tons of code duplication for each table type, or we could end up with a solution that works for all pages but that has to check the current page at runtime if it wants to return the next table (if it's a P4-P2 table) or the actual page (if it's a P1 table).

The first case is really error-prone, and difficult to maintain, while the second one not only continues being error-prone, but it even requires checks at runtime, making it slower. Rust can do better.

The solution is to define a trait that all pages have, let's call it `PageTable`, and a trait that only higher-order tables have (tables that cannot directly return a page but that they need to return another page table). Let's call it `HighTable`. Since all `HighTable` types are also `PageTable`, one trait will inherit from the other:

```
pub trait PageTable {}

pub enum P4 {}
pub enum P3 {}
pub enum P2 {}
pub enum P1 {}

impl PageTable for P4 {}
impl PageTable for P3 {}
impl PageTable for P2 {}
impl PageTable for P1 {}
```

This creates four enumerations representing page table levels. The reason for using enumerations instead of structures is that empty enumerations cannot be instantiated, which will avoid some typos. Then we write the `HighTable` trait:

```
pub trait HighTable: PageTable {
    type NextTable: PageTable;
}

impl HighTable for P4 {
    type NextTable = P3;
}

impl HighTable for P3 {
    type NextTable = P2;
}

impl HighTable for P2 {
    type NextTable = P1;
}
```

As you can see, we add an associated type to each enumeration to represent the next level of paging. But, of course, in the case of the last level, it will not have another page table below.

This allows you to define functions associated to `HighTable` that will not be accessible to a P1 table and so on. And it lets you create a `Page` type that will contain the contents of a `Page` (a byte array, more or less) that is generic over what level it is.

Rust will ensure that you cannot try to get the next table of a P1 table at compile time, and at runtime, these enumerations will disappear, as they are zero-sized. The logic will be safe, though, and checked at compile time with no overhead.

Extra performance tips

Compile-time checks are not the only place where you can benefit from a performance enhancement at no cost. While in `Chapter 1`, *Common Performance Pitfalls*, we saw the common errors people write in Rust, we left the most advanced tips and tricks for this chapter.

Using closures to avoid runtime evaluation

Sometimes, it might seem natural to write code that does not perform as fast as expected. Many times, this is due to Rust doing some extra computations at runtime. An example of an unnecessary computation that someone could write is the following:

```
let opt = Some(123);
let non_opt = opt.unwrap_or(some_complex_function());
```

I have intentionally made this example simply because a real example usually takes really long code. The idea behind it is valid though. When you have an Option or a Result, you have some very useful functions to allow you get the value inside or a default. There is this specific function, the unwrap_or() function, that allows you specify the default value. Of course, you can pass anything you want to that function, but if you require a complex calculation to calculate the default value (and it's not a constant), the code will perform poorly.

This happens because when calling the unwrap_or() function, the value you pass must be calculated beforehand. This does not make much sense if most of the time the value will exist and the computation is not required. A better option is to use unwrap_or_else(). This function accepts a closure that will only be executed if the Option/Result is None/Err respectively. In this concrete case, since some_complex_function() does not have any arguments, you can directly use that as the closure:

```
let opt = Some(123);
let non_opt = opt.unwrap_or_else(some_complex_function);
```

But if the function requires arguments, you will need to build the closure yourself:

```
let opt = Some(123);
let non_opt = opt.unwrap_or_else(|| {
    even_more_complex_function(get_argument())
});
```

This way, you can use a very complicated function, as complicated as you'd like, and you will avoid calling it if there is something inside the Option type. You will also reduce the cyclomatic complexity of the function.

Unstable sorting

There is also an interesting place where some gains can be made. Usually, when you want to sort a vector, for example, stable sorting is used. This means that if two elements have the same ordering, the original ordering will be preserved. Let's see it with an example. Suppose we have a list of fruits we want to order alphabetically, taking into account only their first letter:

```
let mut fruits = vec![
    "Orange", "Pome", "Peach", "Banana", "Kiwi", "Pear"
];
fruits.sort_by(|a, b| a.chars().next().cmp(&b.chars().next()));

println!("{:?}", fruits);
```

This will print exactly the following:

```
["Banana", "Kiwi", "Orange", "Pome", "Peach", "Pear"]
```

And in that order. Even though `Peach` and `Pear` should be before `Pome` if we did the sorting by the whole word, since we only take the first character into account, the ordering is correct. The final order depends on the one at the beginning. If I changed the first list and put `Pome` after `Peach`, the final order would have `Pome` after `Peach`. This is called **stable ordering**.

On the other hand, unstable ordering doesn't try to preserve previous ordering. So, `Pome`, `Peach`, and `Pear` could end up in any order between them. This is consistent with the condition of being ordered by the first letter, but without preserving the original order.

This unstable sorting is actually faster than the stable sorting, and if you don't care about respecting the initial ordering, you can save valuable time doing the sorting operation, one of the most time-consuming operations. A simple example is ordering a list of results alphabetically. In the case of a mismatch, you usually don't care how they were ordered in the database, so it doesn't matter if one comes after the other or the other way around.

To use unstable sorting, you will need to call `sort_unstable()` or `sort_unstable_by()`, depending on whether you want to use the default comparison of each `PartialOrd` element or use your own classifier, if you want a custom one or if the elements in the vector are not `PartialOrd`. Consider the following example using unstable sorting:

```
let mut fruits = vec![
    "Orange", "Pome", "Peach", "Banana", "Kiwi", "Pear"
];
fruits.sort_unstable_by(|a, b|
a.chars().next().cmp(&b.chars().next()));

println!("{:?}", fruits);
```

A possible output for this would be the following, impossible with stable sorting:

```
["Banana", "Kiwi", "Orange", "Pome", "Peach", "Pear"]
```

So, summarizing, if you really need to maintain the ordering of the input, use stable sorting; if not, use unstable sorting, since you will make your program much faster.

Map hashing

Rust also has another development option that allows you to make the hashing of the maps faster. This comes from the idea that when storing information in a `HashMap`, for example, the key gets hashed or a faster lookup. This is great, since it allows using arbitrary long and complex keys, but adds overhead when retrieving a value or inserting a new value, since the hash must be calculated.

Rust allows you to change the hashing method for a `HashMap`, and even create your own. Of course, usually, the best thing is to use the default hashing algorithm, since it has been thoroughly tested and avoids collisions (different keys having the same hash and overwriting one another). The default hasher for Rust is a very efficient hasher, but if you need performance and you are working with a really small `HashMap` or even a somehow predictable `HashMap`, it could make sense to use your own function or even a faster function included in Rust.

But beware—it's very risky to use one of these functions in an environment where a user can provide (or manipulate) keys. They could generate a collision and modify the value of a key they should not have access to. They could even create a denial of service attack using it.

Using a different hashing is as simple as using the `with_hasher()` function when creating the `HashMap`:

```
use std::collections::HashMap;
use std::collections::hash_map::RandomState;

// <u8, u8> as an example, just to make the type inference happy.
let map: HashMap<u8, u8> = HashMap::with_hasher(RandomState::new());
```

Currently, only `RandomState` is available in the standard library; the rest have been deprecated. But you can create your own by implementing the `Hasher` trait:

```
use std::hash::{BuildHasher, Hasher};

#[derive(Clone)]
struct MyHasher {
    count: u64,
}

impl Hasher for MyHasher {
    fn finish(&self) -> u64 {
        self.count
    }

    fn write(&mut self, bytes: &[u8]) {
        for byte in bytes {
            self.count = self.count.wrapping_add(*byte as u64);
        }
    }
}

impl BuildHasher for MyHasher {
    type Hasher = Self;
    fn build_hasher(&self) -> Self::Hasher {
        self.clone()
    }
}
```

This creates the `MyHasher` structure, which contains a count that can be initialized as you wish. The `hash` function is really simple; it just adds all the bytes of the key and returns a `u64` with the sum result. Generating a collision here is pretty easy: you just need to make your bytes sum the same. So `[45, 23]` will have the same hash as `[23, 45]`. But it works as an example of a hasher. The `BuildHasher` trait is also required, and it only needs to return an instance of a `Hasher`. I derived the `Clone` trait and just cloned it.

This can be easily used, as we saw before:

```
use std::collections::HashMap;

let mut map = HashMap::with_hasher(MyHasher { count: 12345 });
map.insert("Hello", "World");
```

This will probably be faster than the default hasher, but it will also be much, much less secure. So be careful about what hash function you use.

Perfect hash functions

If the map is known at compile time, and it does not change during the runtime, there is a very, very fast system that can improve by orders of magnitude the use of maps. It's called **perfect hash functions**, and that's the key to them: they perform the minimum required computation for a hash to know whether it's stored in the hash map. This is because it maps one, and only one, integer for each element. And it has no collisions. Of course, this requires a constant, known hash map at compilation time.

To use them, you will need the phf crate. With this crate, you will be able to define a hash map at compile time in the build.rs file at the same level as the Cargo.toml file and use it with no more overhead than a comparison in your code. Let's see how to configure it.

First, you will need to add the phf_codegen crate as a development dependency. For that, you will need to add a build-dependencies section to your Cargo.toml, with the same syntax as the dependencies section. Then, you will need to create a build.rs file and, inside, you will need something like the following:

```
extern crate phf_codegen;

use std::path::Path;
use std::env;
use std::fs::File;
use std::io::{BufWriter, Write};

fn main() {
    let out_dir = env::var("OUT_DIR").unwrap();
    let path = Path::new(&out_dir).join("phf.rs");
    let mut file = BufWriter::new(File::create(&path).unwrap());

    let map = [("key1", "\"value1\""), ("key2", "\"value2\"")];

    write!(
        &mut file,
```

```
        "static MAP: phf::Map<&'static str, &'static str> =\n"
    ).unwrap();

    let mut phf_map = phf_codegen::Map::new();
    for &(key, value) in &map {
        phf_map.entry(key, value);
    }

    phf_map.build(&mut file).unwrap();
    write!(&mut file, ";\n").unwrap();
}
```

Let's check what is happening here. The build.rs script is run before the compilation starts (if it's present). We have a map that is an array of key/value tuples. It then creates a code generation map and adds entries one by one to the map. This has to be done in a loop, since the compiler stack could overflow due to deep recursion.

It will write into a file, called phf.rs, starting with a line adding a static variable, and then writing the whole map into the file, ending it with a new line. This means that once the compilation starts, a new file named phf.rs will exist that we can use from our code. How? You will need to directly include the file in your code:

```
extern crate phf;

include!(concat!(env!("OUT_DIR"), "/phf.rs"));

fn main() {
    println!("{}", MAP.get("key1").unwrap());
}
```

This will print the value associated to key1, in this case, value1.

 Note that when creating the map in the build.rs file, the values are written directly, so if you want to put a string, you need to add the quotation marks and escape them. This enables you to add enumeration variants, for example, or to write code directly for values.

Once you have learned how to use compile-time hash maps, you should understand the different kinds of collections the standard library allows you to use, since it will be crucial to the speed and memory footprint of your application.

Standard library collections

Rust's standard library has eight different collection types in the `std::collections` module. They are divided into sequences, maps, sets, and a binary heap that does not fit in any group. The most well known ones are arguably `HashMap` and `Vec`, but each of them has a use case, and you should know about them to use the proper one in each moment.

The official standard library documentation is really good, so you should check it thoroughly. In any case, though, I will introduce the types so that you can familiarize yourself with them. Let's start with sequences.

Sequences

The most-used dynamic sequence in Rust and in most languages is the vector, represented in Rust as `Vec`. You can add elements to the back of a vector with the `push()` method, and get the last element back with the `pop()` method. You can also iterate through the vector and, by default, it will go from front to back, but you can also reverse the iterator to go from back to front. In general, a vector in Rust can be compared to a stack, since it's primarily a LIFO structure.

Vectors are really useful when you want to add new elements to a list, and when you are fine with working with indexes in slices to get the elements. Remember that vectors can be referenced as slices, and can be indexed with ranges. An interesting thing is that you can convert a vector into a boxed slice, that is similar to an array, but allocated in heap instead of a stack. You only have to call the `into_boxed_slice()` method. This is useful when you have finished growing the vector and want it to occupy less RAM. A vector has a capacity, a length, and a pointer to the elements, while a boxed slice will only have the pointer and the length, avoiding some extra memory usage.

Another useful sequence is the `VecDeque` sequence. This structure is a FIFO queue, where you can append elements to the back of the queue using the `push_back()` method, and pop elements from the front by using `pop_front()`. This can be used as a buffer since it can be consumed from the front while you continue adding elements to the back. Of course, to use it as a buffer crossing thread boundaries, you will need to lock it with a `Mutex`, for example. Iterations in these queues go from front to back, the same way as in vectors. It's implemented with a growable ring buffer.

Finally, the `LinkedList` is another sequential list where its peculiarity is that instead of having a chunk of elements in the memory, each element gets linked to the one before and the one after so that there is no need for an index. It's easy to iterate, and easy to remove any element in the list without leaving gaps or having to reorder the memory, but in general, it's not very memory-friendly and requires more CPU consumption.

You will, most of the time, prefer a `Vec` or a `VecDeque`. `LinkedLists` are usually only a good option when many inserts and removes have to be done in the middle of the sequence, since in that case, `Vecs` and `VecDeques` will have to reorder themselves, which takes a lot of time. But if you will usually only change the structure of the list from the back, a `Vec` is the best option; if you will also change it from the front, a `VecDeque`. Remember that in both you can read any element easily by indexing, it's just that it's more time-consuming to remove or add them in the middle of the list.

Maps

There are two kinds of maps: `HashMap` and `BTreeMap`. The main difference between them is how they order themselves in memory. They have similar methods to insert and retrieve elements, but their performance changes a lot depending on the operation.

`HashMap` creates an index, where for every key a hash points to the element. That way, you do not need to check the whole key for every new `insert`/`delete`/`get` operation. You simply hash it and search it in the index. If it exists, it can be retrieved, modified, or deleted; if it doesn't, it can be inserted. It is pretty fast to insert new elements. It's as simple as adding it to the index. Retrieving it is also pretty much the same: just get the value if the hashed index exists; all operations are done in $O(1)$. You cannot append one `HashMap` to another, though, because their hashing algorithms will be different, or at least be in different states.

`BTreeMap`, on the other hand, does not create indexes. It maintains an ordered list of elements and, that way, when you want to insert or get a new element, it does a binary search. Check whether the key is bigger than the key in the middle of the list. If it is, divide the second half of the list into two and try it again with the element of the middle of the second half; if it's not, do the same with the first half.

That way, you don't have to compare each element with all elements in the map, and you can quickly retrieve them. Adding new elements is a similarly costly algorithm, and all operations can be done in $O(\log n)$. You can also append another `BTreeSet` to this one, and the elements will be reordered for the search to be as fast as possible.

Sets

Both `HashMap` and `BTreeMap` have their set counterparts, called `HashSet` and `BTreeSet`. Both are implemented with the same idea in mind: sometimes you don't need a key/value store, but just an element store, where you can retrieve the list of the elements by iterating through them, or where you can check whether an element is inside just by comparing it to the ones inside.

Their approach is the same as with the case of their map counterparts, and you can think of them as their counterpart maps but with a null value, where only keys are the ones doing the job.

Summary

In this chapter, you learned how to use compile-time checks to your advantage. You learned how Rust's type system can help you create complex and safe behaviour without runtime overhead. You learned how to create state machines and how to make your code less error-prone.

You also learned about some extra performance enhancements that complement those of `Chapter 1`, *Common Performance Pitfalls*. You learned about unstable sorting and map hashing, including perfect hash functions created at compile time, and how to create compile-time hash maps that will have no runtime overhead.

Finally, you learned about the collections in the standard library, how they are classified, and which type of collection you should use depending on the situation. You learned about sequences, maps, and sets, and how they can be adapted for your code.

In `Chapter 3`, *Memory Management in Rust*, we will talk about memory management in Rust. Even if, in Rust, you do not need to manually allocate and de-allocate memory, there are still plenty of things you can do to improve your memory footprint.

Memory Management in Rust 3

Until now, we have always talked about how the Rust compiler handles the memory by itself, and how that makes it memory-safe and gives us some extra superpowers without the fear of creating memory vulnerabilities. Nevertheless, there is no limit to what you can accomplish by using unsafe scopes, and even by using safe code.

We will check all the configuration and metaprogramming options that Rust gives us regarding memory management and see how we can improve our code by using both safe and unsafe code.

In this chapter, we will be looking into the following topics:

- Learning the rules of the borrow checker
- Binding lifetimes
- Memory representation
- Data representation for FFI with C/C++
- Shared pointers
- Reference counted pointers

Mastering the borrow checker

To ensure memory and thread safety, Rust's borrow checker has three simple rules. They are enforced all through the code except in unsafe scopes. Here they are:

- Each binding will have an owner
- There can only be one owner for a binding
- When the owner goes out of the scope, the binding gets dropped

These three rules seem simple enough, but they have a great implication on how we code. The compiler can know beforehand when an owner goes out of scope, so it will always know when to drop/destruct a binding/variable. This means that you can write your code without having to think about where you create variables, where you call destructors, or whether you have already called a destructor or you are calling it twice.

Of course, this comes with an additional learning curve that can sometimes be difficult to catch up. The second rule is what most people find difficult to manage. Since there can only be one owner at a time, sharing information sometimes becomes somewhat difficult.

Let's see an example of this behavior with a known type, the `Vec` type:

```
let mut my_vector = vec![0, 16, 34, 13, 95];
my_vector.push(22);
println!("{:?}", my_vector);
```

This will print the following:

```
[0, 16, 34, 13, 95, 22]
```

At the end of the current scope (the `main()` function, for example), the vector will be dropped by calling its destructor. In this case, it will simply deallocate the memory cleanly and then destroy itself.

Allocations

For a variable to be growable (so that it can occupy different amounts of space in the memory at different times), it needs to be allocated on the heap, and not on the stack. The stack works faster, since on the loading of the program, it gets assigned to it. But the heap is slower, since for each allocation you need to perform a system call to the kernel, which means you will need a context switch (to kernel mode) and back (to user mode). This makes things too slow.

Vectors (and other standard library structures) have an interesting way of allocating that memory so that they perform as efficiently as possible. Let's check the algorithm it uses to allocate new memory with this code:

```
let mut my_vector = vec![73, 55];
println!(
    "length: {}, capacity: {}",
    my_vector.len(),
    my_vector.capacity()
```

```
    );

    my_vector.push(25);
    println!(
        "length: {}, capacity: {}",
        my_vector.len(),
        my_vector.capacity()
    );

    my_vector.push(33);
    my_vector.push(24);
    println!(
        "length: {}, capacity: {}",
        my_vector.len(),
        my_vector.capacity()
    );
```

The output should be something along these lines:

```
length: 2, capacity: 2
length: 3, capacity: 4
length: 5, capacity: 8
```

This means that, at the beginning, the vector will have allocated only the space required by our first two elements. But as soon as we push a new one, it will allocate space for two new elements, so that with the fourth push it won't need to allocate more memory. When we finally insert a fifth element, it allocates space for another four, so that it does not need to allocate until it gets to the ninth.

If you follow the progression, the next time it will allocate space for 8 more elements, making the capacity grow to 16. This is dependent on the first allocation, and if we had started the vector with 3 elements, the numbers would be 3, 6, 12, 24,... We can, in any case, force the vector to pre-allocate a given number of elements with two functions, reserve() and reserve_exact(). The former will reserve space for at least the given number of elements, while the latter will reserve space exactly for the given number of elements. This is really useful when you know the size of the input, so that it doesn't need to allocate once and again. It will just allocate once.

Mutability, borrowing, and owning

There are also rules about mutability in Rust, that prevent data races between threads. Let's see them:

- All bindings are immutable by default
- There can be unlimited immutable borrows of a binding at the same time
- There can only be one mutable borrow of a binding at most at a given point in time
- If there is a mutable borrow, no immutable borrows can coexist at a given point in time

They are fairly simple to understand. You can read the contents of a binding from as many places as you would like, but if you want to modify a binding, you must somehow ensure that no readers or other writers exist. This, of course, prevents data races, but makes your coding a bit more troublesome.

Let's see this with a couple of examples. Let's first define these two functions:

```
fn change_third(slice: &mut [u32]) {
    if let Some(item) = slice.get_mut(2) {
        *item += 1
    }
}

fn print_third(slice: &[u32]) {
    if let Some(item) = slice.get(2) {
        println!("Third element: {}", item);
    }
}
```

The `change_third()` function requires a mutable u32 slice that will use to add 1 to the third element if the slice has at least three elements. The second will print that element. You can then use this `main()` function to test it:

```
fn main() {
    let mut my_vector = vec![73, 55, 33];
    print_third(&my_vector);
    change_third(&mut my_vector[..]);
    print_third(&my_vector);
}
```

As you can see, since the two functions borrow the vector (one of them mutably and the other one immutably), you can continue using the vector in the main() function. This means that the ownership of the vector is in the main() function.

If we had a function that took ownership of the vector, we wouldn't be able to use it later. Consider changing the change_third() function for this one:

```
fn change_third(mut slice: Vec<u32>) {
    if let Some(item) = slice.get_mut(2) {
        *item += 1
    }
}
```

In this case, the function receives the argument and takes ownership of the vector (there is no slicing or referencing on the function declaration). Of course, we will need to change the call to the function:

```
change_third(my_vector);
```

The issue is that the program will no longer compile. After we give the ownership of the vector to the change_third() function, there will no longer be a my_vector variable in the main() function. The error that the Rust compiler shows is really clarifying, and it will even point out where the issue is:

```
ror[E0382]: use of moved value: `my_vector`
 --> src/main.rs:17:18
  |
      change_third(my_vector);
                   --------- value moved here
      print_third(&my_vector);
                  ^^^^^^^^^^^ value used here after move
  |
  = note: move occurs because `my vector` has type `std::vec::Vec<u32>`, which does not implement the `Copy` tra
```

In conclusion, if you need to continue using the variable after using it to call a function, pass it by reference, let the function borrow your variable but not own it. If you don't, and you prefer the new function to have absolute control over the variable (even to drop it), pass it by value. This doesn't apply to Copy types, as we saw in Chapter 1, *Common Performance Pitfalls*, since, in that case, the whole object gets copied to the new function.

References can be a little difficult to manage though. We sometimes require a structure to have a referenced value, but since the structure won't have ownership of the variable to drop it, it will have to make sure that the owner of the variable doesn't do it while it is still in use. For this, we have lifetimes.

Lifetimes

Every variable, structure attribute, and constant has a lifetime in Rust. Most of them can be elided, since we usually know that a constant has a static lifetime (it will always be there for us), or that most of the variables have the lifetime of its scope. Nevertheless, there is sometimes a place where we need to specify that lifetime. Let's check the following structures:

```
struct Parent<'p> {
    age: u8,
    child: Option<&'p Child>,
}

struct Child {
    age: u8,
}
```

As you can see, the parent has a reference to the child, but we added two letters preceded by a single quote. These are lifetime specifications, and what means is that the reference to the child has to live at least while the parent exists. Let's see this behavior with a simple `main()` function:

```
fn main() {
    let child = Child { age: 10 };
    let parent = Parent {
        age: 35,
        child: Some(&child),
    };

    println!("Child's age: {} years.", parent.child.unwrap().age);
}
```

This will print that the child is 10 years old. The child gets dropped at the end of the `main` function, so the reference is valid while the parent exists. But let's create a small inner scope to see if we can trick the compiler. Inner scopes are explicit scopes that you can create by using curly braces. All variables defined in there will be dropped at the end of the inner scope, and if an expression is added at the end without a semicolon, it will be the value of the scope, and can be assigned to any variable.

Let's try to add a `child` to a `parent` that will be dropped at an inner scope:

```
let mut parent = Parent {
    age: 35,
    child: None,
};
```

```
    {
        let child = Child { age: 10 };
        parent.child = Some(&child);
    }

    println!("Child's age: {} years.", parent.child.unwrap().age);
```

If we try to compile this, the compiler will tell us that `child` does not live long enough. The compiler has understood that we told it in the structure that `child` had to live at least as long as the `Parent` structure, and since, in this case, it knows that the variable defined inside the inner scope will be dropped there, it will complain at compile time and not let you add it to the `parent`.

This can be extended to functions. Let's consider a very simple function that returns a reference to the oldest child of the two provided:

```
fn oldest_child(child1: &Child, child2: &Child) -> &Child {
    if child1.age > child2.age {
        child1
    } else {
        child2
    }
}
```

This will not compile, since it needs a lifetime parameter. This means that the compiler does not know whether the return child will live as long as `child1` or as long as `child2`. We don't know either, so we will specify that all lifetimes must be at least as long as the current function, and then the rest is the problem of our caller:

```
fn oldest_child<'f>(child1: &'f Child, child2: &'f Child) -> &'f Child {
    if child1.age > child2.age {
        child1
    } else {
        child2
    }
}
```

This just declares a new lifetime (declared before the first parenthesis before the arguments) that we call `f`, that will be the lifetime of the function. We then specify that all references must live at least as long as the function.

Memory representation

Apart from managing the references, ownerships, allocations, and copies, we can also manage the memory layout of those structures we saw earlier, and we can do it by using both safe and unsafe code. Let's first understand how Rust manages the memory. Think of the following structure:

```
struct Complex {
    attr1: u8,
    attr2: u16,
    attr3: u8,
}
```

Alignment

When accessing the attributes from memory, they need to be aligned so that their position in memory is a multiple of their size, 16 bits in this case. That way, when we try to get each attribute, we will only need to add 16 bits to the base address of the structure, multiplied by the attribute. This makes information retrieval much more efficient, and it's done by the compiler automatically. The main issue with it is that for each attribute to be 16-bit aligned, the compiler would need to pad 8 bits for each of the first and third attributes.

This means that the structure gets converted to the following:

```
struct Complex {
    attr1: u8,
    _pad1: u8,
    attr2: u16,
    attr3: u8,
    _pad2: u8,
}
```

But, in this concrete case, both `attr1` and `attr3` have 8 bits, so they do not need to be 16-bit aligned; they could be 8-bit aligned and work properly. This means that we could move the first attribute to the end and, that way, it would be something like having two 16-bit aligned attributes, and the second one would contain two 8-bit aligned attributes:

```
struct Complex {
    attr2: u16,
    attr1: u8,
    attr3: u8,
}
```

This does not require extra padding and thus the structure will occupy 32 bits (instead of 48 as before). This is a typical optimization that has to be done manually in C/C++, messing up our order of attributes, but in Rust we can do better. The compiler knows about this, and it will reorder the fields the best it can to have a better memory footprint, so you can put the attributes in the order you'd like.

But, if the compiler already does this automatically, what is this doing in a performance optimization book? Well, there is a situation where you want to avoid this behavior.

Let's face it, not all of the software is written in Rust yet, and in the case of high-performance libraries, it's common that we have to use C dependencies. Luckily, Rust can seamlessly integrate with any C-compatible interface at no cost. But you will have a problem if you move structures between the Rust and C codes.

As we discussed, Rust will reorder the fields, which means that the structure in C and in Rust might not have attributes positioned the same way. We can tell Rust not to change the order of the fields, though, by using the `repr` attribute with the `C` value:

```
#[repr(C)]
struct Complex {
    attr3: u8,
    attr2: u16,
    attr1: u8,
}
```

This will make the structure compatible with C. We can also tell Rust not to add padding to attributes, and therefore make the structure minimal size even if its alignment could be better. Note that this will break the code for platforms that require aligned structures. If you still want to use it, you can simply use the `packed` form of representation:

```
#[repr(packed)]
struct Complex {
    attr3: u8,
    attr2: u16,
    attr1: u8,
}
```

Complex enumerations

If you know about C/C++ enumerations, you know that each element represents a value, and that you can use them to avoid remembering the proper integers from the set of possible values. They are not strongly typed, though, so you can mix different enumerations. And they can only store one integer.

Once again, Rust can do better, and we can create complex enumerations where we cannot only have strong typing (we won't mix enumerations) but we will even be able to have more than integers in enumerations. As you can see in the following `Color` enumeration, we can have inner data, and even attributes:

```
enum Color {
    Red,
    Blue,
    Green,
    Other { r: u32, g: u32, b: u32 },
}
```

As you can see, in this case, the enumeration can have one of four values, but in the case of the last one, it will have three numbers associated. This gives you almost infinite possibilities, where you can safely represent any data structure. Check out, for instance, this implementation of *any JSON value* by the `Serde` crate, one of the most-used crates in the ecosystem:

```
pub enum Value {
    Null,
    Bool(bool),
    Number(Number),
    String(String),
    Array(Vec<Value>),
    Object(Map<String, Value>),
}
```

A value in a JSON structure can either be null, a Boolean (and with the information whether it's `true` or `false`), a number (that will be another enumeration to know whether it's positive, negative, or float point), a string, with the text information, an array of values, or a whole JSON object with its keys as strings and values.

There are two caveats with this approach, though. For comparison between the different variants of an enumeration, they must be tagged. This means that they will need to occupy some extra space just to differentiate between them at runtime.

The second problem is that the size of the enumeration type (without taking into account the tag) will be the size of the biggest option. So if you have 10 options that can be stored in 1 byte, but another one needs 10 bytes, the enumeration will have 10 bytes (plus the tag) independently of the variant being stored. This works this way because it works as a `union` (in C/C++ language), where all variants share the same representation.

To mitigate this, an option is for big objects to be references. We can do this in two ways. The first way is by borrowing the color, in which case the compiler will force us to not return the enumeration from any function where the color was created (remember, the reference would be destroyed at the end of the scope):

```
enum Color<'c> {
    Red,
    Blue,
    Green,
    Other(&'c Rgb),
}

struct Rgb {
    r: u32,
    g: u32,
    b: u32,
}
```

And if we want to avoid that, we can simply store that element in the heap by boxing it (yes, this will slow performance). It depends whether you require a lower RAM consumption or an improved speed. To store an element in the heap, you will need to use the Box type, as you can see here:

```
enum Color {
    Red,
    Blue,
    Green,
    Other(Box<Rgb>),
}
```

Unions

There is also another type of union that is not tagged. If the types in the union are not Copy, you will need to use the untagged_unions feature and compile the code with the nightly compiler. This can be avoided by deriving the Copy trait in the structures used inside the union, but you shouldn't do this for big structures, as we discussed earlier:

```
union Plant {
    g: Geranium,
    c: Carnation,
}

#[derive(Copy, Clone)]
struct Geranium {
```

```
        height: u32,
    }

    #[derive(Copy, Clone)]
    struct Carnation {
        flowers: u8,
    }
```

In this particular example, the `Plant` can be a `Geranium` or a `Carnation`. Or more precisely, it will be both at the same time. The `Plant` will have the size of the biggest structure in it, and it won't have any extra padding for a tag describing which of the two variants it is.

This means that when writing one of the fields of the union, you will change the rest of the fields too. When creating the union, you will need to specify only one field, and since the compiler won't know which variant it is at compile time, you will need to read the values using an unsafe block, as you can see in the next piece of code, since reading an unset value ends up being undefined behavior:

```
    fn main() {
        let mut my_plant = Plant {
            c: Carnation { flowers: 15 },
        };
        my_plant.g = Geranium { height: 300 };
        let height = unsafe { my_plant.g }.height;

        println!("Height: {}", height);
    }
```

In this example, we first create a `Plant` that is a `Carnation`, and then we convert it to a `Geranium`. That change does not need an unsafe block, since the `Plant` will always have 32 bits, the size of the `Geranium`, so it can be assigned with perfect memory safety.

When we retrieve the height, though, we need to specify that we want to read the `Plant` as a `Geranium`, and then get the height. In this case, it works perfectly, since we changed the `Plant` to be a `Geranium`. If we tried to get the plant as a `Carnation` in this example, it would trigger undefined behavior. This means that the number of flowers can be a random number depending on the layout of the union. Still, this is not a security vulnerability, since the `u8` we will get for the number of flowers will be one of the bytes of the `Geranium` height, it will just feel random (in my case, it says 44 flowers).

But in any case, this is particularly great for interfacing with C (FFI). If we use the `#[repr(C)]` attribute in the union, it will be structured exactly the same way as in C, so we will be able to send the union to a C library without needing to think about how to emulate a C union.

Shared pointers

One of Rust's most criticized problems is that it's difficult to develop an application with shared pointers. As we have seen before, it's true that due to Rust's memory safety guarantees, it might be difficult to develop those kinds of algorithms, but as we will see now, the standard library gives us some types we can use to safely allow that behavior.

The cell module

The standard library has one interesting module, the `std::cell` module, that allows us to use objects with interior mutability. This means that we can have an immutable object and still mutate it by getting a mutable borrow to the underlying data. This, of course, would not comply with the mutability rules we saw before, but the cells make sure this works by checking the borrows at runtime or by doing copies of the underlying data.

Cells

Let's start with the basic `Cell` structure. A `Cell` will contain a mutable value, but it can be mutated without having a mutable `Cell`. It has mainly three interesting methods: `set()`, `swap()`, and `replace()`. The first allows us to set the contained value, replacing it with a new value. The previous structure will be dropped (the destructor will run). That last bit is the only difference with the `replace()` method. In the `replace()` method, instead of dropping the previous value, it will be returned. The `swap()` method, on the other hand, will take another `Cell` and swap the values between the two. All this without the `Cell` needing to be mutable. Let's see it with an example:

```
use std::cell::Cell;

#[derive(Copy, Clone)]
struct House {
    bedrooms: u8,
}

impl Default for House {
```

```rust
    fn default() -> Self {
        House { bedrooms: 1 }
    }
}

fn main() {
    let my_house = House { bedrooms: 2 };
    let my_dream_house = House { bedrooms: 5 };

    let my_cell = Cell::new(my_house);
    println!("My house has {} bedrooms.", my_cell.get().bedrooms);

    my_cell.set(my_dream_house);
    println!("My new house has {} bedrooms.", my_cell.get().bedrooms);

    let my_new_old_house = my_cell.replace(my_house);
    println!(
        "My house has {} bedrooms, it was better with {}",
        my_cell.get().bedrooms,
        my_new_old_house.bedrooms
    );

    let my_new_cell = Cell::new(my_dream_house);

    my_cell.swap(&my_new_cell);
    println!(
        "Yay! my current house has {} bedrooms! (my new house {})",
        my_cell.get().bedrooms,
        my_new_cell.get().bedrooms
    );

    let my_final_house = my_cell.take();
    println!(
        "My final house has {} bedrooms, the shared one {}",
        my_final_house.bedrooms,
        my_cell.get().bedrooms
    );
}
```

As you can see in the example, to use a `Cell`, the contained type must be `Copy`. If the contained type is not `Copy`, you will need to use a `RefCell`, which we will see next. Continuing with this `Cell` example, as you can see through the code, the output will be the following:

```
My house has 2 bedrooms.
My new house has 5 bedrooms.
My house has 2 bedrooms, it was better with 5
Yay! my current house has 5 bedrooms! (my new house 2)
My final house has 5 bedrooms, the shared one 1
```

So we first create two houses, we select one of them as the current one, and we keep mutating the current and the new ones. As you might have seen, I also used the `take()` method, only available for types implementing the `Default` trait. This method will return the current value, replacing it with the default value. As you can see, you don't really mutate the value inside, but you replace it with another value. You can either retrieve the old value or lose it. Also, when using the `get()` method, you get a copy of the current value, and not a reference to it. That's why you can only use elements implementing `Copy` with a `Cell`. This also means that a `Cell` does not need to dynamically check borrows at runtime.

RefCell

`RefCell` is similar to `Cell`, except that it accepts non-`Copy` data. This also means that when modifying the underlying object, it cannot simply copy it when returning it, it will need to return references. The same way, when you want to mutate the object inside, it will return a mutable reference. This only works because it will dynamically check at runtime whether a borrow exists before returning a mutable borrow, or the other way around, and if it does, the thread will panic.

Instead of using the `get()` method as in `Cell`, `RefCell` has two methods to get the underlying data: `borrow()` and `borrow_mut()`. The first will get a read-only borrow, and you can have as many immutable borrows in a scope. The second one will return a read-write borrow, and you will only be able to have one in scope to follow the mutability rules. If you try to do a `borrow_mut()` after a `borrow()` in the same scope, or a `borrow()` after a `borrow_mut()`, the thread will panic.

There are two non-panicking alternatives to these borrows: `try_borrow()` and `try_borrow_mut()`. These two will try to borrow the data (the first read-only and the second read/write), and if there are incompatible borrows present, they will return a `Result::Err`, so that you can handle the error without panicking.

Both `Cell` and `RefCell` have a `get_mut()` method, that will get a mutable reference to the element inside, but it requires the `Cell`/`RefCell` to be mutable, so it doesn't make much sense if you need the `Cell`/`RefCell` to be immutable. Nevertheless, if in a part of the code you can actually have a mutable `Cell`/`RefCell`, you should use this method to change the contents, since it will check all rules statically at compile time, without runtime overhead.

Interestingly enough, `RefCell` does not return a plain reference to the underlying data when we call `borrow()` or `borrow_mut()`. You would expect them to return `&T` and `&mut T` (where `T` is the wrapped element). Instead, they will return a `Ref` and a `RefMut`, respectively. This is to safely wrap the reference inside, so that the lifetimes get correctly calculated by the compiler without requiring references to live for the whole lifetime of the `RefCell`. They implement `Deref` into references, though, so thanks to Rust's `Deref` coercion, you can use them as references.

The rc module

The `std::rc` module contains reference-counted pointers that can be used in single-threaded applications. They have very little overhead, thanks to counters not being atomic counters, but this means that using them in multithreaded applications could cause data races. Thus, Rust will stop you from sending them between threads at compile time. There are two structures in this module: `Rc` and `Weak`.

An `Rc` is an owning pointer to the heap. This means that it's the same as a `Box`, except that it allows for reference-counted pointers. When the `Rc` goes out of scope, it will decrease by 1 the number of references, and if that count is 0, it will drop the contained object.

Since an `Rc` is a shared reference, it cannot be mutated, but a common pattern is to use a `Cell` or a `RefCell` inside the `Rc` to allow for interior mutability.

Rc can be downgraded to a Weak pointer, that will have a borrowed reference to the heap. When an Rc drops the value inside, it will not check whether there are Weak pointers to it. This means that a Weak pointer will not always have a valid reference, and therefore, for safety reasons, the only way to check the value of the Weak pointer is to upgrade it to an Rc, which could fail. The upgrade() method will return None if the reference has been dropped.

Let's check all this by creating an example binary tree structure:

```
use std::cell::RefCell;
use std::rc::{Rc, Weak};

struct Tree<T> {
    root: Node<T>,
}

struct Node<T> {
    parent: Option<Weak<Node<T>>>,
    left: Option<Rc<RefCell<Node<T>>>>,
    right: Option<Rc<RefCell<Node<T>>>>,
    value: T,
}
```

In this case, the tree will have a root node, and each of the nodes can have up to two children. We call them left and right, because they are usually represented as trees with one child on each side. Each node has a pointer to one of the children, and it owns the children nodes. This means that when a node loses all references, it will be dropped, and with it, its children.

Each child has a pointer to its parent. The main issue with this is that, if the child has an Rc pointer to its parent, it will never drop. This is a circular dependency, and to avoid it, the pointer to the parent will be a Weak pointer.

Summary

In this chapter, you have learned how the borrow checker works. You now understand the rules that your code must follow to compile, and how little tricks can make your code much faster without having to worry about making the compiler happy.

You also learned about the memory representation of structures and enumerations in Rust and how to make your Rust code compatible with the C/C++.

Finally, you understood how Rust manages shared pointers for complex structures where the Rust borrow checker can make your coding experience much more difficult.

In Chapter 4, *Lints and Clippy*, we will learn about linting and a surprisingly good linting tool called **Clippy**. With these lints, you will be able to find many of the issues we saw at compile time.

4
Lints and Clippy

Up until now, we needed to check all the details of the code by ourselves. This can often get out of control, since we cannot be checking each line of code. In this chapter, you will learn about the lints Rust brings us, both the ones enabled by default and the ones you can enable yourself.

Moreover, you will learn about a great tool, Clippy, that will give you many more lints you can use, and that can help you write much better code. In many cases, it will lint about performance pitfalls. In other cases, they will be potential errors or idiomatic conventions. It will also help you clean your code.

In this chapter, you will learn about the following topics:

- Linting in Rust
- Default lints
- Using and configuring Clippy
- Extra Clippy lints

Using Rust compiler lints

The Rust compiler, at the time of writing, has 70 lints. We will not check all 70, but we will take a look at the most relevant ones. Let's first start by learning how to configure a lint. We will take `unused_imports` as an example. The compiler will warn you for this lint by default. The compilation will continue, but it will show a warning in the command line, or in the editor if it's configured to show Rust compilation warnings.

We can change this behavior, and we can change it for each scope. The options are `allow`, `warn`, `deny`, and `forbid` the lint. If we allow the lint, no more warnings will appear. If we warn, compilation warnings will appear, and if we deny or forbid, the program won't compile if it finds something that triggers the lint. The difference between `deny` and `forbid` is that the former can be overridden down the line, while the latter can't. So we can have a module that denies one behavior, but in one particular function, we want to allow it.

This configuration can be applied at crate level, by putting `#![deny(unused_imports)]`, for example, at the top of the `lib.rs` or `main.rs` file. It can also be applied to any scope, even scopes you might create inside functions. If it has an exclamation mark (`!`) after the hash, it will affect the current scope; if not, it will affect the scope just next to it. Let's see what lints the Rust compiler gives us.

Lints

In this section, we will check the lints that allow the behavior by default, and that you will probably want to add at least a warning for in most cases.

Avoiding anonymous parameters

Anonymous parameters have been deprecated. This allowed you to specify traits without requiring binding names in traits:

```
trait MyTrait {
    fn check_this(String);
}
```

This is a deprecated legacy feature that might get removed in future versions, so you should probably avoid using this syntax. In order to warn or deny this syntax in your code base, you will need to use this syntax: `#![warn(anonymous_parameters)]`.

Avoiding heap allocated box pointers

Rust allocates space in the stack by default, since it's much faster than using the heap. Nevertheless, sometimes, when we do not know the size of objects at compile time, we need to use the heap to allocate new structures. Rust makes this explicit by using the `Vec`, `String`, and `Box` types, for example. The last one allows us to put in the heap any kind of object, which is usually a bad idea, but sometimes it's a must.

Check out, for example, the following code:

```
fn main() {
    let mut int = Box::new(5);
    *int += 5;
    println!("int: {}", int);
}
```

This code compiles perfectly, and it tells us that the integer is 10 (5 + 5). The main issue with this is that it does a heap allocation, doing a system call that needs to find the space in the heap and so on. But we already know that an integer has a fixed size at compile time, so we should be using the stack for this.

These kinds of errors can be avoided by warning every Box usage using #![warn(box_pointers)]. But beware: this will warn every usage of a boxed type, so you probably want to allow this in many places explicitly.

Avoiding missing implementations

There are a couple of traits we probably want many of our types to implement. The first of them is the Debug trait. The Debug trait should probably be implemented by all of our types, since it enables a developer to print debug information about our structures, enumerations, and so on. Moreover, it allows a user of our API to derive the Debug trait in structures using our API types by only adding an attribute.

We can enforce the implementation of this trait for all of our types by adding #![warn(missing_debug_implementations)]. The only detail is that this trait will only check for types exposed in our API. So, it will only work for pub types.

Another interesting trait is the Copy trait. Sometimes, we create a small structure with a couple of integers that would work best if copied in certain cases, as we saw in the previous chapters. The problem is that if we forget about implementing it, we might end up doing excessive referencing, making our code slower. We can solve this by adding this lint: #![warn(missing_copy_implementations)].

This lint has a couple of caveats though. It will only work for pub types, as in the case for the Debug implementation lint, and it will lint all structures that all of its members are Copy types. This means that if we have a really big structure that we wouldn't like to copy around, we will need to allow the lint for that particular structure.

Enforcing documentation

This is arguably the most important lint of all, and it's a pity that it's `allow` by default. Whenever we create an API, we must document what the API does. This will make it much, much easier for new developers to use it. The `#![warn(missing_docs)]` lint will make sure that at least all of your public API has some documentation. I personally usually have this as a warning during the development and change it to `deny` or even `forbid` once the project enters into production.

Pointing out trivial casts

Sometimes, we might explicitly cast an element to a type that the compiler should cast automatically. This sometimes happens when we use traits, but it can also happen because we changed the type of an element to a new type and we didn't change the castings. To clean these kinds of behavior, we have the `trivial_casts` and `trivial_numeric_casts` lints. Let's see it as an example:

```
#![warn(trivial_casts, trivial_numeric_casts)]

#[derive(Default, Debug)]
struct MyStruct {
    a: i32,
    b: i32,
}

fn main() {
    let test = MyStruct::default();
    println!("{:?}", (test as MyStruct).a as i32);
}
```

In this case, we first cast `test` as a `MyStruct`, but it's already a `MyStruct`, so this is redundant and makes the code much less readable, and in consequence, more error-prone. Then we cast its `a` attribute as an `i32`, but it's already an `i32`, so once again, redundant information. The first is not common, but the second could be found if we use this parameter for a function that only accepts an `i32`, and our structure had `i16` in a previous implementation, for example.

In any case, these kinds of castings are not good practice, since it could be that we had changed the `a` attribute for an `i64`, and we would be silently losing precision. We should use `i32::from()` so that if we change it for an `i64`, it will simply stop compiling. This gets automatically linted with the Clippy tool we will see later.

It is a good idea to enable these two lints anyway, since it will help us find these kinds of errors. The `trivial_casts` lint will lint us for non-numeric type/trait casts, while `trivial_numeric_casts` will lint the numeric casts.

Linting unsafe code blocks

In some situations, especially if we are using extremely low-level programming, sometimes used for high-performance computing, we will need to perform some pointer arithmetics or even **Single Instruction, Multiple Data (SIMD)** intrinsics that will require unsafe scopes. This might be the case in some specific functions or pieces of code, but in general, we should avoid unsafe scopes.

A rule of thumb is this: if you are not working on performance-critical code, do not use them. If you are, use them very carefully and only in places where there is no other option to improve performance. This means that usually intrinsic code can be wrapped in one module or function.

To make sure nobody uses unsafe code outside the scope where we want it to be shown, we can lint all unsafe scopes by using the `unsafe_code` lint. Let's see it as an example:

```
#![warn(unsafe_code)]

fn main() {
    let test = vec![1, 2, 3];
    println!("{}", unsafe { test.get_unchecked(2) });
}
```

If you remember from Chapter 1, *Common Performance Pitfalls*, the `get_unchecked()` function in a slice will get the element at the given index without checking the bounds of the slice, making it go faster. This also means that if the index is out of bounds, you could get from a memory leak to a segmentation fault.

In this example, when compiling this piece of code, a warning will tell us that we are using unsafe code. We can allow it for this particular function if it's 100% required, or we can change the code. An example fixing the issue above while still using unsafe code can be seen here:

```
#![deny(unsafe_code)]

fn main() {
    let test = vec![1, 2, 3];
    println!("{}", get_second(&test));
}
```

```
#[allow(unsafe_code)]
fn get_second(slice: &[i32]) -> i32 {
    *unsafe { slice.get_unchecked(1) }
}
```

In this example, the crate won't compile if we add an unsafe scope outside the get_second() function. In any case, this function is not safe, as it will not check any bounds of the slice being sent to it; we should probably add an assert!(), or at least a debug_assert!(), to the length of the slice at the beginning of the function.

Unused lints

Let's face it, we sometimes forget to remove a dependency we are no longer using, or we forget that the write() method returns the number of bytes written. This usually is not a big deal. The first will simply make our compilation slower, while the second, in most cases, will simply not change our code.

But since we do not want to have unused dependencies, or we don't want to forget that we might not have written the whole buffer to a file, that's where the next lints come to help us. Let's start with the first one, the unused_extern_crates lint. This lint will mark the external crates that are not being used in our code. This can be useful to remove dependencies we are no longer using, so I usually configure it to warn while I'm starting the development and change it to forbid once my crates go to production or the dependencies are not changing in every commit.

The second lint you should know about is the unused_results lint. By default, the compiler will warn about unused results for Result<T, E> return values. That is an important detail because it could be that an I/O operation failed, for example, and you should act accordingly. There are other cases, though, where the Rust compiler won't warn, but that can be almost as dangerous as the previous ones. The Write and Read traits, for example, will return the number of bytes written and read, respectively, and you should probably be aware of that number.

This lint will make sure you always take into account any return value, except for the empty tuple (). This can sometimes be annoying, but you can explicitly discard a result by using the underscore binding, which is shown as follows:

```
#![warn(unused_results)]

fn main() {
    let _ = write_hello();
}
```

```
fn write_hello() -> usize {
    unimplemented!()
}
```

There are also a couple of lints that will make your code much more readable: `unused_qualifications` and `unused_import_braces`. The first will detect places where you are using extra qualifications for some elements:

```
#![warn(unused_qualifications)]

#[derive(Debug)]
enum Test {
    A,
    B,
}

fn main() {
    use Test::*;

    println!("{:?}", Test::A);
    println!("{:?}", B);
}
```

This example of code will warn us that in the first `println!()` we do not need to use the `Test::` qualification, as we are already importing all values inside the `Test` enumeration. The second `println!()` will not warn us since we are not specifying any extra qualifications. This will make the code more readable, potentially reducing errors.

The second lint, the `unused_import_braces` lint, will check for places where we are importing only one element with import braces:

```
#![warn(unused_import_braces)]

#[derive(Debug)]
enum Test {
    A,
    B,
}

#[derive(Debug)]
enum Test2 {
    C,
    D,
}

fn main() {
    use Test::{A, B};
```

```
    use Test2::{C};

    println!("{:?}, {:?}, {:?}", A, B, C);
}
```

Even though the Rust formatter will automatically remove the braces around the C variant of the `Test2` import, if we do not use the formatter, this is an interesting lint that will alert that we do not require those braces and that removing them we will make the code cleaner.

Variant size differences

As we saw in the previous chapters, the size of an enumeration will be the size of the biggest element plus the tag, but, as we discussed, this can be troublesome if we have many small variants and one has a bigger size: all variants will occupy the whole space for the biggest one. We saw that an option would be to move the big variant to a heap allocation.

We can detect enumerations with variants significantly bigger than the rest with the `variant_size_differences` lint. It will check for enumerations where a variant is at least three times bigger than the rest:

```
#![warn(variant_size_differences)]

enum Test {
    A(u8),
    B(u32),
}
```

 Note that it will not work for unions and that if we have middle-sized variants, even if the difference between the biggest one and the smallest one is more than three times, the lint will not alert us.

Lint groups

The Rust compiler lets us configure some of the aforementioned lints in groups. For example, the `unused` group will contain many of the `unused_` kind of lints. The `warnings` group will contain all the lints that have been configured to warn, and so on.

Lint groups can be used the same way as lints, by specifying what you want to happen when the compiler catches that behavior:

```
#[deny(warnings)]
```

You can check out the rest of the built-in lints by running `rustc -W help`. It will show the ones we have talked about and the other lints that are `warn` or `deny` by default.

Clippy

If there is a tool that will help you sanitize your code the most, it is Clippy. At the time of writing, Clippy provides 208 extra lints, most of them really useful to avoid interesting pitfalls such as the `unwrap_or()` usage that we discussed in Chapter 2, *Extra Performance Enhancements*, or to avoid non-idiomatic code. Of course, we will not see all of them here, and you will find a comprehensive list of all of them in the Clippy lint documentation at `https://rust-lang-nursery.github.io/rust-clippy/master/`.

Since many of them already warn or even deny by default, we will check some of the ones that are allowed by default but that could be really useful to improve the code quality of your application and even its performance.

Installation

Installing Clippy is pretty easy: you will need to install Rust nightly by running `rustup toolchain install nightly`, then you can install Clippy by running `cargo +nightly install clippy`.

Note that since Clippy requires a nightly compiler to build, and since it uses compiler intrinsics, some Rust nightly compiler updates make it unusable. Those issues are usually fixed in a couple of days and a new Clippy version gets released, but meanwhile, you can select a previous nightly version by appending a previous date to the nightly toolchain: `rustup toolchain install nightly-YYYY-MM-DD`.

Once the correct toolchain is installed, Clippy will be installed perfectly. To use it, you will need to go to your project and run `cargo clippy` instead of the usual `cargo check` or `cargo build` commands. This will run all Clippy lints and show you the results.

Configuration

Even if we will check individual lints in the next section, we will now see how we can configure the whole Clippy execution. Clippy will read the `clippy.toml` file at the same level as the `Cargo.toml` file and act accordingly.

Some lints have configuration parameters. For instance, the cyclomatic complexity lint will alert you whenever a function has more than 25 branches. As we saw in Chapter 1, *Common Performance Pitfalls*, this is bad practice, since it will make the optimizations of the code much harder for the compiler, creating less performant code.

However, you can change the threshold that creates the warning. 25 is a fair amount of branches, but depending on your product, you would prefer not to have more than 20 branches or to be able to have up to 30, for example. The setting that changes this behavior in the `clippy.toml` is the `cyclomatic-complexity-threshold`:

```
cyclomatic-complexity-threshold = 30
```

Clippy will also warn you, for example, when it finds names that could be the name of a structure or enumeration in the documentation without the proper (`` ` ``) characters showing that they are code. This can have false positives in cases such as your software being called `MyCompanyInc`, for example, where Clippy will think it's a `struct` or an `enum`. There is a configuration parameter for this case too. You can check all of them in the Clippy wiki at `https://rust-lang-nursery.github.io/rust-clippy/master/`.

If we want to add Clippy lints to our project, when we compile without Clippy, Rust will warn us that those lints are unknown. Of course, those have been defined by Clippy, but the compiler does not know this. Clippy sets a `cargo-clippy` feature by default, and when configuring the lints, we can use it to remove the unknown lints warning:

```
#![cfg_attr(feature = "cargo-clippy", forbid(deprecated))]
```

This way, when we run `cargo clippy`, the lint will be taken into account, but when running `cargo check`, it won't.

Lints

From those 208 lints currently available in Clippy, we will analyze only some of them that are configured as `allow` by default. The rest can be checked at the Clippy wiki at `https://rust-lang-nursery.github.io/rust-clippy/master/`, but you should take note of these ones, since they will not show an alert by default.

Casting

Casting numbers is sometimes a dangerous operation. We could lose precision, lose sign, truncate numbers, and so on. Clippy gives us some very useful lints that can avoid these situations. Of course, often you do not care about these behaviors since you might know they won't happen or they could be intended behavior.

Nevertheless, I have found these lints useful even if you only activate them on one occasion to check the places where these casts take place and set them to allow by default when usual testing.

The lints are the following:

- `cast_possible_truncation`
- `cast_possible_wrap`
- `cast_precision_loss`
- `cast_sign_loss`

Bad practice

Clippy also gives us lints that will detect bad coding practices. You should, for example, not import enumeration variants, since enumeration variants should always be prefixed with the actual enumeration. To lint against this practice, you can use the `enum_glob_use` lint.

Other code practices that might create issues are the panicking `From` and `Into` trait implementations. By definition, these traits must never fail, and using `unwrap()`, `expect()`, `panic!()`, or `assert!()` functions and macros can panic the function. This can be the desired behavior in an application, even though it's bad practice (you should use `TryInto` and `TryFrom` traits, or create a new function if developing with the stable compiler).

But the main issue is when developing software such as kernels that could cause the whole OS to panic. You can detect these issues by using the `fallible_impl_from` lint.

We talked about iterators in Chapter 1, *Common Performance Pitfalls*, and as we saw, we sometimes have useful functions to wrap `filter()` and `map()`. This improves readability, and concatenations of these functions can be detected by using the `filter_map` lint.

Sometimes, we write conditionals that might not be straightforward to understand, sometimes because we do negations in conditions with else branches or because we add lots of conditions that mess up our comparisons. We have two Clippy lints that will point out these situations: if_not_else and nonminimal_bool.

The first will detect a negation in a conditional, and suggest changing the condition to a positive one and changing the else and the if code sections. The second will check for Booleans that can be simplified to remove redundancy and clean up the code.

Some match statements can also be improved when there are only two branches and one of them does not require any parameters, such as when dealing with Option types. In this case, it's cleaner to change them for an if let expression with an else that will also reduce the indenting of the comparison. These points of failure can be shown by using the single_match_else lint.

Another interesting couple of lints will check for places where you might be adding 1 to an integer just to make comparisons or ranges inclusive. Let's see an example:

```
let max = 10;
for i in 0..max + 1 {
    println!("{}", i);
}
```

That code only adds 1 to be able to print the 10 too. You can create an inclusive range of nightly Rust by using an equals symbol after the two range periods (..=):

```
#![feature(inclusive_range_syntax)]

fn main() {
    let max = 10;
    for i in 0..=max {
        println!("{}", i);
    }
}
```

The lint that will point out this error is called range_plus_one, while the one that will detect comparisons such as a < b+1, that can be replaced by a <= b, is called int_plus_one.

There are also times where we might change the name of a variable or misspell it and break our code, even if it seems to compile. Other times, we might create variables with too similar names and end up mixing them up. This can be avoided by using the similar_names lint.

Another bad practice is to include the name of an enumeration in a variant of the enumeration, or a structure containing the name of the current module. Since names can be qualified, repetition is not required and adds a lot of text. This will be warned by default, but not in public APIs. You can control that with the `stutter` and the `pub_enum_variant_names` lints.

Finally, the same way the Rust compiler gave us a `missing_docs` lint that would point out missing public documentation, the `missing_docs_in_private_items` Clippy lint will do the same for private items. This is great to enforce documentation of the whole code base.

Performance lints

If you are reading this book, these two lints will probably be the ones you will find more important than the ones Clippy does not warn by default. The first is pretty simple: if you want to share an integer between threads, using a `Mutex` is a really bad idea if you do not need to use it as a synchronization variable.

Usually, things such as counters will be much faster by using atomic types. Only pointer-sized atomics and booleans are stable at the time of writing, but the rest are also coming and can now be used in nightly Rust. You can spot this issue with the `mutex_integer` lint.

Also, you might be tempted to use `std::mem::forget()` to enable sending data to C APIs, or to be able to do some strange memory tricks. This can be fine (even though it can lead to memory leaks), but can sometimes prevent running destructors. If you want to make sure that your `Drop` types never get forgotten, use the `mem_forget` lint.

If you are worried about infinite iterators that could hang your applications, you should use the `maybe_infinite_iter` lint, which will find those. It will not detect stopping conditions, so it could show too many false positives.

We might also find ourselves adding debug information when developing by using `print!()` macros and debug formatting. Once the application goes into production, a good way to avoid these logs staying in the code base is to use the `print_stdout` and `use_debug` lints.

Unwraps

Rust allows you to unwrap `Results` and `Options`, at the cost of panicking if they are `Err(_)` or `None` respectively. This should be avoided in any production code, and either use `expect()` to add an information message or use error chaining with the `?` operator, for example. You can also match them and control the error.

To avoid those unnecessary panics, you can use the `result_unwrap_used`, `option_unwrap_used`, `option_map_unwrap_or_else`, `option_map_unwrap_or`, and `result_map_unwrap_or_else` lints.

Shadowing

In Rust, you can shadow a variable by creating another `let` binding with the same name. This is usually okay, except when we maybe only wanted to mutate a variable, for example. In general, you should avoid this practice and only use it where it helps readability.

You can use the `shadow_unrelated`, `shadow_same`, and `shadow_reuse` lints and warn this behavior by default, then allow it for specific situations.

Integer overflow

Sometimes, when we do operations with integers, we do not take overflows, underflows, and wrappings into account. C will let you do this by default, while Rust will panic when running in debug mode. In release mode, though, these integer overflows can be a big problem.

You can use the `integer_arithmetic` lint that will suggest using one of the `wrapping_...()` or `saturating_...()` methods of the integer to make sure you know what the outcomes of the operation are.

Lint groups

There are two lint groups in Clippy. The `clippy` lint group will control all the lints that warn by default, and you can, for example, deny all of them. The `clippy_pedantic` group will control the rest of the lints as a group, but making all of them warn, for example, will make your compilation results full of warnings, due to false positives.

To use them, you simply need to use the group of lints as a lint:

```
#![deny(clippy)]
```

You can check the rest of the lints and configuration options in the Clippy wiki at `https://rust-lang-nursery.github.io/rust-clippy/master/`.

Summary

In this chapter, you learned how to configure the different lints that Rust and the Clippy tool give us. With them, you can get warnings of much more specific grain options that affect performance and code quality.

We covered the lints that you will not see by default, making your exploration journey much easier. In `Chapter 5`, *Profiling Your Rust Application*, we will learn about other tools; in this case, to profile your application and find performance bottlenecks that are not straightforward to see.

Profiling Your Rust Application

5

One of the elementary steps to understand why your application is going slower than expected is to check what your application is doing at a low level. In this chapter, you will understand the importance of low-level optimization, and learn about some tools that will help you find where your bottlenecks are.

In this chapter, you will learn about the following topics:

- How the processor works at low level
- CPU caches
- Branch prediction
- How to fix some of the most common bottlenecks
- How to use Callgrind to find your most-used code
- How to use Cachegrind to see where your code might be performing poorly in the cache
- Learn how to use OProfile to know where your program spends most of its execution time

Understanding the hardware

To understand what our software is doing, we should first understand how the compiled code is running in our system. We will, therefore, start with how the **Central Processing Unit (CPU)** works.

Understanding how the CPU works

The CPU is in charge of running the central logic of your application. Even if your application is a graphics application running most of its workload in the GPU, the CPU is still going to be governing all that process. There are many different CPUs, some faster than others for certain things, others that are more efficient and consume less power, sacrificing their computing power. In any case, Rust can compile for most CPUs, since it knows how they work.

But our job here is to figure out how they work by ourselves, since sometimes the compiler won't be as efficient at improving our machine code as we are. So, let's get to the center of the processing, where things get done.

The processor has a set of instructions it knows how to execute. We can ask it to perform any kind of instruction in that set, but we have a limitation: in most cases, it can only work with what's called a **register**. A register is a small location near the **arithmetic and logical unit (ALU)** inside the CPU. It can contain one variable, as big as the processor word size; nowadays, that is 64 bits most of the time, but it can be 32, 16, or even 8 in some embedded processors.

Those registers go as fast as the processor itself, so information can be modified in them without having to wait for anything (well, just for the actual instructions to execute). This is great; in fact, you might be wondering, why do we even need RAM if we have registers?

Well, the answer is simple: price. Having more registers in a CPU is very costly. You cannot have much more than a couple of dozen registers (in the best case scenario), since the processor wiring would get very complicated. Taking into account that for each instruction and register you will have dedicated data lines and control lines, this is very costly.

So, an external memory is required, one that can be freely accessed without requiring you to read all the memory sequentially, and still being very fast. **Random Access Memory (RAM)** is there for you. Your program will be loaded from RAM and will use RAM to store data that will need to be manipulated during the software execution. Of course, that software in RAM has to be loaded from the hard or solid state disk to RAM before being usable.

The main issue with RAM is that even if it's much, much faster than even the fastest SSD out there, it's still not as fast as the processor. The processor can execute tens of instructions while waiting for the RAM to get some data into one of the processor's registers to be able to operate with them. So, to avoid having the processor waiting every time it needs to load or store something in RAM, we have caches.

Speeding up memory access with the cache

The first level of cache, also known as the L1 cache, is a cache located almost as close as the registers to the ALU. The L1 cache is almost as fast as a register (about three times slower), and it has a very interesting property. Its internal structure can be represented as a lookup table. It will have two columns: the first will contain a memory address in the RAM, while the second will contain the contents of that memory address. When we need to load something from the RAM to a register, if it's already in the L1 cache, it will be almost immediate.

And not only that, this cache is usually divided in two very differentiated areas: the data cache and the instructions cache. The first will contain information about variables that the program is using, while the second will contain the instructions the program will execute. This way, since we know how the program is being executed, we can preload the next instructions in the instructions cache and execute them without having to wait for the RAM. In the same way, since we know what variables will be required in the execution of the program, we can preload them in the cache.

But this cache has some problems too. Even if it's three times slower than the processor, it is still too expensive. Also, there is not much physical space so close to the processor, so its size is limited usually to about 32 KiB. Since most software requires more than that size, and we want it to execute fast without having to wait for the RAM, we usually have a second level of cache, called the L2 cache, that also runs at the processor's clock speed, but being farther away from the L1 cache makes its signal arrives with a higher latency.

The L2 cache is thus almost as fast as the L1 cache and usually has up to 4 MiB of space. Instructions and data are combined. This is still not enough for many operations your software might do. Remember you will require all the data you are using, and in image processing, that might be millions of pixels with their value. So, for that, some high-end processors have an L3 cache in this case, farther away and with a slower clock, but still much faster than the RAM. Sometimes, this cache can be up to 32 MiB at the time of writing.

But still, we know that even in processors such as the Ryzen processors, with more than 40 MiB of combined caches, we will need more space. We have the RAM, of course, since in the end, the cache is just a copy of the RAM we have close to the processor for faster use. For every new piece of information, we will need to load it from RAM to the L3 cache, then the L2, then the L1, and finally a register, making the process slower.

For this, processors have highly complex algorithms programmed in pure silicon, in hardware, that are able to predict what memory locations are going to be accessed next, and preload the locations in bursts. This means that if the processor knows you will access variables stored from address 1,000 to 2,000 in the RAM, it will request the RAM to load the whole batch of the memory in the L3 cache, and when the time to use them approaches, the L2 cache will copy the data from the L3, and so will the L1 from the L2. When your program asks for that memory location's value, it will magically be in the L1 cache already, and be extremely fast to retrieve.

Cache misses

But how well does this work? Is it possible to have 100% efficiency? Well, no. Sometimes, your software will do something the processor wasn't built to predict, and the data will not be in the L1 cache. This means that the processor will ask the L1 cache for the data, and this L1 cache will see that it doesn't have it, losing time. It will then ask the L2, the L2 will ask the L3, and so on. If you are lucky, it will be on the second level of cache, but it might not even be on the L3 and thus your program will need to wait for the RAM, after waiting for the three caches.

This is what is called a cache miss. How often does this happen? Depending on how optimized your code and the CPU are, it might be between 2% and 5% of the time. It seems low, but when it happens, the whole processor stops to wait, which means that even if it doesn't happen many times, it has a huge performance impact, making things much slower. And as we saw, it's not only the loss of time of having to wait for the slower storage, it's also the lookup time in the previous storage that is lost, so in cache misses, it would have been faster to just ask the RAM directly (if the value wasn't in any cache).

How can you fix it?

It is not easy to fix this situation. Cache misses happen sometimes because you use big arrays only once, for example, in scenarios such as video buffers. If you are streaming some data, it might happen that the data is not yet in the cache and that it will no longer be used after using it once. This creates two problems. First, the time you need it, it's still in some area of the RAM, creating a cache miss. And second, once you load it into the cache, it will occupy most of the cache, forgetting about other variables you might require and creating more cache misses. This last effect is called **cache pollution**.

The best way to avoid this kind of behavior is to use smaller buffers, but this creates other problems, such as the data requiring constant buffering, so you will need to see what is best for your particular situation. If it's not caused by buffers, it might be that you are creating too many variables and only use them once. Try to find out whether you can reuse information, or whether you can change some executions for loops. But be careful, since some loops can affect branch prediction, as we will see later.

Cache invalidation

There is another big issue with caches, called **cache invalidation**. Since, usually, in new processors, you use multithreaded applications, it sometimes happens that one thread changes some information in memory and that the other threads need to check it. As you might know, or as you will see in Chapter 10, *Multithreading*, Rust makes this perfectly safe at compile time. Data races won't happen, but it won't prevent cache invalidation performance issues.

A cache invalidation happens in the case that some information in the RAM gets changed by another CPU or thread. This means that if that memory location was cached in any L1 to L3 caches, somehow it will need to be removed from there, since it will have old values. This is usually done by the storage mechanism. Whenever a memory address gets changed, any cache pointing to that memory address gets invalidated. This way, the next instruction trying to read the data from that address will create a cache miss, thus making the cache refresh and get data from the RAM.

This is pretty inefficient, in any case, since every time you change a shared variable, that variable will require a cache refresh in the rest of the threads it gets used. In Rust, for that, you will be using an Arc. To try to avoid this kind of performance pitfall, you should try to share as little as possible between threads, and if messages have to be delivered to them, it might sometimes make sense to use structures in the std::sync::mpsc module, as we will see in Chapter 10, *Multithreading*.

CPU pipeline

Instruction sets get more and more complex, and processors have faster and faster clock speeds, which sometimes makes most CPU instructions require more than one clock tick to execute. This is usually because the CPU needs to first understand what instruction is being executed, understand its operands, produce the meaningful signals to get those operands, perform the operations, and then save those operations. And no more than one step can be done per clock tick.

This is usually solved in processors by creating a CPU pipeline. This means that when a new instruction comes in, while that instruction gets analyzed and executed, the next instruction comes to the CPU to get analyzed. This has some complications, as you might imagine.

First, if an instruction requires the output of a previous instruction, it might need to sometimes wait for the result of another instruction. It might also sometimes happen that the instruction being executed is a jump to another place in the memory so that new instructions need to be fetched from the RAM and the pipeline needs to be removed.

Overall, what this technique achieves is to be able to execute one instruction per clock cycle in ideal conditions (once the pipeline is full). Most new processors do this, since it enables much faster execution without requiring a clock speed improvement, as we can see in this diagram:

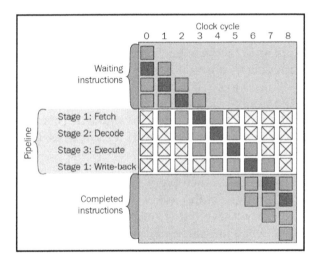

Another extra benefit from this approach is that dividing the instruction processing makes each step easier to implement, and not only that. Since each section will be physically smaller, electrons at light speed will be able to synchronize the whole step circuit in less time, making it possible for the clock to run faster.

In any case, though, dividing each instruction execution into more steps increases the complexity of the CPU wiring, since it has to fix potential concurrency issues. In the event that an instruction requires the output of the previous one to work, four different things can happen. As a first, and bad, option, it could happen that the behavior gets undefined. This is not what we want, and fixing this complicates the wiring of the processor.

The most important wiring piece to fix this is to first detect it. This on its own will make the wiring more complex. Once the CPU can detect the potential issue, the easiest fix is to simply wait for the output without advancing the pipeline. This is called **stalling**, and will hurt the performance of the CPU, but it will work properly.

Some processors will handle this by adding some extra input paths that will contain previous results, in case they need to be used, but this will greatly increase the complexity of the pipeline. Another option would be to detect some safety instructions and make them run before the instruction that requires the output of the previous one. This last option is called **out of order execution** and will also increase the complexity of the CPU.

So, in conclusion, to improve the speed of a CPU, apart from making its clock run faster, we have the option to create a pipeline of instructions. This will make it possible to run one instruction per clock tick (ideally) and sometimes even increase the clock speed. It will increase the complexity of the CPU, though, making it much more expensive.

And what are the pipelines of current processors like, you might ask? Well, they come in different lengths and behaviors, but in the case of some high-end Intel chips, pipelines can be larger than 30 steps. This will make them run really fast, but greatly increase their complexity and price.

When you develop applications, a way to avoid slowing down the pipeline will be to try to perform operations that do not require previous results first, and then use the generated results, even though this, in practice, is very difficult to do, and some compilers will actually do it for you.

Branch prediction

There is one situation that we didn't see how to solve, though. When our processor receives a conditional jump instruction, depending on the current state of the processor flags, the next instruction to execute will be one or another. This means that we cannot anticipate some instructions and load them into the pipeline. Or can we?

There are multiple ways of somehow predicting what code will be run next without doing the computation of the last instructions. The simplest way, and one used in old processors, was to statically decide which branches will load the next instructions and which will load instructions at the jump address.

Some processors would do that by deciding that some type of instructions were more likely to jump than others. Other processors would look into the jump address. If the address was lower, they would load the instructions at the target address into the pipeline, if not, they would load the ones at the next address. For example, in loops, it's much more likely to loop back to the beginning of the loop more times than continuing the flow of the program.

In both preceding cases, the decision was made statically, when developing the processor, and the actual program execution wouldn't change the way pipeline loading would work. A much-improved approach, a dynamic one, was to count how many times the processor would jump for a given conditional jump.

The first time the processor gets to the branch, it won't know whether the code will jump or not, so it will probably load the next instruction to the pipeline. If it jumps, the next instruction will be canceled and new instructions will be loaded in the pipeline. This will make the processor wait for as many cycles as the pipeline has stages.

In this old method, we would have put the counter of jumps for those instructions to 1, and the counter of no jumps to 0. The next time the program gets to the same jump, seeing the counter, the processor will start loading the instructions that come from the jump into the pipeline, instead of the next instructions.

Once the calculation has been done, if the processor actually needs to jump, it already has the instructions in the pipeline. If not, it will need to load the next instructions into it. In both cases, the respective counter would go up by 1.

This means that, for example, in a long `for` loop, the jump counter will increase to a high number, since it will, most of the time, have to jump back to the beginning of the loop, and only after the last iteration will it continue the flow of the application. This means that for all except the first and the last iteration, there will be no empty pipeline and the branch will be predicted properly.

These counters are actually a bit more complex since they would saturate at 1 or 2 bits, meaning that the counter could indicate whether the last time the branch was taken or not, or how sure the processor was that the next time the branch would be taken. The counter could be 0, if it usually never takes the branch, 1, if it might take it, 2, if it many times takes the branch or 3 if it takes it almost always. This means that a branch that gets taken only some of the time will have a better prediction. Some benchmarks have shown that the accuracy can be as high as 93.5%.

It's amazing how a simple counter will make branch prediction much more efficient, right? Well, of course, this has big limitations. In code, that branching depends on some condition, but where patterns can be seen (an `if` condition that returns true on almost every second call, for example), counters will fail enormously, since they will have no clue of the pattern.

For this kind of behavior, complex adaptive prediction tables get used. It will store the last *n* occurrences of the `jump` instruction in a table, and see whether there is a pattern. If there is, it will group the outcomes in groups of the number of elements in the pattern, and better predict this kind of behavior. This increases the accuracy up to 97% in some cases.

There are many different branch prediction techniques, and depending on the pipeline size, it will make more sense to use more complex predictors or simpler ones. If the processor has a 30-stage pipeline, failing to predict a branch will end up in a 30-cycle delay for the next instruction. If it has 2 stages, it will only lose 2 cycles. This means that more complex and expensive pipelines will also require more complex and expensive branch predictors.

The relevance of branch prediction for our code

This book is not about creating processors, so you might think that all this branch prediction theory does not make sense for our use case of improving the efficiency of our Rust code. But the reality is that this theory can make us develop more efficient applications.

First, knowing that patterns in conditional execution will probably be detected after two passes by new and expensive processors will make us try to use those patterns if we know that our code will be mainly used by newer processors. On the other hand, if we know that our code will run in a cheaper or older processor, we might optimize its execution by maybe writing the result of the pattern condition sequentially if possible (in a loop) or by trying to group conditions in other ways.

Also, we have to take into account compiler optimizations. Rust will often optimize loops to the point of copying some code 12 times if it knows it will always be executed that number of times, to avoid branching. It will also lose some optimization prediction if we have many branches in the same code generation unit (a function, for example).

This is where Clippy lints such as **cyclomatic complexity** enter into play. They will show as functions where we are adding too many branches. This can be fixed by dividing such functions into smaller ones. The Rust compiler will better optimize the given function, and if we have link-time optimizations enabled, it might even end up in the same function, in the end, making the processor branchless.

We shouldn't completely rely on hardware branch prediction, especially if our code is performance-critical, and we should develop taking into account how the processor will optimize it too. If we know for sure which processor will be running our code, we might even decide to learn the branch prediction techniques of the processor from the developer manual and write our code accordingly.

Profiling tools

You might be wondering how we will detect bottlenecks such as these ones in our application. We all know that not all developers will take such low-level details into account, and even if they do, they might forget to do it in some critical code that the program needs to run many times in a row. We cannot check the whole code base manually but, fortunately, there are some profiling tools that will give us information about our software.

Valgrind

Let's first start with a tool that will help you find where your software spends more time. **Valgrind** is a tool that helps to find bottlenecks. Two main tools inside Valgrind will give us the statistics we need to find out where to improve our code. It's included in most Linux distributions. There are Windows alternatives, but if you have access to a Linux machine (even if it's a virtual one), Valgrind will really make the difference when getting results.

The easiest way to use it is to use `cargo-profiler`. This tool is in `crates.io`, but it's no longer updated, and the version in GitHub has some much-needed fixes. You can install it by running the following command:

```
cargo install --git https://github.com/kernelmachine/cargo-profiler.git
```

Once installed, you can use it by running `cargo profiler callgrind` or `cargo profiler cachegrind`, depending on the Valgrind tool you want to use. Nevertheless, `cargo-profiler` does not compile with source annotations by default, so it might make sense to use the `cargo rustc` command to compile with a -g flag, and then run Valgrind directly in those binaries:

```
cargo rustc --release --bin {binary_name} -- -g
```

Callgrind

Callgrind will show statistics about the most-used functions in your program. To run it, you will need to run `cargo profiler callgrind {args}`, where `args` are the arguments to your executable. There is an interesting issue here though. Rust uses `jemalloc` as the default allocator, but Valgrind will try to use its own allocator to detect calls. There is a way to use Valgrind's allocator, but it will only work in nightly Rust.

You will need to add the following lines to your `main.rs` file:

```
#![feature(alloc_system)]
extern crate alloc_system;
```

This will force Rust to use the system allocator. You might need to add `#![allow(unused_extern_crates)]` to the file so that it doesn't alert you for an unused crate. An interesting flag for Valgrind is `-n {num}`. This will limit the results to the `num` most relevant ones. In the case of Callgrind, it will only show the most-used functions. An optional `--release` flag will tell `cargo profiler` if you want to profile the application in release mode instead of doing it in debug mode.

Let's see an output of the Callgrind tool:

```
[razican@laptop super]$ cargo profiler callgrind -n 20 --release mmanager

Compiling super-analyzer in release mode...

Profiling super-analyzer with callgrind...

Total Instructions...2,295,834,932

193,169,402 (8.4%) ???:__memcpy_avx_unaligned_erms
-------------------------------------------------------------
170,265,249 (7.4%) ???:regex::dfa::Fsm
-------------------------------------------------------------
124,701,782 (5.4%) lib.rs:abxml::visitor::Executor
-------------------------------------------------------------
117,346,136 (5.1%) ???:<regex::pikevm
-------------------------------------------------------------
116,132,541 (5.1%) ???:abxml::visitor::Executor
-------------------------------------------------------------
104,604,710 (4.6%) ???:sha1::Sha1State
-------------------------------------------------------------
100,475,629 (4.4%) lib.rs:regex::dfa::Fsm
-------------------------------------------------------------
98,810,150 (4.3%) lib.rs:regex::exec::ExecNoSync
-------------------------------------------------------------
97,010,957 (4.2%) ???:sha2::sha256_utils
```

Let's analyze what this means. I only selected the top functions, but we can already see lots of information. The most-used function is a system call for a memory copy. This means that this program is copying lots of data in memory between one position and another. Fortunately, at least it uses an efficient system call, but maybe we should check whether we need so much copying for its job.

The second most-used function is something called `Executor` in the `abxml` module/crate. You might think the `regex` reference is more used because it's in the second position, but the `Executor` seems to be divided since it seems that some of the references lost their initial `lib.rs` (third and fifth elements seem the same). It seems that we use that function a lot, or that at least it's taking most of our CPU time.

We should ask ourselves if this is normal. Should it spend so much time on that function? In the case of this program, the SUPER Android Analyzer (`http://superanalyzer.rocks/`), it uses that function to get the resources of the application. It makes sense that most of the time it would be actually analyzing the application instead of decompressing it (and in fact, we are not being shown the use of a Java dependency that takes 80% of the time). But it seems that the decompression of the resources of the `apk` file takes a lot of time.

We could check if there is something that could be optimized in that function or in descendant functions. It makes sense that if we could optimize 10% of that function, we would gain a lot of speed in the application.

Another option would be to check our regular expression usage, as we can see that many instructions are used to check regular expressions and compile them. An improvement in the regular expression engine would also make a difference.

We finally see that the SHA-1 and SHA-256 algorithm execution take a lot of time too. Do we need them? Could they be optimized? Maybe by using the native algorithm implementations often found in newer processors, we could speed up the execution. It might make sense to create a pull request in the upstream crate.

As you can see, Callgrind gives us tons of valuable information about the execution of our program, and we can at least see where it makes sense to spend time trying to optimize the code. In this particular case, hashing algorithms, regular expressions, and resource decompression take most of the time; we should try to optimize those functions. On the other hand, for example, one of the lesser-used functions is the XML emitter. So even if we find out how to optimize that function by 90%, it won't really make a difference. If it's an easy optimization, we can do it (better something than nothing), but if it will take us a long time to implement, it probably makes no sense to do it.

Cachegrind

We have talked at length about caches in this chapter, but is there a way to see how our application is performing in this sense? There actually is. It's called **Cachegrind**, and it's part of Valgrind. It's used in the same way as Callgrind, with `cargo profiler`. In the case of the same preceding application, the `cargo profiler` failed to parse Cachegrind's response, so I had to run Valgrind directly, as you can see in the following screenshot:

```
[razican@laptop super]$ valgrind --tool=cachegrind target/release/super-analyzer mmanager
==3735== Cachegrind, a cache and branch-prediction profiler
==3735== Copyright (C) 2002-2017, and GNU GPL'd, by Nicholas Nethercote et al.
==3735== Using Valgrind-3.13.0 and LibVEX; rerun with -h for copyright info
==3735== Command: target/release/super-analyzer mmanager
==3735==
--3735-- warning: L3 cache found, using its data for the LL simulation.

Starting analysis of mmanager.
Application decompressed.
Jar file generated.
Application decompiled.
Results struct created.
Warning: Seems that the package in the AndroidManifest.xml is not the same as the application ID provided. Provided application id: mmanager
, manifest package: com.mmahillo.mmanager movil
If you need more information, try to run the program again with the -v flag.
Manifest analyzed.
Source code analyzed.

HTML report generated.
==3735==
==3735== I   refs:      2,295,958,721
==3735== I1  misses:          975,497
==3735== LLi misses:           21,855
==3735== I1  miss rate:         0.04%
==3735== LLi miss rate:         0.00%
==3735==
==3735== D   refs:      1,051,162,017  (677,839,058 rd   + 373,322,959 wr)
==3735== D1  misses:       22,599,328  ( 15,920,599 rd   +   6,678,729 wr)
==3735== LLd misses:          687,372  (    313,680 rd   +     373,692 wr)
==3735== D1  miss rate:          2.1% (        2.3%      +        1.8%   )
==3735== LLd miss rate:          0.1% (        0.0%      +        0.1%   )
==3735==
==3735== LL  refs:         23,574,825  ( 16,896,096 rd   +   6,678,729 wr)
==3735== LL  misses:          709,227  (    335,535 rd   +     373,692 wr)
==3735== LL miss rate:          0.0% (        0.0%      +        0.1%   )
```

This was my second or third run, so some information might have already been cached. But still, as you can see, 2.1% of the first-level data cache missed, which is not so bad, given that the second-level cache had that data most of the time (it only missed 0.1% of the time).

Instruction data was fetched properly at the level 1 cache almost all the time, except for 0.04% of the time. There was almost no miss at level 2. Cachegrind can also give us more valuable information with some flags though.

Using `--branch-sim=yes` as an argument, we can see how the branch prediction worked:

```
==4362== Branches:        447,186,237  (432,629,103 cond + 14,557,134 ind)
==4362== Mispredicts:      14,900,049  (  8,107,732 cond +  6,792,317 ind)
==4362== Mispred rate:           3.3% (        1.9%     +       46.7%   )
```

As we can see, 3.3% of the branches were not predicted properly. This means that an interesting improvement could be done if branches were more predictable, or if some loops were unrolled, as we saw previously.

This, by itself, tells us nothing about where we could improve our code. But using the tool creates a `cachegrind.out` file in the current directory. This file can be used by another tool, `cg_anotate`, that will show improved stats. Running it, you will see the various stats on a per-function basis, where you can see which functions are giving the cache more trouble, and go there to try to fix them.

In the case of SUPER, it seems that the resource decompress is giving more cache misses. It might make sense, though, since it's reading new data from a file and reading that data almost all the time from memory for the first time. But maybe we can check those functions and try to improve the fetching, by using buffers, for example, if they are not being used.

OProfile

OProfile is another great tool that can give us interesting information about our program. It's also only available for Linux, but you will find a similar tool for Windows too. Once again, if you can get a Linux partition to check this, your results will probably be more in line with what you will read next. To install it, install the `oprofile` package of your distribution. You might also need to install the generic Linux tools (`linux-tools-generic` in Ubuntu).

OProfile is not of much help without source annotations, so you should first compile your binary with them by using the following command:

```
cargo rustc --release --bin super-analyzer -- -g
```

You will need to be root to do the profiling, as it will directly get the kernel counters for it. Don't worry; once you profile the application, you can stop being root. To profile the application, simply run `operf` with the binary and the arguments to profile:

```
[root@laptop super]# operf target/release/super-analyzer mmanager
operf: Profiler started

Starting analysis of mmanager.
Application decompressed.
Jar file generated.
Application decompiled.
Results struct created.
Warning: Seems that the package in the AndroidManifest.xml is not the same as the application ID provided. Provided application id: mmanager
, manifest package: com.mmahillo.mmanager_movil
If you need more information, try to run the program again with the -v flag.
Manifest analyzed.
Source code analyzed.

HTML report generated.
* * * * WARNING: Profiling rate was throttled back by the kernel * * * *
The number of samples actually recorded is less than expected, but is
probably still statistically valid.  Decreasing the sampling rate is the
best option if you want to avoid throttling.

Profiling done.
```

This will create an `oprofile_data` directory in the current path. To make some sense from it, you can use the `opannotate` command. This will show a bunch of stats, with some of the source code present, with how much time the CPU spends in each place. In the case of our Android analyzer, we can see that the rule processing takes quite a lot of time:

```
              :       'check: for rule in rules {
  2 4.2e-04 :           if manifest.is_some() && rule.max_sdk().is_some() &&
              :               rule.max_sdk().unwrap() < manifest.as_ref().unwrap().min_sdk()
              :           {
              :               continue 'check;
              :           }
              :
              :           let filename = path.as_ref().file_name().and_then(|f| f.to_str());
              :
              :           if let Some(f) = filename {
  5   0.0011 :               if !rule.has_to_check(f) {
              :                   continue 'check;
              :               }
              :           }
              :
              :           for permission in rule.permissions() {
              :               if manifest.is_none() ||
              :                   !manifest
              :                       .as_ref()
              :                       .unwrap()
              :                       .permission_checklist()
              :                       .needs_permission(*permission)
              :               {
              :                   continue 'check;
              :               }
              :           }
              :
  1 2.1e-04 :           'rule: for m in rule.regex().find_iter(code.as_str()) {
              :               for white in rule.whitelist() {
```

In this case, this is probably reasonable. It makes sense that a piece of software that is supposed to analyze a file with rules would spend lots of time analyzing that file with those rules. But, nevertheless, it also means that in that code, we could find some optimization that could make a difference.

With OProfile, we could find some areas where the program is spending more time than it should. Maybe we would find a bottleneck in an unexpected area. That is why it's important to use these kinds of tools.

Summary

In this chapter, you learned how the processor really works. You understood the multiple hacks we have in the hardware so that everything runs much, much faster than it would if the CPU was always waiting for the RAM. You also got a grasp of the most common performance issues and some information on how to fix them.

Finally, you learned about the Callgrind, Cachegrind, and OProfile tools, which will help you find those bottlenecks so that you can fix them easily. They will even show where in your source code you can find the slowdowns.

In `Chapter 6`, *Benchmarking*, you will learn how to benchmark your application. It is especially interesting to compare it to other applications or to a previous version of your own application. You will learn how to spot changes that make your application slower.

6
Benchmarking

We have learned how to profile our application and how to find and fix the main bottlenecks, but there is another step in this process: checking whether our changes have improved the performance.

In this chapter, you will learn how to benchmark your application so that you can measure your improvements. This can meet two objectives: firstly, to check whether a new version of your application runs faster than an older version, and secondly, if you are creating a new application to solve a problem an existing application already solves, to compare the efficiency of your creation to the existing application.

In this context, you will learn about the following topics in this chapter:

- Selecting what to benchmark
- Benchmarking in nightly Rust
- Benchmarking in stable Rust
- Continuous integration for benchmarks

Selecting what to benchmark

Knowing whether your program improves efficiency for each change is a great idea, but you might be wondering how to measure that improvement or regression properly. This is actually one of the bigger deals of benchmarking since, if done properly, it will clearly show your improvements or regressions but, if done poorly, you might think your code is improving while it's even regressing.

Depending on the program you want to benchmark, there are different parts of its execution you should be interested in benchmarking. For example, a program that processes some information and then ends (an analyzer, a CSV converter, a configuration parser...), would benefit from a whole-program benchmark. This means it might be interesting to have some test input data and see how much time it takes to process it. It should be more than one set, so that you can see how the performance changes with the input data.

A program that has an interface and requires some user interaction, though, is difficult to benchmark this way. The best thing is to take the most relevant pieces of code and benchmark them. In the previous chapter, we learned how to find the most relevant pieces of code in our software. With profiling techniques, we can understand which functions and code pieces impact the execution of our application the most, so we can decide to benchmark those.

Usually, you will want to mostly have fine-grained benchmarks. This way, you will be able to detect a change in one of the small pieces of code that affect the overall performance of the application. If you have broader benchmarks, you might know that the overall performance of one part of the application has regressed, but it will be difficult to tell what in the code has made that happen.

In any case, as we will see later, having continuous integration for benchmarks is a good idea, creating alerts if a particular commit regresses the performance. It's also important for all benchmarks to run in as similar as possible environments. This means that the computer they are running on should not change from one run to the next, and it should be running only the benchmarks, so that the results are as real as possible.

Another issue is that, as we saw in the previous chapter, the first time we run something in a computer, things go slower. Caches have to be populated, branch prediction needs to be activated, and so on. This is why you should run benchmarks multiple times, and we will see how Rust will do this for us. There is also the option to warm caches up for some seconds and then start benchmarking, and there are libraries that do this for us.

So, for the rest of the chapter, you should take all this into account. Create small micro-benchmarks, select the most relevant sections of your code to benchmark, and run them in a known non-changing environment.

Also, note that creating benchmarks does not mean that you should not write unit tests, as I have seen more than once. Benchmarks will only tell you how fast your code runs, but you will not know whether it does it properly. Unit testing is out of the scope of this book, but you should test your software thoroughly before even thinking about benchmarking it.

Benchmarking in nightly Rust

If you search online for information on how to benchmark in Rust, you will probably see a bunch of guides on how to do it in nightly Rust, but not many on how to do it in stable Rust. This is because the built-in Rust benchmarks are only available on the nightly channel. Let's start by explaining how the built-in benchmarks work, so that we can then find out how to do it in stable Rust.

First of all, let's see how to create benchmarks for a library. Imagine the following small library (code in `lib.rs`):

```
//! This library gives a function to calculate Fibonacci numbers.

/// Gives the Fibonacci sequence number for the given index.
pub fn fibonacci(n: u32) -> u32 {
    if n == 0 || n == 1 {
        n
    } else {
        fibonacci(n - 1) + fibonacci(n - 2)
    }
}

/// Tests module.
#[cfg(test)]
mod tests {
    use super::*;

    /// Tests that the code gives the correct results.
    #[test]
    fn it_fibonacci() {
        assert_eq!(fibonacci(0), 0);
        assert_eq!(fibonacci(1), 1);
        assert_eq!(fibonacci(2), 1);
        assert_eq!(fibonacci(10), 55);
        assert_eq!(fibonacci(20), 6_765);
    }
}
```

As you can see, I added some unit tests so that we can be sure that any modifications we make to the code will still be tested, and checked that the results were correct. That way, if our benchmarks find out that something improves the code, the resulting code will be (more or less) guaranteed to work.

The `fibonacci()` function that I created is the simplest recursive function. It is really easy to read and to understand what is going on. The Fibonacci sequence, as you can see in the code, is a sequence that starts with 0 and 1, and then each number is the sum of the previous two.

As we will see later, recursive functions are easier to develop, but their performance is worse than iterative functions. In this case, for each calculation, it will need to calculate the two previous numbers, and for them, the two before, and so on. It will not store any intermediate state. This means that, from one calculation to the next, the last numbers are lost.

Also, this will push the stack to the limits. For each computation, two functions have to be executed and their stack filled, and, in each of them, they have to recursively create new stacks when they call themselves again, so the stack usage grows exponentially. Furthermore, this computation could be done in parallel since, as we discard previous calculations, we do not need to do them sequentially.

In any case, let's check how this performs. For this, we'll add the following code to the `lib.rs` file:

```
/// Benchmarks module
#[cfg(test)]
mod benches {
    extern crate test;
    use super::*;
    use self::test::Bencher;

    /// Benchmark the 0th sequence number.
    #[bench]
    fn bench_fibonacci_0(b: &mut Bencher) {
        b.iter(|| (0..1).map(fibonacci).collect::<Vec<u32>>())
    }

    /// Benchmark the 1st sequence number.
    #[bench]
    fn bench_fibonacci_1(b: &mut Bencher) {
        b.iter(|| (0..2).map(fibonacci).collect::<Vec<u32>>())
    }

    /// Benchmark the 2nd sequence number.
    #[bench]
    fn bench_fibonacci_2(b: &mut Bencher) {
        b.iter(|| (0..3).map(fibonacci).collect::<Vec<u32>>())
    }
```

```
/// Benchmark the 10th sequence number.
#[bench]
fn bench_fibonacci_10(b: &mut Bencher) {
    b.iter(|| (0..11).map(fibonacci).collect::<Vec<u32>>())
}

/// Benchmark the 20th sequence number.
#[bench]
fn bench_fibonacci_20(b: &mut Bencher) {
    b.iter(|| (0..21).map(fibonacci).collect::<Vec<u32>>())
}
}
```

You will need to add `#![feature(test)]` to the top of the `lib.rs` file (after the first comment).

Let's first understand why we created these benchmarks. We are testing how long it takes for the program to generate the numbers with index 0, 1, 2, 10, and 20 of the Fibonacci sequence. But, the issue is that if we directly provide those numbers to the function, the compiler will actually run the recursive function itself, and directly only compile the resulting number (yes, **Low Level Virtual Machine** (**LLVM**) does this). So, all benchmarks will tell us that it took 0 nanoseconds to calculate, which is not particularly great.

So, for each number we add an iterator that will yield all numbers from 0 to the given number (remember that ranges are non-inclusive from the right), calculate all results, and generate a vector with them. This will make LLVM unable to precalculate all the results.

Then, as we discussed earlier, each benchmark should run multiple times so that we can calculate a median value. Rust makes this easy by giving us the `test` crate and the `Bencher` type. The `Bencher` is an iterator that will run the closure we pass to it multiple times.

As you can see, the map function receives a pointer to the `fibonacci()` function that will transform the given `u32` to its Fibonacci sequence number. To run this, it's as simple as running `cargo bench`. And, the result is:

```
running 6 tests
test tests::it_fibonacci ... ignored
test benches::bench_fibonacci_0  ... bench:          19 ns/iter (+/- 0)
test benches::bench_fibonacci_1  ... bench:          19 ns/iter (+/- 0)
test benches::bench_fibonacci_10 ... bench:         931 ns/iter (+/- 120)
test benches::bench_fibonacci_2  ... bench:          24 ns/iter (+/- 2)
test benches::bench_fibonacci_20 ... bench:     115,248 ns/iter (+/- 6,402)

test result: ok. 0 passed; 0 failed; 1 ignored; 5 measured; 0 filtered out
```

So, this is interesting. I selected those numbers (0, 1, 2, 10 and 20) to show something. For the 0 and the 1 numbers the result is straightforward, it will just return the given number. From the second number onward, it needs to perform some calculations. For example, for the number 2, it's just adding the previous two, so there is almost no overhead. For the number 10 though, it has to add the ninth and the eighth, and for each of them, the eighth and the seventh, and the seventh and the sixth respectively. You can see how this soon gets out of hand. Also, remember that we discard the previous results for each call.

So, as you can see in the results, it gets really exponential for each new number. Take into account that these results are on my laptop computer, and yours will certainly be different, but the proportions between one another should stay similar. Can we do better? Of course we can. This is usually one of the best learning experiences to see the differences between recursive and iterative approaches.

So, let's develop an iterative `fibonacci()` function:

```
pub fn fibonacci(n: u32) -> u32 {
    if n == 0 || n == 1 {
        n
    } else {
        let mut previous = 1;
        let mut current = 1;
        for _ in 2..n {
            let new_current = previous + current;
            previous = current;
            current = new_current;
        }
        current
    }
}
```

In this code, for the first two numbers, we simply return the proper one, as before. For the rest, we start with the sequence status for the number 2 (0, 1, 1), and then iterate up to number n (remember that the range is not inclusive on the right). This means that for the number 2, we already have the result, and for the rest, it will simply add the two numbers again and again until it gets the result.

In this algorithm, we always remember the previous two numbers, so we do not lose information from one call to the next. We also do not use too much stack (we only need three variables for the number 2 onward and we do not call any function). So it will require less allocation (if any), and it should be much faster.

Also, if we give it a much bigger number, it should scale linearly, since it will calculate each previous number only once, instead of many times. So, how much faster is it?

```
running 6 tests
test tests::it_fibonacci ... ignored
test benches::bench_fibonacci_0   ... bench:              20 ns/iter (+/- 0)
test benches::bench_fibonacci_1   ... bench:              20 ns/iter (+/- 0)
test benches::bench_fibonacci_10  ... bench:              21 ns/iter (+/- 0)
test benches::bench_fibonacci_2   ... bench:              21 ns/iter (+/- 0)
test benches::bench_fibonacci_20  ... bench:             149 ns/iter (+/- 6)

test result: ok. 0 passed; 0 failed; 1 ignored; 5 measured; 0 filtered out
```

Wow! The results have really changed! We now see that, at least until the 10th number, the processing time is constant and, after that, it will only go up a little bit (it will multiply by less than 10 for calculating 10 more numbers). If you run `cargo test`, you will still see that the test passes successfully. Also, note that the results are much more predictable, and the deviation from test to test is much lower.

But, there is something odd in this case. As before, 0 and 1 run without doing any calculation, and that's why it takes so much less time. We could maybe understand that for the number 2, it will not do any calculations either (even though it will need to compare it to see if it has to run the loop). But, what happens with number 10?

In this case, it should have run the iteration seven times to calculate the final value, so it should definitely take more time than not running the iteration even once. Well, an interesting thing about the LLVM compiler (the compiler Rust uses behind the scenes) is that it is pretty good at optimizing iterative loops. This means that, even if it could not do the precalculation for the recursive loop, it can do it for the iterative loop. At least seven times.

How many iterations can LLVM calculate at compile time? Well, it depends on the loop, but I've seen it do more than 10. And, sometimes, it will unroll those loops so that if it knows it will be called 10 times, it will write the same code 10 times, one after the other, so that the compiler does not need to branch.

Does this defeat the purpose of the benchmark? Well, partly, since we no longer know how much difference it makes for the number 10, but for that, we have the number 20. Nevertheless, it tells us a great story: if you can create an iterative loop to avoid a recursive function, do it. You will not only create a faster algorithm, but the compiler will even know how to optimize it.

Benchmarking in stable Rust

Until now, we have seen how to benchmark our code using the nightly release channel. This is because Rust requires the `test` nightly feature for benchmarks to run. It's where the `test` crate and the `Bencher` types can be found. If you still want to be able to use the stable compiler for everything except benchmarks, you can put all your benchmarks in the `benches` directory. The stable compiler will ignore them for normal builds, but the nightly compiler will be able to run them.

But, if you really want to use the stable compiler to run benchmarks, you can use the `bencher` crate. You can find it in `crates.io`, and using it is really similar to using the built-in nightly benchmarks, since this crate is just a stable port of the benchmarking library.

To use it, you will need to first change the `Cargo.toml` file to make sure it looks like the following after the package metadata and dependencies:

```
[lib]
name = "test_bench"
path = "src/lib.rs"
bench = false

[[bench]]
name = "example"
harness = false

[dev-dependencies]
bencher = "0.1.4"
```

Here, we create a benchmark with an example name, and specify not to create a harness around it. Then, create the `benches/example.rs` file with the following content:

```
//! Benchmarks

#[macro_use]
extern crate bencher;
extern crate test_bench;
use test_bench::*;
use self::bencher::Bencher;

/// Benchmark the 0th sequence number.
fn bench_fibonacci_0(b: &mut Bencher) {
    b.iter(|| (0..1).map(fibonacci).collect::<Vec<u32>>())
}

/// Benchmark the 1st sequence number.
```

```
fn bench_fibonacci_1(b: &mut Bencher) {
    b.iter(|| (0..2).map(fibonacci).collect::<Vec<u32>>())
}

/// Benchmark the 2nd sequence number.
fn bench_fibonacci_2(b: &mut Bencher) {
    b.iter(|| (0..3).map(fibonacci).collect::<Vec<u32>>())
}

/// Benchmark the 10th sequence number.
fn bench_fibonacci_10(b: &mut Bencher) {
    b.iter(|| (0..11).map(fibonacci).collect::<Vec<u32>>())
}

/// Benchmark the 20th sequence number.
fn bench_fibonacci_20(b: &mut Bencher) {
    b.iter(|| (0..21).map(fibonacci).collect::<Vec<u32>>())
}

benchmark_group!(
    benches,
    bench_fibonacci_0,
    bench_fibonacci_1,
    bench_fibonacci_2,
    bench_fibonacci_10,
    bench_fibonacci_20
);
benchmark_main!(benches);
```

And, finally, remove the benchmark module. This will create a benchmark for each of the previous functions. The main difference is that you need to import the crate you are benchmarking, you do not add the #[bench] attribute to each function, and you use two macros to make the benchmark run. The benchmark_group! macro will create a group of benchmarks with the first argument for the macro as its name and with the given functions. The benchmark_main! macro will create a main() function that will run all the benchmarks.

Let's look at the results:

```
running 5 tests
test bench_fibonacci_0  ... bench:           33 ns/iter (+/- 0)
test bench_fibonacci_1  ... bench:           32 ns/iter (+/- 1)
test bench_fibonacci_10 ... bench:           72 ns/iter (+/- 3)
test bench_fibonacci_2  ... bench:           31 ns/iter (+/- 1)
test bench_fibonacci_20 ... bench:          215 ns/iter (+/- 5)

test result: ok. 0 passed; 0 failed; 0 ignored; 5 measured
```

As you can see, this approach does not give us beautiful colors and it adds some extra overhead to the native method, but the results are still equivalent. In this case, we can see that the 10th number will actually not be calculated at compile time. This is because, on stable Rust, using an external crate, the compiler is not able to compute everything at compile time. Still, it gives us really good information about how different each option's performance is.

Continuous integration for benchmarks

Once we know how to benchmark (and I will use the nightly way from now on), we can set up our continuous integration environment so that we can get alerts when a performance regression occurs. There are multiple ways of achieving something like this, but I will be using the Travis-CI infrastructure, some Bash, and a Rust library to do it.

Travis-CI integration

Let's first start by thanking the great work of Lloyd Chan and Sunjay Varma, who were the first to suggest this approach. You can find the code we will be using in Sunjay's blog (`http://sunjay.ca/2017/04/27/rust-benchmark-comparison-travis`). Nevertheless, it makes sense to check it, understand it, and see how it works.

The idea is simple: on Travis-CI builds, you can build against multiple Rust channels. When a pull request is received when building against the nightly channel, let's run all the benchmarks and then compare them to benchmarks we will run on the pull request target branch. Finally, output the comparison results in Travis-CI's build logs.

Let's start by configuring our Travis-CI build script. For that, we will need a `.travis.yml` file similar to the following one in our repository:

```
language: rust
dist: trusty # Use a little more updated system
os:
  - linux # Build for Linux
  - osx # Build also for MacOS X

# Run builds for all the supported trains
rust:
  - nightly
  - beta
  - stable
  - 1.16.0 # Minimum supported version
```

```
# Load travis-cargo
before_script:
  - export PATH=$PATH:~/.cargo/bin

# The main build
script:
  - cargo build
  - cargo package
  - cargo test

after_success:
  # Benchmarks
  - ./travis-after-success.sh
```

Let's see what this code does. First of all, if you never used Travis-CI for your continuous integration, you should know that the `.travis.yml` YAML file contains the build configuration. In this case, we tell Travis-CI that we want to build a Rust project (so that it sets up the compiler by itself) and we tell it that we want to build against nightly, beta, and stable release channels. I usually like to add the minimum supported Rust version, mostly to know when it breaks, so that we can advertise the minimum Rust compiler version in our documentation.

We then export the `cargo` binary path so that we can add `cargo` binaries by installing them in the build. This will be needed for the benchmark comparison script. Then, we tell Travis-CI to build the library/binary crate, we tell it to package it to check that a valid package will be generated, and we finally run all the unit tests. So far, nothing too different from a normal Travis-CI Rust build.

Things change once we get to the `after-success` section. We call a shell script that we haven't defined yet. This script will contain the logic of the benchmark comparison.

Before writing all the code, let's first learn about a library that will make things much easier for us. I'm talking about the `cargo-benchcmp`, `cargo` binary. This executable can read outputs from Rust benchmarks and compare them. To install it, you only need to run `cargo install cargo-benchcmp`. It also has some great command-line arguments that can help us get the output we want.

To get the results of a benchmark in a file, it's as simple as doing `cargo bench > file`. In this case, we will have two benchmarks, the *control* benchmark, a benchmark that we decide will be the reference; and a *variable* benchmark, the one we want to compare. Usually, a pull request will have the target branch as a control benchmark and the pull request branch as a variable benchmark.

Using the executable is as easy as running `cargo benchcmp control variable`. This will show a great output with a side-by-side comparison. You can ask the tool to filter the output a bit, since you probably don't want to see tens of benchmarks with really similar values, and you are probably interested in big improvements or regressions.

To see the improvements, add the `--improvements` flag to the command line and, to see the regressions, add the `--regressions` flag. You can also set up a threshold as a percentage, and benchmarks that change below that threshold won't show, to avoid non-changing benchmarks. For that, use the `--threshold {th}` syntax, where `{th}` is a number higher than 0 representing the percentage change that should be taken into account.

Now we understand this, let's see the code that will be in the `travis-after-success.sh` file:

```bash
#!/usr/bin/env bash

set -e
set -x

if [ "${TRAVIS_PULL_REQUEST_BRANCH:-$TRAVIS_BRANCH}" != "master" ]
&& [ "$TRAVIS_RUST_VERSION" == "nightly" ]; then
    REMOTE_URL="$(git config --get remote.origin.url)"

    # Clone the repository fresh...
    cd ${TRAVIS_BUILD_DIR}/..
    git clone ${REMOTE_URL} "${TRAVIS_REPO_SLUG}-bench"
    cd "${TRAVIS_REPO_SLUG}-bench"

    # Bench the pull request base or master
    if [ -n "$TRAVIS_PULL_REQUEST_BRANCH" ]; then
      git checkout -f "$TRAVIS_BRANCH"
    else # this is a push build
      git checkout -f master
    fi
    cargo bench --verbose | tee previous-benchmark
    # Bench the current commit that was pushed
    git checkout -f "${TRAVIS_PULL_REQUEST_BRANCH:-$TRAVIS_BRANCH}"
    cargo bench --verbose | tee current-benchmark

    cargo install --force cargo-benchcmp
    cargo benchcmp previous-benchmark current-benchmark
fi
```

Let's see what this script is doing. The `set -e` and `set -x` commands will simply improve how the commands are shown in Travis-CI build logs. Then, only for nightly, it will clone the repository in a new location. If it's a pull request, it will clone the base branch; if not, it will clone the master branch. Then, it will run benchmarks in both places and compare them using `cargo-benchcmp`. This will show the results in the build logs.

This script can, of course, be modified to suit any needs and, for example, use a different branch to the master branch as a default branch, or filter the output of the comparison, as we saw earlier.

Benchmark statistics with Criterion

If we want to know more about benchmark comparison, there is no better library than **Criterion**. It will generate statistics that you can use to compare benchmarks from multiple commits, and not only that, it will also enable you to show plots if you have `gnuplot` installed. It requires Rust nightly to run.

Let's see how to use it. First, you will need to add Criterion as a dependency in your `Cargo.toml` file and create a benchmarks file:

```
[dev-dependencies]
criterion = "0.1.1"

[[bench]]
name = "example"
harness = false
```

Then, you will need to create a benchmark. I will be using the Fibonacci function that we saw earlier to demonstrate the behavior. The way to declare the benchmarks is almost exactly the same as the Rust stable `bencher` crate. Let's write the following code in the `benches/example.rs` file:

```
//! Example benchmark.

#[macro_use]
extern crate criterion;
extern crate test_bench;

use criterion::Criterion;
use test_bench::fibonacci;

fn criterion_benchmark(c: &mut Criterion) {
    Criterion::default().bench_function("fib 20", |b| b.iter(||
```

```
        fibonacci(20)));
}

criterion_group!(benches, criterion_benchmark);
criterion_main!(benches);
```

If we now run `cargo bench`, we will see a similar output to this one (with the recursive version):

```
        Running target/release/deps/example-9b142967dfe3d030
Gnuplot not found, disabling plotting
Gnuplot not found, disabling plotting
Benchmarking fib 20
> Warming up for 3.0000 s
> Collecting 100 samples in estimated 5.1532 s
> Found 15 outliers among 99 measurements (15.15%)
  > 7 (7.07%) high mild
  > 8 (8.08%) high severe
> Performing linear regression
  >   slope [42.534 us 42.837 us]
  >    R^2  0.9607553 0.9601474
> Estimating the statistics of the sample
  >    mean [42.597 us 43.979 us]
  > median [42.342 us 42.495 us]
  >     MAD [167.25 ns 318.09 ns]
  >      SD [572.62 ns 5.5562 us]
```

As you can see, we get tons of information here. First, we see that Criterion warms the processor for three seconds so that it can load the caches and set up branch prediction. Then, it gets 100 measurements of the function, and it shows us valuable information about the sample.

We can see how much time it takes to run an iteration (about 42 microseconds), the mean and the median of the sample, the number of outliers (significantly different samples), and a slope with its R^2 function. Until now, it only gives some extra information regarding the benchmark. If you check the current directory, you will see that it created a `.criterion` folder, which stores previous benchmarks. You can even check the JSON data.

Let's run the benchmark again, by replacing the recursive function with the iterative function:

```
        Running target/release/deps/example-9b142967dfe3d030
Gnuplot not found, disabling plotting
Gnuplot not found, disabling plotting
Benchmarking fib 20
> Warming up for 3.0000 s
> Collecting 100 samples in estimated 5.0001 s
> Found 14 outliers among 99 measurements (14.14%)
  > 9 (9.09%) high mild
  > 5 (5.05%) high severe
> Performing linear regression
  >    slope [17.409 ns 17.527 ns]
  >      R^2  0.9658139 0.9647010
> Estimating the statistics of the sample
  >     mean [17.449 ns 17.565 ns]
  > median [17.367 ns 17.437 ns]
  >      MAD [69.862 ps 143.94 ps]
  >       SD [180.77 ps 419.19 ps]
fib 20: Comparing with previous sample
> Performing a two-sample t-test
  > H0: Both samples have the same mean
  > p = 0
  > Strong evidence to reject the null hypothesis
> Estimating relative change of statistics
  >     mean [-99.960% -99.959%]
  > median [-99.959% -99.959%]
  > mean has improved by 99.96%
  > median has improved by 99.96%
```

Wow! Lots more data! Criterion compared this new benchmark with the previous one and saw that there is strong evidence to reject that this improvement is just a statistical anomaly. The benchmarks have improved by 99.96%!

As you can see, Criterion gives us a better informative approach than the built-in benchmarks for statistical analysis. Running this tool once in a while will show us how the performance of our application changes.

The library allows for function comparison, graph creation, and more. It can be configured for each benchmark, so you will be able to fine-tune your results according to your needs. I recommend you check the official documentation of the project for further insights (https:/ /crates.io/crates/criterion).

To include this in your Travis-CI builds, it's as simple as modifying the previous shell script. Just call `cargo bench` instead of `cargo benchcmp` and make sure that you move the `.criterion` folder to where you run the benchmarks (since it downloads two repositories).

Summary

In this chapter, you learned how to benchmark your Rust application. You saw the different options and found out what was best for your particular needs. You also learned about some libraries that will help you compare the results of the benchmarks and even how to use them in your continuous integration environment.

For the next chapter, you will enter the world of metaprogramming by learning about Rust's macro system and the macros built in to the standard library.

7

Built-in Macros and Configuration Items

Now that we know how to improve our code efficiency, we can learn how to make it work on multiple platforms and how to make sure we take advantage of all possible native optimizations, while we make the code faster and easier to implement. Metaprogramming allows us to do all that with really easy code snippets, and you probably know some of these features.

In this chapter, you will learn how to use the following macros and configuration items built in with the compiler and the standard library:

- Attributes
- Crate features
- Macros
- Nightly functionality

Understanding attributes

Rust allows us to conditionally compile certain parts of the code depending on what we call attributes. These attributes can be applied to either complete crates/modules or to specific functions, scopes, or even structure fields or enumeration variants. We saw some examples when we talked about Clippy, but these attributes allow for so much more that we will now look at them in depth.

Let's first see how an attribute works. An attribute that you want to apply to the whole current module/crate will be written like this: `#![{attribute}]`. Ones that apply to the scope/function/field/variant next to it will be written like this: `#[{attribute}]`. Note that the first has the `!` symbol between the hash tag and the attribute.

You have probably seen attributes such as `#[macro_use]` or `#[derive(Debug)]` somewhere in some code. The first one will allow using macros from an external crate, while the second one will derive the `Debug` trait in the given structure or enumeration. Let's start by checking what can we avoid typing thanks to the derivation of traits.

Trait derivations

There are two types of trait derivations: built-in derives and custom derives. We will talk about the second ones in Chapter 9, *Creating Your Own Macros*, but let's see what deriving can help us achieve. Let's imagine the following structure:

```
struct MyData {
    field1: String,
    field2: u64,
}
```

It's recommended that every structure implements the `Debug` trait so that if, for example, we need to debug what is happening with some part of the code, we can use the `println!("{:?}", element);` syntax. It should show the contents of the fields, so we could imagine something like the following:

```
use std::fmt;

impl fmt::Debug for MyData {
    fn fmt(&self, f: &mut fmt::Formatter) -> fmt::Result {
        write!(
            f,
            "MyData {{ field1: \"{}\", field2: {} }}",
            self.field1, self.field2
        )
    }
}
```

This will print the field information. For example, suppose we have the following code:

```
fn main() {
    let data = MyData {
        field1: "This is my string".to_owned(),
        field2: 4402,
    };

    println!("Data: {:?}", data);
}
```

We will receive this output:

```
Data: MyData { field1: "This is my string", field2: 4402 }
```

This is good, since it enables us to get information about our structure, but it's difficult to maintain and adds a lot of boilerplate code to our code base. Let's suppose we have a 20-field structure, and we need to remove 2 fields, and add 4 new ones. This rapidly escalates to a big mess. We will need to modify the trait implementation, maybe change the order of the fields, and so on.

This is where the `#[derive]` attribute comes into play: it will write that code for us, and if we change our structure it will rewrite that code. And, even better, it will not pollute our code base, since that code will be written at compile time. The whole `Debug` trait implementation can be replaced by adding `#[derive(Debug)]` to the beginning of the structure:

```
#[derive(Debug)]
struct MyData {
    field1: String,
    field2: u64,
}
```

And, if we run the program again, we will see that nothing has changed. There are multiple traits that can be derived: comparison traits (`PartialEq`, `Eq`, `PartialOrd`, and `Ord`), `Copy`, `Clone`, `Hash`, `Default` and, as we saw, `Debug`. Let's see what each of these traits does. We already talked about the `Debug` trait, so let's start with comparison traits.

The first two derivable traits are `PartialEq` and `Eq`. Both of them make it possible to use the `==` and the `!=` operators with the structure, but how do they work?

`PartialEq` is meant to describe a partial equivalence relation, which means that if *A* is partially equal to *B*, *B* is partially equal to *A*, and if, in that example, *B* is partially equal to *C*, *A* is also partially equal to *C*, since the property is symmetric and transitive.

When derived for structures or enumerations, it will only be available if all members of the structure or enumeration already implement PartialEq, and it will consider two structures or enumerations equal if all of their fields are equal.

The Eq trait requires an extra condition, and it cannot be checked at compile time. It requires that *A* is equal to *A*. This might sound strange if we are talking about structures with simple fields, but there is a simple type in the standard library that shows the opposite behavior. The floating point types (f32 and f64) do not respect this when they are **NaN** (**Not a Number**). Two NaN are not equal, even if both of them are NaN.

To derive the Eq trait, it requires all the fields in the structure or enumeration to implement Eq. This means that you will not be able to implement Eq for any structure or enumeration containing a floating point number. This trait does not require any method implementation, it just tells the compiler that the structure or enumeration is always equal to itself, without any extra code.

The next two traits, PartialOrd and Ord, work similarly to PartialEq and Eq, but they add the ability to compare two elements to know their order, so it allows you to use the <, <=, => and > operators with the structure or enumeration. Both require that if *A* < *B* and *B* < *C*, then *A* < *C* (and the same for == and >), and that if *A* > *B*, then *A* < *B* is false. The Ord trait also requires that one and only one of *A* < *B*, *A* == *B*, or *A* > *B* is true.

As an extra point of information, the PartialOrd trait adds a partial_cmp() function, while the Ord trait adds the cmp() function. Both return an Ordering, but for the first function, it is optional (Option<Ordering>) and for the second one, it is mandatory. This is because a partial comparison could not have any defined order for a particular value; remember the NaN case for floats.

Implementing this function for structures that contain only PartialOrd or Ord fields is pretty easy: define which is the most relevant field for ordering and compare them between structures, then, if equal, compare the next relevant field. This can be avoided by using #[derive(PartialOrd)] or #[derive(PartialOrd, Ord)].

The derivation will compare fields from first to last, so make sure you put the most relevant fields first. In the case of enumerations, it will consider first variants *smaller* than latest variants. If you want to change that, you can either change the order of fields or variants, or implement the trait yourself. You might also want to only compare one of the fields of a structure and consider the rest irrelevant. In this case, you will need to implement the trait yourself.

To implement any of these traits, you can simply compare the fields one by one. Note that Ord requires Eq, so we need to implement PartialEq to check only the day, month, and year and then derive Eq. You can check the details of the implementation as follows:

```
use std::cmp::Ordering;

#[derive(Eq)]
struct DateNotes {
    day: u8,
    month: u8,
    year: i32,
    comment: String,
}

impl PartialEq for DateNotes {
    fn eq(&self, other: &Self) -> bool {
        self.day == other.day && self.month == other.month &&
self.year == other.year
    }
}

impl Ord for DateNotes {
    fn cmp(&self, other: &Self) -> Ordering {
        match self.year.cmp(&other.year) {
            Ordering::Equal => match self.month.cmp(&other.month) {
                Ordering::Equal => self.day.cmp(&other.day),
                o => o,
            },
            o => o,
        }
    }
}

impl PartialOrd for DateNotes {
    fn partial_cmp(&self, other: &Self) -> Option<Ordering> {
        Some(self.cmp(other))
    }
}
```

In this example, we compare the date by first checking the year. If the year is the same, we compare the month, and if the month is equal, we compare the day. We do not check which comments are associated to the date because we do not need to. The PartialOrd trait implementation only returns the result from the Ord trait wrapped in an Option::Some.

The next two, the `Copy` and `Clone` traits, allow for a structure to be copied in memory. This means that you will be able to copy, one by one, all the contents of the instance to another instance. The `Clone` trait enables this by adding the `clone()` method, which usually only calls the `clone()` method of each of the fields. It can run any arbitrary code, though, and you never know whether it will be expensive to clone the object or not. This is why using it requires an explicit call to the `clone()` method.

The `Copy` trait, on the other hand, makes it implicit to copy one element. It means that, for example, when moving a variable to a function, if it's a `Copy` variable, you will be able to still use it after the move, because only a copy of it will be moved. We saw some examples of the benefits and drawbacks of this approach in `Chapter 1`, *Common Performance Pitfalls*.

You cannot implement the `Copy` trait, though, since Rust requires it to be extremely inexpensive and it's implemented using compiler intrinsics. So, you can safely use a `Copy` type knowing it will not be expensive to copy it, but you cannot implement it by yourself. You can derive it though. Deriving `Copy` for a structure or an enumeration requires the structure or enumeration to implement `Clone` (you can derive it too if all elements inside implement `Clone`) and all elements inside to implement `Copy`.

So, you can derive `Copy` for a structure with basic types such as the following:

```
#[derive(Clone, Copy)]
struct MyData {
    field1: u64,
    field2: f64,
    field3: i32,
}
```

But, you cannot derive it for structures with complex non-copyable types:

```
#[derive(Clone)]
struct MyData {
    field1: String,
    field2: Vec<u32>,
    field3: i32,
}
```

You can derive `Clone` in most cases, though, since most of the standard library types implement it. But, remember that the `clone()` method is usually expensive and should not be used too much. In fact, it's commonly said that if you use the `clone()` method directly, you are probably doing something wrong, and in most cases, it's true that other methods, such as `to_owned()` or `into()`, will do the trick more efficiently.

`to_owned()` will get the owned version of a variable, which in slices and strings means only to `memcpy()` the heap. The `into()` method, on the other hand, will use the specialized conversion implementation so that it produces the best output code. Both of them will change the type of the variable. Finally, `clone()` is usually generic, which means it will call `clone()` for each of its member attributes, making it slower sometimes.

Let's now talk about the `Hash` trait. This trait enables the use of the given structure or enumeration as a key in hashed structures such as `HashMap`. It gives us the possibility to hash the structure with a `Hasher` to get a hash of the information contained. A `Hasher` is a trait that receives input such as bytes or numbers, and once you call `finish()` on it, it will return a `u64` with the hash value.

Since `Hasher` is a trait, implementation details are not provided by the trait itself, but as we saw in `Chapter 2`, *Extra Performance Enhancements*, some default implementations are provided in the standard library: `SipHasher`, `SipHasher13`, `SipHasher24`, and `DefaultHasher`. We have already seen some differences between them.

The main idea behind the `Hash` trait is that it enables hashing any structure and does not limit `HashMap` keys, for example, to be bytes or numbers. You could implement the trait yourself for your structure (if you want to fine-tune how the hashing is done), but if what you want is to simply be able to use your structure or enumeration as a key in a `HashMap`, you can simply derive the `Hash` trait and the compiler will write that code for you.

Not only that, you will probably want to also implement the `Eq` trait for it since, for `HashMap` keys, it's required. If you implement it yourself, you will need to make sure that if $A = B$ then *hash(A) = hash(B)*, which might not be trivial. The best thing is to simply derive both. Let's check this example code with the structure we defined earlier:

```
use std::collections::HashMap;

#[derive(Clone, Hash, PartialEq, Eq)]
struct MyData {
    field1: String,
    field2: Vec<u32>,
    field3: i32,
}

fn main() {
    let key1 = MyData {
        field1: "myField".to_owned(),
        field2: vec![0, 1, 2],
        field3: 1898,
```

```
    };

    let key2 = key1.clone();

    let key3 = MyData {
        field1: "myField2".to_owned(),
        field2: vec![5, 3, 1],
        field3: 2345,
    };

    let mut map = HashMap::new();
    map.insert(key1, "MyFirst");

    assert!(map.get(&key2).is_some());
    assert!(map.get(&key3).is_none());
}
```

Here, we first derive Hash, PartialEq, and Eq in the MyData structure, then we create two identical keys and a different one. I used clone for easier understanding, but creating another one with the same values would work too. We add a value to the map using the first key and check whether we can retrieve the element with the clone of the key without any issues. If we try with a different key, though, we won't be able to get the value. You can also check that if the MyData structure does not implement Eq or Hash, you won't be able to use the HashMap with it as a key.

As before, the only requirement for a structure to derive Hash is that all of its members already implement it, and most of the standard library types implement Hash. The default implementation will simply hash all attributes one by one with the given Hasher, which is what you would probably implement manually. An example of this implementation could be the following:

```
use std::hash::{Hash, Hasher};

impl Hash for MyData {
    fn hash<H>(&self, state: &mut H)
    where
        H: Hasher,
    {
        self.field1.hash(state);
        self.field2.hash(state);
        self.field3.hash(state);
    }
}
```

As you can see, it's simple code, but you will keep everything cleaner and easier to maintain if you derive it. Implementing it yourself, though, can help you deal with fields that do not implement `Hash`, custom hashing techniques or avoiding some fields to be hashed for a little better performance if the comparison of the structure is still valid without taking them into account.

Finally, the last trait that you can derive out of the box with Rust is the `Default` trait. This trait gives the structure, or enumeration, a `default()` method that will create a structure with default values. These default values are, for example, 0 for numbers, empty strings for strings, empty vectors for vectors, and so on. It's usually used as a placeholder for future calculations.

If you have a structure where you would like to have a default value, you can implement the `Default` trait. And, doing it can be as simple as giving a value to each of the attributes. If you don't need particular default value (all zeros is OK with you), you will probably prefer to simply derive the `Default` trait. Let's check an example with the `MyData` structure:

```
#[derive(Debug, Default)]
struct MyData {
    field1: String,
    field2: Vec<u32>,
    field3: i32,
}

fn main() {
    let test1 = MyData {
        field1: "sth".to_owned(),
        ..Default::default()
    };
    let test2 = MyData::default();

    println!("test1: {:?}", test1);
    println!("test2: {:?}", test2);
}
```

As you can see, I derived the `Default` trait (and the `Debug` trait, just to print the structure). This allows to create the `test2` variable by only calling `MyData::default()`. You can also call `Default::default()` if you give a type hint for the variable:

```
let test3: MyData = Default::default();
```

As you can see, if some fields of a structure implement `Default`, you can use the trait to complete the fields you don't want to specify, as you can see with the `test1` variable. Simply specify the non-default fields, and then, after the last comma, add a couple of periods (`..`) and then `Default::default()`, so that the compiler uses the `Default` trait to fill the other fields. You can use any function that is generic over the rest of the fields with this syntax.

As you can see, the `Default` trait is a pretty useful trait and if you don't need any special treatment of any field for the default value of your structure, deriving it is a great idea. A potential implementation that you would be avoiding by doing this is the following:

```
impl Default for MyData {
    fn default() -> Self {
        Self {
            field1: Default::default(),
            field2: Default::default(),
            field3: Default::default(),
        }
    }
}
```

As you can see, deriving it makes your work much easier. You can use this implementation, though, to customize any of the fields for a default instance of your structure, which could be a good idea if, for example, you would like all your structures to have the string field set to `"This is my data"` by default. Implementing it yourself will also enable you to customize it if any of your fields do not implement `Default`, which is rarely the case if using types of the standard library.

Crate features

The second, very interesting, attribute use is to enable crate features. These features might encapsulate some functionality that some people using the crate don't need, therefore making it optional to compile. The Rust compiler will remove any unused code during the compilation, but not having some part of the code compile from the beginning will speed up the process.

You can define crate features in the `Cargo.toml` file by using the `[features]` section. You can specify some default features for the crate that will be built if nothing is specified:

```
[features]
default = ["add"]
add = []
multiply = ["expensive_dependency"]
```

In this example, two features have been defined, the `add` feature and the `multiply` feature. The `add` feature does not have any extra dependency, but the `multiply` feature depends on the `expensive_dependency` crate. By default, only the `add` feature will be built. If this were a binary crate, you could specify which features to build with the `--features` command-line option for `cargo`:

```
cargo build --features "multiply"
```

If you want to opt out of default features, simply run it with the `--no-default-features` command-line option. If you want to use a crate that has features as a dependency for your project, you can specify which features to include when declaring the dependency in the `Cargo.toml` file:

```
[dependencies.my_dep]
version = "1.0"
default-features = false
features = ["nice_feat"]
```

The `[section.subsection]` syntax is only so that we do not need to add an inline object to the `dependencies` section. In this case, it opts out of the default features and requests the `nice_feat` feature.

But, how does this look in the code? Let's see. If we have an `add` feature as we saw before, we might add an attribute to enable one function, or module, only for that case:

```
#[cfg(feature = "add")]
pub fn add(a: i32, b: i32) -> i32 {
    a + b
}
```

This will only be compiled when the `add` feature is requested. We already saw a similar syntax when using `cargo clippy`, since it will request the `cargo-clippy` feature from our crate, enabling us to cherry-pick the lints.

Configuration attributes

The final type of attributes are `#[cfg]` attributes. These attributes are incredibly powerful, enabling us to compile certain parts of the code depending on the target we are compiling to. For example, we might want to use a specific Windows function and have a backup one for the rest, or we might want the code to do different things in little- and big-endian machines.

The syntax is pretty easy. For example, if you want to check the system architecture, you can use `#[cfg(target_arch = "arm")]`, and instead of ARM, you can check for `"x86"`, `"x86_64"`, `"mips"`, `"powerpc"`, `"powerpc64"`, or `"aarch64"` too. To compile something only for FreeBSD, we can use `#[cfg(target_os = "freebsd")]`. You can compare the `target_os` configuration attribute with `"windows"`, `"macos"`, `"ios"`, `"linux"`, `"android"`, `"freebsd"`, `"dragonfly"`, `"bitrig"`, `"openbsd"`, or `"netbsd"`.

If you only care about Windows/Unix differences, you can use `#[cfg(target_family = "windows")]` or `#[cfg(target_family = "unix")]`, or even directly `#[windows]` and `#[unix]`. This can be specified further by using `#[cfg(target_env = "gnu")]`, or `"msvc"`, or `"musl"`. The endianness of the system can be checked with `#[cfg(target_endian = "little")]` or `#[cfg(target_endian = "big")]`, and the pointer width (32 or 64 bits) with `#[cfg(target_pointer_width = "32")]` or `#[cfg(target_pointer_width = "64")]` respectively.

More complex details can also be checked, such as whether the target has atomic integer types, and what size those atomic integers are. For example, to check whether the target platform has atomic 8 bit integers, you will use `#[cfg(target_has_atomic = "8")]`. You can check for 8, 16, 32, 64, and pointer width integers (with `"ptr"`). You can even check the vendor of the target architecture by checking `#[cfg(target_vendor = "apple")]`. You can check for `"apple"`, `"pc"`, or `"unknown"`.

Finally, a couple of attributes let you know whether you are doing a test (using `#[test]`) and whether the debug assertions are turned on (using `#[debug_assertions]`). The first one could be useful if you want to change any particular behavior only for tests (not recommended; tests should run the same code as in production), and the second one lets you, for example, add some debug information if the application was compiled in debug mode.

You can set/use a configuration item selectively by using `#[cfg_attr(a, b)]`. This will have the same effect as doing `#[b]`, but will only do something if `a` is true. If it's false, it will be like nothing was written. This is useful, for example, if you want to enable or disable lints depending on other attributes, or if you want to derive a trait only for certain targets, and implement it for the rest.

You can also check these configuration attributes in the code inside the logic by using the `cfg!()` macro. Simply use the same syntax as with attributes:

```
if cfg!(target_pointer_width = "32") {
    do_something();
}
```

Macros

One of the most useful Rust functionalities is its macro ecosystem. You probably already know the `println!()` macro, but there are many more. These macros allow you to write complex boilerplate code (such as `stdio` handling in the `println!()` case) in a simple way and without having to add a ton of boilerplate code. Let's check out some of the most used ones.

Console printing

When you need to lock the standard I/O interface, then write bytes to it, and finally flush it for each call, the `print!()` and `println!()` macros allow you to do that by just giving them a formatting static string and a series of parameters. Not only that, you can use the whole `std::fmt` module to specify number precision, format things in debug mode, and so on.

Similar macros exist for the standard error output interface or `stderr`. They are called `eprint!()` and `eprintln!()`, and allow you to easily print in `stderr` with the same format as `print!()` and `println!()`. The four macros use the syntax from the `format!()` macro, which we will see next.

String formatting

Creating strings is easy: you just call `String::new()` and then use a static string or add characters to it. Sometimes, you might want easier access to how the string gets created. If you, for example, want the string to say `Hello {user}!`, even though you can probably do something such as creating a `String` with `Hello` in it, then appending the username and then the exclamation mark, this is not ideal.

This is where the `std::fmt` module comes in handy, with its `format!()` macro and all of its formatting options. These options apply to console printing, string formatting, and even buffer writing with `write!()` and `writeln!()` macros. You can find the complete guide in the `std::fmt` module documentation at the standard library documentation, by running `rustup doc --open`.

Compilation environment

You can check environment variables at compile time by using the `env!("VAR")` and `option_env!("VAR")` macros. The first will retrieve the environment variable as `&'static str`. If the variable is not defined, the compilation will fail. The `option_env!()` macro avoids this by returning an `Option::None` if the environment variable is not set and an `Option::Some(&'static str)` if the variable is set:

```
const THE_KEY: &str = env!("KEY");
```

Loading byte arrays and strings at compile time

You can load various types of constants at compile time. The `include_bytes!()` macro will create a byte (`u8`) array with the contents of the specified file. The `include_str!()` macro, on the other hand, will get the contents of the file as a string and create a `&static str`. Both will make the compilation fail if the file does not exist at compile time.

You can also use the `include!()` macro that will include the code of the given file and add it to the current file at compile time. The compilation will also fail if the code in that file is not valid Rust code:

```
const CRATE_CONFIG: &str = include_str!("../Cargo.toml");
```

Code paths

Some paths should never be traversed and, in our code, that is usually a condition for our code to work properly. If we are receiving bad input data, we might want to return an error, but if our library is being misused, we might prefer to panic. Sometimes, we also want to make sure that it's impossible for a variable to be out of some bounds once it gets to the logic of our function, to avoid security flaws, for example. In those cases, the `unreachable!()` macro, or even the explicit `panic!()` macro, can help us.

There is another path that might not be ready to be traversed yet. While our crate is being implemented, we can use the `unimplemented!()` macro, as we saw before in some examples, to indicate that the code we are writing is not implemented. This will enable the code to compile but, if executed, it will panic with the *not yet implemented* message.

Checking preconditions and postconditions

When testing, and even in our everyday code, we probably want to have some preconditions to our functions, or we might want to check some postconditions. We use assertions for this. They come in two variants, debug assertions and normal assertions.

Normal assertions will always be checked, but will slow down your production code since they need to run every time. Debug assertions will only run when compiling in debug mode, so you will be able to catch errors then, and the production code will run without performance issues.

In general, you should use all the debug assertions you can, and use normal assertions only in places where you receive output from the user or another crate (if building a library).

The three macros are `assert!()`, `assert_eq!()`, and `assert_ne!()`, and their debug counterparts are `debug_assert!()`, `debug_assert_eq!()`, and `debug_assert_ne!()`. The first accepts a Boolean returning expression as the first argument and an optional second argument can contain a message that will be printed when panicking if the first argument is false.

The other two macros accept two arguments that will be compared between them and a third optional comment string. The `assert_eq!()` macro will panic if the two elements are different and the `assert_ne!()` will panic if they are equal.

Others

There are many more macros. We have already used some of them, such as the `cfg!()` and `vec![]` macros. You can also cause an explicit compile error with the `compile_error!("message")` macro, or use the `file!()`, `line!()`, and `column!()` macros to get the current position in the code, or even the `module_path!()` macro to get the current module.

If you want to know more, open the standard library documentation by running `rustup doc --open` and check out the rest of the macros there.

Nightly Rust

Nightly Rust can speed up your code even more in certain situations. If you don't need compatibility with stable Rust, you might want to check all the nightly features. In some cases, such as kernel development, it's impossible to get all the required functionality using stable Rust. You can use nightly Rust by overriding the default compiler:

```
rustup override add nightly
```

Or, you can call cargo with the +nightly flag. These methods will only work if you use rustup to manage your Rust installation, which you probably should if you have the option.

To use nightly features, you will need to use the #![feature] attribute at the crate level. For example, if you want to use the conservative_impl_trait feature, you will need to add #![feature(conservative_impl_trait)] to the beginning of your main.rs or lib.rs files.

Let's see some of the most interesting unstable features. Note that these features will probably change rapidly, and they might have already changed by the time you read this book. Always check the latest Rust's unstable feature list (https://doc.rust-lang.org/unstable-book/the-unstable-book.html) to get the latest information. There are dozens of features and it's impossible to check all of them in this chapter, but here you can find an explanation of the most relevant ones so that you understand what can they do for you and how you can use them to improve the performance of your applications.

Conservative trait return

This feature enables you to directly return a trait from a function. This means that in stable Rust, you will need to write this if you want to return a type that implements a trait without specifying the type:

```
fn iterate_something() -> Box<Iterator<Item = u32>> {
    unimplemented!()
}
```

This means that, before returning the iterator, you will need to move all of its information to the heap (this is done easily, but is costly with Box::new()) and then return it. This should not be necessary, since Rust should be able to know what type you are returning at compile time and allocate stack accordingly, then only let you use the trait, since it's what you specified beforehand.

Well, this has already been implemented in nightly Rust, but you will need to use the
`conservative_impl_trait` feature:

```
#![feature(conservative_impl_trait)]

fn iterate_something() -> impl Iterator<Item = u32> {
    (0..3).into_iter()
}
```

This allows Rust to use the stack directly, which will avoid a costly allocation and make
your code faster.

Constant functions

The `const_fn` feature enables you to declare some functions as constant so that they can
receive constant arguments at compile time and be executed then instead of at runtime. This
is particularly useful for constructors or for constants that need to create an object as soon as
possible.

For this last option, we have the `lazy_static!{}` macro, as we will see in the next chapter,
but this macro runs all of its code at its first use, and not at compile time. Doing it at
compile time would make compilations take a bit longer, but when running, it would not
require computing anything as everything would already be a constant. It seems that not
all `lazy_static!{}` cases can be solved with `const_fn`, though.

Let's see what it looks like:

```
#![feature(const_fn)]

const FIRST_CONST: MyData = MyData::new(23, 275);
const SECOND_CONST: MyData = MyData::new(336, 7);

#[derive(Debug)]
struct MyData {
    field1: u32,
    field2: f32,
}

impl MyData {
    pub const fn new(a: u32, b: u32) -> MyData {
        MyData {
            field1: a / b,
            field2: b as f32 / a as f32,
        }
```

```
        }
    }

    fn main() {
        println!("FIRST_CONST: {:?}", FIRST_CONST);
        println!("SECOND_CONST: {:?}", SECOND_CONST);

        let third = MyData::new(78, 22);
        println!("third: {:?}", third);
    }
```

In this case, as you can see, we created two constants that use the `MyData::new()` method to create them. The same method is then used at runtime in the `main()` function. The things you can do in a constant function are very limited. You cannot, for example, create bindings, and if you call another function or macro, it must also be constant. But you can still do pretty complex operations that won't affect the performance of the application. As you can imagine, this is the output of this code:

```
FIRST_CONST: MyData { field1: 0, field2: 11.956522 }
SECOND_CONST: MyData { field1: 48, field2: 0.020833334 }
third: MyData { field1: 3, field2: 0.2820513 }
```

Inline assembly and naked functions

This might be one of the most interesting nightly features of Rust. Using `#[feature(asm)]`, we will get a new macro, `asm!()`, which we will be able to use in our code. With this macro, we can write inline assembly to perform fine-grained operations in the code if we need further performance optimizations.

The exact syntax is still being worked on, but it already enables you to write arbitrary assembly code within your functions. This is a must for kernel development, for example, where access to CPU features can only be done by direct CPU instructions. Make sure you thoroughly test this code, since it will be unsafe to use it.

Furthermore, `#[feature(naked_functions)]` allows you to add the `#[naked]` attribute to a function. This will remove some boilerplate assembly that gets added before and after each function so that you can write plain assembly code. Many times, this is essential for using some CPU intrinsics.

Using bigger integers

The `i128_type` feature gives us the `i128` and `u128` integers, which work the same way as `i64` and `u64` types, but with 128 bits instead of 64, which gives them more capacity. They have the same API as the rest of the integers, so you can perform the same kind of operations. Sometimes it's great to have a bigger, full-precision integer and, in this case, since it uses LLVM intrinsics, the type is almost as lightweight as a `u64` or `i64` (more or less double the processing time in a 64-bit machine; it should be around the same in a 128-bit machine). A simple example is given in the main documentation:

```
#![feature(i128_type)]

fn main() {
    assert_eq!(1u128 + 1u128, 2u128);
    assert_eq!(u128::min_value(), 0);
    assert_eq!(u128::max_value(),
            340282366920938463463374607431768211455);

    assert_eq!(1i128 - 2i128, -1i128);
    assert_eq!(i128::min_value(),
            -170141183460469231731687303715884105728);
    assert_eq!(i128::max_value(),
            170141183460469231731687303715884105727);
}
```

Single instruction multiple data

The **single instruction multiple data** (**SIMD**) CPU features have revolutionized the way operations are performed in our CPUs. Using processor-specific features, we can now run the same operation with multiple inputs simultaneously. Let's suppose that we need to add four numbers in pairs. We could first add the first two and then the second two, and get the two results. SIMD allows us to compute both results at the same time, by applying that adding operation to both pairs at the same time.

This requires assembly, though, and even though LLVM does the best job it can to use as much SIMD as possible, it's sometimes not enough for some high-performance applications. We could use inline assembly, of course, but it's not rare to mess things up when using assembly, and you will need to rewrite it for each target, so a SIMD specific frontend is being developed.

The API is still a work in progress, but check the `simd` feature to get a grasp on how it will be done. It seems, for now, that an external crate will be developed with all the intrinsics. You will be able to generate groups of data and apply simultaneous operations to every element in supporting processors.

Allocation API

Some specific projects require the ability to change the default heap allocation algorithm. Rust uses jemalloc by default for targets that allow it. As we saw in previous chapters, one of the features of this allocator is that, in collections, it will allocate the multiple of two of the last allocations.

You can change that by using the `alloc`, `allocator_api`, `alloc_jemalloc`, and `alloc_system` features. The last two specify the global allocator of the crate, which, in cases such as kernel development, must be specified and some functions implemented so that collections work. The other two allow for more customized allocator manipulation, even giving you the option to change the allocator for each collection.

Compiler plugins

To finish with this list, we will talk about the compiler plugins. These plugins can be used by adding `#![feature(plugin)]` to the top of the `main.rs` or `lib.rs` files, as with the rest of the nightly features. If you want to actually create a plugin, you will need to use the `plugin_registrar` and `rustc_private` features.

The unstable feature list has an interesting guide to create plugins, which will be extended in *Chapter 9*, *Creating Your Own Macros*. You will need to use the `libsyntax` crate, along with the internals of the compiler syntax, and the compiler internals themselves, so that you can parse the **advanced source tree (AST)** tokens, and perform the operations required by your plugin.

Plugins enable big syntax extensions to the language, which can let you run arbitrary Rust code inside a macro or derive any kind of boilerplate code. We will see a real example of a crate that makes heavy use of plugins to create a great web development experience in the next chapter.

Some of these features might not get stabilized in the short term, some might change a lot, and some might not even get implemented, even though I doubt it will happen for the list you just read. These changes could make your code obsolete from one day to the next, so you have to make sure that, if you use some of these features, you can maintain an always changing ecosystem.

Summary

In this chapter, we started with metaprogramming by learning about attributes and macros. Both of them will help you write less code and make sure that you get the best possible implementation for trivial details.

We then learned about nightly Rust and how some nightly features give us new language extensions that can greatly help improve the efficiency, performance, and clarity of our code.

In the next chapter, we will see how crates in `crates.io` bring new macros and plugins to the ecosystem, and we will go through the most-used ones that improve the performance and development time for your applications.

8
Must-Have Macro Crates

One of the most useful features of Rust is its crate ecosystem. In languages such as C/C++, it's sometimes troublesome to find the proper library to use, and then it can be difficult to actually use it. This is almost straightforward in Rust, and in this chapter, we will see some of the most interesting crates, which give us great metaprogramming primitives:

- **Serde**: Data serialization and deserialization support
- **Nom**: Zero-copy byte-level parser creation
- **Lazy static**: Lazily initialized static variables
- **Derive builder**: Derive the common builder pattern for your structures
- **Failure**: Easy error handling
- **Log and env_logger**: Logging for your software
- **CLAP**: Creating command-line interfaces
- **Maud**: Compile-time templates with huge performance
- **Diesel**: MySQL/MariaDB, PostgreSQL, and SQLite database management, and ORM
- **Rocket**: Nightly only high-performance web framework

Working with external data

Sometimes, we do not have complete control of our software stack. Usually, if you want to create a project, you will need to contact external data sources, which can lead to many issues, since achieving compatibility between your code and external APIs or sources can be difficult. Moreover, it can lead to performance loss, which we should avoid as much as possible. Let's check some efficient and easy-to-use solutions.

Data serialization and deserialization

When it comes to data serialization and deserialization in Rust, there is no doubt we are talking about serde (`https://crates.io/crates/serde`). Serde, from *serialization and deserialization*, gives us a unique tool to be able to transform our data structures to JSON, TOML, XML, or any other serializable format. Let's see how it works.

We start with a simple structure:

```
struct MyData {
    field1: String,
    field2: u32,
    field3: Vec<u8>,
}
```

And we add serde and serde_derive as dependencies to our `Cargo.toml` file:

```
[dependencies]
serde = "1.0.0"
serde_derive = "1.0.0"
```

Then, in our `main.rs` file, we just need to import the crates using `extern crate` and derive the `Serialize` trait for our structure:

```
extern crate serde;
#[macro_use]
extern crate serde_derive;

#[derive(Debug, Serialize)]
struct MyData {
    field1: String,
    field2: u32,
    field3: Vec<u8>,
}
```

Now, we will need a *frontend* for our serializable structure. This is because serde by itself only gives our structure the ability to be serialized, but not the language into which it will get serialized. Let's use JSON as an example, since it's a very well-known object notation language. We first add the dependency to the `Cargo.toml` file:

```
serde_json = "1.0.0"
```

Then, we import it in our `main.rs` file and check the data serialization:

```
extern crate serde_json;

fn main() {
    let example = MyData {
        field1: "Test field".to_owned(),
        field2: 33_940,
        field3: vec![65, 22, 96, 43],
    };

    let json = serde_json::to_string_pretty(&example)
                .expect("could not generate JSON string");
    println!("{}", json);
}
```

If we execute `cargo run`, we will see that the output of this code is the following:

```
{
  "field1": "Test field",
  "field2": 33940,
  "field3": [
    65,
    22,
    96,
    43
  ]
}
```

This is a perfectly formatted and prettified JSON structure. OK, so how can we convert that string back into our data structure? We need to derive `Deserialize`:

```
#[derive(Debug, Serialize, Deserialize)]
struct MyData {
    field1: String,
    field2: u32,
    field3: Vec<u8>,
}

fn main() {
    let example = MyData {
        field1: "Test field".to_owned(),
        field2: 33_940,
        field3: vec![65, 22, 96, 43],
    };

    let json = serde_json::to_string_pretty(&example)
```

```
                    .expect("could not generate JSON string");
        println!("JSON:");
        println!("{}", json);

        let example_back: MyData = serde_json::from_str(&json)
                            .expect("could not parse JSON string");
        println!("Back from JSON:");
        println!("{:?}", example_back);
    }
```

This will give us this output:

```
JSON:
{
  "field1": "Test field",
  "field2": 33940,
  "field3": [
    65,
    22,
    96,
    43
  ]
}
Back from JSON:
MyData { field1: "Test field", field2: 33940, field3: [65, 22, 96, 43] }
```

This means that we can go back and forward, from JSON to a memory structure, really easily! But, of course this only works for direct structure <-> object serialization/deserialization. It won't work if any of them have different fields or names for fields. Or does it?

Well, not directly of course, but we can ask serde to modify some parameters of our structure when serializing or deserializing it. For example, since in Rust we should use snake case for our structure fields, and *pascal* case for enumeration and structure names, we might think it's not possible to deserialize structures with pascal case fields or enumerations with snake case variants.

Thankfully, the serde crate provides some attributes to personalize this behaviour. For example, let's suppose we want to represent the following structure in Rust:

```
{
    "FirstData": 56,
    "SecondData": "hello, world",
    "ThirdData": -1.23
}
```

We have to first create a Rust structure that will hold this information, like this:

```
struct MyData {
    first_data: u32,
    second_data: String,
    third_data: f32,
}
```

And then, we derive the appropriate traits. To rename the fields, we need to use the #[serde] attribute with the rename_all directive at the structure level, as you can see in the following code snippet:

```
extern crate serde;
#[macro_use]
extern crate serde_derive;
extern crate serde_json;

#[derive(Debug, Serialize, Deserialize)]
#[serde(rename_all = "PascalCase")]
struct MyData {
    first_data: u32,
    second_data: String,
    third_data: f32,
}

fn main() {
    let json = r#"{
        "FirstData": 56,
        "SecondData": "hello, world",
        "ThirdData": -1.23
    }"#;

    let in_rust: MyData = serde_json::from_str(json)
                            .expect("JSON parsing failed");
    println!("In Rust: {:?}", in_rust);

    let back_to_json = serde_json::to_string_pretty(&in_rust)
                        .expect("Rust to JSON failed");
    println!("In JSON: {}", back_to_json);
}
```

When you run it, you will see that the output is exactly as expected:

```
In Rust: MyData { first_data: 56, second_data: "hello, world", third_data: -1.23 }
In JSON: {
  "FirstData": 56,
  "SecondData": "hello, world",
  "ThirdData": -1.23
}
```

You can choose between `"lowercase"`, `"PascalCase"`, `"camelCase"`, `"snake_case"`, `"SCREAMING_SNAKE_CASE"`, and `"kebab-case"`. You can also rename one particular field, which is especially useful if the original structure has a reserved keyword (such as `type`). In this case, you can use `#[serde(rename = "type")]` in the field and use the name you want in your Rust structure.

Serializing and deserializing complex structures

In some cases, you might want to serialize or deserialize complex data structures. Most of the time, you will have a crate that does this for you (such as the *chrono* crate for dates and times). But in some cases this is not enough. Suppose you have a data structure that has a field that can take a value of either 1 or 2, and that each of them means something different. In Rust, you would use an enumeration for it, but we may not always have control of external APIs, for example.

Let's look at this structure:

```
{
    "timestamp": "2018-01-16T15:43:04",
    "type": 1,
}
```

And let's say we have some code, almost ready to compile, which represents this structure:

```
#[derive(Debug)]
enum DateType {
    FirstType,
    SecondType,
}

#[derive(Debug, Serialize, Deserialize)]
struct MyDate {
    timestamp: NaiveDateTime,
    #[serde(rename = "type")]
    date_type: DateType,
}
```

As you can see, we will need to define that `NaiveDateTime` structure. We will need to add the following to our `Cargo.toml` file:

```
[dependencies.chrono]
version = "0.4.0"
features = ["serde"]
```

And then add the imports at the top of the `main.rs` file:

```
extern crate chrono;
use chrono::NaiveDateTime;
```

The only thing left is to implement `Serialize` and `Deserialize` for `DateType`. But what if this enumeration is not part of our crate and we cannot modify it? We can, in this case, specify a way of making it work by using a function in our crate, adding the function name as a serde `deserialize_with` attribute in the `MyDate` type:

```
#[derive(Debug, Serialize, Deserialize)]
struct MyDate {
    timestamp: NaiveDateTime,
    #[serde(rename = "type",
            deserialize_with = "deserialize_date_type")]
    date_type: DateType,
}
```

Then, we will need to implement that function. It is required that the function has the following signature:

```
use serde::{Deserializer, Serializer};

fn deserialize_date_type<'de, D>(deserializer: D)
    -> Result<DateType, D::Error>
    where D: Deserializer<'de>
{
    unimplemented!()
}

fn serialize_date_type<S>(date_type: &DateType, serializer: S)
    -> Result<S::Ok, S::Error>
    where S: Serializer
{
    unimplemented!()
}
```

Then, it's as simple as using the `Deserializer` and `Serializer` traits. You can get the full API documentation by running `cargo doc`, but we will find out how to do it for this particular case. Let's start with the `Serialize` implementation, since it's simpler than the `Deserialize` implementation. You will just need to call the `serialize_u8()` (or any other integer) method with the appropriate value, as you can see in the following code snippet:

```
fn serialize_date_type<S>(date_type: &DateType, serializer: S)
    -> Result<S::Ok, S::Error>
    where S: Serializer
{
    use serde::Serializer;

    serializer.serialize_u8(match date_type {
        DateType::FirstType => 1,
        DateType::SecondType => 2,
    })
}
```

As you can see, we just serialize an integer depending on the variant of the date type. To select which integer to serialize, we just match the enumeration. The `Deserializer` trait uses the visitor pattern, though, so we also need to implement a small structure that implements the `Visitor` trait. This is not very difficult, but can be a bit complex the first time we do it. Let's check it out:

```
fn deserialize_date_type<'de, D>(deserializer: D)
    -> Result<DateType, D::Error>
    where D: Deserializer<'de>
{
    use std::fmt;
    use serde::Deserializer;
    use serde::de::{self, Visitor};

    struct DateTypeVisitor;

    impl<'de> Visitor<'de> for DateTypeVisitor {
        type Value = DateType;

        fn expecting(&self, formatter: &mut fmt::Formatter)
            -> fmt::Result
        {
            formatter.write_str("an integer between 1 and 2")
        }

        fn visit_u64<E>(self, value: u64)
            -> Result<Self::Value, E>
```

```
            where E: de::Error
    {
        match value {
            1 => Ok(DateType::FirstType),
            2 => Ok(DateType::SecondType),
            _ => {
                let error =
                    format!("type out of range: {}", value);
                Err(E::custom(error))
            }
        }
    }

    // Similar for other methods, if you want:
    //    - visit_i8
    //    - visit_i16
    //    - visit_i32
    //    - visit_i64
    //    - visit_u8
    //    - visit_u16
    //    - visit_u32
    }

    deserializer.deserialize_u64(DateTypeVisitor)
}
```

As you can see, I implemented the `visit_u64()` function for `Visitor`. This is because `serde_json` seems to use that function when serializing and deserializing integers. You can implement the rest if you want `Visitor` to be compatible with other serialization and deserialization frontends (such as XML, TOML, and others). You can see that the structure and the `Visitor` trait implementations are defined inside the function, so we do not pollute the namespace outside the function.

You will be able to test it with a new `main()` function:

```
fn main() {
    let json = r#"{
        "timestamp": "2018-01-16T15:43:04",
        "type": 1
    }"#;

    let in_rust: MyDate = serde_json::from_str(json)
                            .expect("JSON parsing failed");
    println!("In Rust: {:?}", in_rust);
```

```
        let back_to_json = serde_json::to_string_pretty(&in_rust)
                            .expect("Rust to JSON failed");
        println!("In JSON: {}", back_to_json);
    }
```

It should show the following output:

```
In Rust: MyDate { timestamp: 2018-01-16T15:43:04, date_type: FirstType }
In JSON: {
  "timestamp": "2018-01-16T15:43:04",
  "type": 1
}
```

You can of course implement the `Serialize` and `Deserialize` traits for full structures and enumerations, if the `serde` attributes are not enough for your needs. Their implementation is close to the ones seen in these functions, but you will need to check the API for more complex data serialization and deserialization. You can find a great guide at `https://serde.rs/` explaining the specific options for this crate.

Parsing byte streams

Sometimes, you might want to parse byte streams or byte slices to get valuable data. An example could be parsing a TCP byte stream to get HTTP data. Thanks to `Rust` and the `Nom` crate, we have an extremely efficient parser generator, which will not add extra overhead by copying data within your crate.

With the `Nom` crate, you create functions that will read the input data byte by byte and return the parsed data. The aim in this section is not to master the `Nom` crate, but to understand its power and point you to the appropriate documentation. So, let's see the adapted example from Zbigniew Siciarz's **24 days of Rust** (`https://siciarz.net/24-days-rust-nom-part-1/`), where he showed a short example of how to parse the first line of the HTTP protocol. You can read more complex tutorials on his blog.

Let's first define what the first line of the protocol looks like:

```
    let first_line = b"GET /home/ HTTP/1.1\r\n";
```

As you can see, the `first_line` variable is a byte array (denoted by the `b` before the string). It just has the method as the first word, in this case `GET`, but it could be `POST`, `PUT`, `DELETE`, or any of the rest methods. We will stick to these four for simplicity. Then, we can read the URL the client is trying to get, and finally, the HTTP protocol version which will be `1.1` in this case. The line ends with a carriage return and a new line.

`Nom` uses a macro called `named!()`, where you define a parser function. The name of the macro comes from the fact that you are giving a name to the function and then its implementation.

If we want to start checking the first HTTP line, we will need to parse the `request` method. To do that, we have to tell the parser that the first line can be any of the possible `request` methods. We can do this by using the `alt!()` macro with multiple `tag!()` macros, one per protocol. Let's add `Nom` to our `Cargo.toml` file and start coding the method parsing:

```
#[macro_use]
extern crate nom;

named!(parse_method,
    alt!(
        tag!("GET") |
        tag!("POST") |
        tag!("PUT") |
        tag!("DELETE")
    )
);

fn main() {
    let first_line = b"GET /home/ HTTP/1.1\r\n";
    println!("{:?}", parse_method(&first_line[..]));
}
```

This will output the following:

```
Ok(([32, 47, 104, 111, 109, 101, 47, 32, 72, 84, 84, 80, 47, 49,
46, 49, 13, 10], [71, 69, 84]))
```

What is happening here? This seems like just a bunch of numbers, one after the other. Well, as we mentioned earlier, `Nom` works byte by byte, and does not care (unless we tell it) about the string representation of things. In this case, it has correctly found a `GET`, bytes 71, 69, and 84 in ASCII, and the rest is still not parsed. It returns a tuple with the unparsed data first and the parsed data second.

We can tell Nom that we want to read the actual GET string by mapping the result to the str::from_utf8 function. Let's change the parser accordingly:

```
named!(parse_method<&[u8], &str>,
    alt!(
        map_res!(tag!("GET"), str::from_utf8) |
        map_res!(tag!("POST"), str::from_utf8) |
        map_res!(tag!("PUT"), str::from_utf8) |
        map_res!(tag!("DELETE"), str::from_utf8)
    )
);
```

As you can see, apart from adding the map_res!() macro, I had to specify that the parse_method returns &str after parsing the input, since Nom assumes that your parsers will return byte slices by default. This will output the following:

```
Ok(([32, 47, 104, 111, 109, 101, 47, 32, 72, 84, 84, 80, 47, 49,
46, 49, 13, 10], "GET"))
```

We can even create an enumeration and map it directly, as you can see here:

```
#[derive(Debug)]
enum Method {
    Get,
    Post,
    Put,
    Delete,
}

impl Method {
    fn from_bytes(b: &[u8]) -> Result<Self, String> {
        match b {
            b"GET" => Ok(Method::Get),
            b"POST" => Ok(Method::Post),
            b"PUT" => Ok(Method::Put),
            b"DELETE" => Ok(Method::Delete),
            _ => {
                let error = format!("invalid method: {}",
                                    str::from_utf8(b)
                                        .unwrap_or("not UTF-8"));
                Err(error)
            }
        }
    }
}

named!(parse_method<&[u8], Method>,
```

```
        alt!(
            map_res!(tag!("GET"), Method::from_bytes) |
            map_res!(tag!("POST"), Method::from_bytes) |
            map_res!(tag!("PUT"), Method::from_bytes) |
            map_res!(tag!("DELETE"), Method::from_bytes)
        )
    );
```

We can combine multiple parsers and create variables in one parser that will be reused in the next one. This is useful, for example, when some parts of the data contain information for parsing the rest. This is the case with the HTTP content length header, which lets you know how much you should parse later. Let's use it to parse the complete request:

```
use std::str;

#[derive(Debug)]
struct Request {
    method: Method,
    url: String,
    version: String,
}

named!(parse_request<&[u8], Request>, ws!(do_parse!(
    method: parse_method >>
    url: map_res!(take_until!(" "), str::from_utf8) >>
    tag!("HTTP/") >>
    version: map_res!(take_until!("\r"), str::from_utf8) >>
    (Request {
        method,
        url: url.to_owned(),
        version: version.to_owned()
    })
)));

fn main() {
    let first_line = b"GET /home/ HTTP/1.1\r\n";
    println!("{:?}", parse_request(&first_line[..]));
}
```

Let's see what's happening here. We created the structure to store the line data and then we created a parser by using the `ws!()` macro (which will automatically consume spacers between tokens). The `do_parse!()` macro allows us to create a sequence of many parsers.

We call the `parse_method()` parser we just created for the request method and then we just store the other two strings as variables. We then just need to create the structure with the variables. Note that I also changed the call in the `main()` function. Let's see the result:

```
Ok(([], Request { method: Get, url: "/home/", version: "1.1" }))
```

As we can see, there are no more bytes to parse, and the `Request` structure has been properly generated. You can generate parsers for extremely complex structures and you could, for example, parse the URL to get the segments, or the version number to get the major and minor version numbers, and so on. The only limitations are your needs.

In this case, we did some copying when calling `to_owned()` for the two strings, but we needed it if we wanted to generate an owned field. You can use explicit lifetimes to avoid a lot of copying if you require faster processing.

Learning about useful small crates

While data handling probably creates some of the most bug-prone code, we should also learn about some small libraries that make our lives much easier. This is the case for the following crates, where some macros can prevent us from writing lots of error-prone or potentially non-optimal code, making our final executables faster and easier to develop.

Creating lazily evaluated statics

We have seen in previous chapters how, in nightly Rust, it is possible to call some trivial constant functions that are evaluated at compile time. Nevertheless, this might not be enough for our needs, and we might not even want to use nightly Rust.

In this case, we can use a great crate, and the macro with the same name—`lazy_static`. This macro allows us to create static variables that will run the code to be generated on their first use. Let's check it, for example, for a `HashMap`. Creating a `HashMap` or adding values to it cannot be done during compile time. As we saw in previous chapters, this can be improved by using the `phf` crate. But what if we want to add values to the `HashMap` based on some environment variable? This is where `lazy_static!{}` comes in:

```
#[macro_use]
extern crate lazy_static;

use std::collections::HashMap;
```

```
lazy_static! {
    static ref MY_MAP: HashMap<&'static str, &'static str> = {
        use std::env;

        let mut map = HashMap::new();
        if let Ok(val) = env::var("GEN_MAP") {
            if val == "true" {
                map.insert("firstKey", "firstValue");
                map.insert("secondKey", "secondValue");
            }
        }

        map
    };
}


fn main() {
    for (key, value) in MY_MAP.iter() {
        println!("{}: {}", key, value);
    }
}
```

As you can see, we create a `HashMap` at runtime the first time we use it, so it will not be defined until we call `MyMap.iter()`, and if we were to use it again, it wouldn't need to be recreated. Not only that, it depends on the `GEN_MAP` environment variable. So, if we run the program with `cargo run`, it won't show anything; but if we run it with `GEN_MAP=true cargo run`, it will show the two key-values.

Under the hood, this will create a new type that implements `Deref` to `HashMap`. This will call to the `initialize()` function the first time it tries to get to the underlying type, generating the actual `HashMap`. This is very efficient if you only want one initialization of something you will be using more than once.

Avoiding boilerplate code for the builder pattern

This one is pretty straightforward. If you know about the builder pattern, you will know that it's a very useful pattern to create structures. We can avoid writing the whole new builder structure by using the `derive_builder` crate. So, let's add it to our `Cargo.toml` file and check how it works:

```
#[macro_use]
extern crate derive_builder;
```

```
use std::path::PathBuf;

#[derive(Default, Debug, Builder)]
#[builder(setter(into), default)]
struct MyData {
    field1: u8,
    field2: PathBuf,
    field3: String,
}


fn main() {
    let data = MyDataBuilder::default()
                .field2("path/to/file.png")
                .field3("Some string")
                .build().unwrap();

    println!("{:?}", data);
}
```

As you can see, we just added `#[derive(Build)]` to the structure and added some extra parameters, such as allowing the use of default values for non-initialized fields and allowing generic parameters (`Into<T>`) for setters. Note that it requires the structure to implement the `Default` trait.

This enables us to initialize the structure with mere `&str` variables, for example, and then the builder will do the rest. As you can see, it will create a `{your_structure}Builder` structure that you will use to build the main one. Make sure you check all the little options that let you adapt the builder to your needs on the crate page at `crates.io`.

Managing errors

If you have used multiple libraries in Rust, you will probably have noticed that managing errors is not straightforward. We have the awesome `?` operator, but if a function has multiple errors, it's not so easy to use. We can create our own error types, have variants for each of them, and have an `Into` trait implementation for each of the errors we might encounter. This is a tedious approach, but until recently it was the only way.

Luckily, we have a crate that can help us with that. This crate provides us with a `Fail` trait, which already guarantees thread safety and already provides default conversion implementations from all standard library error types. It also gives us some macros that help us with some boilerplate code. Let's see an example of how this would work:

```
extern crate failure;

use std::fs::File;
use std::io::Read;

use failure::{Error, ResultExt};

fn main() {
    match read_file() {
        Err(e) => {
            eprintln!("Error: {}", e);

            for cause in e.causes().skip(1) {
                eprintln!("Caused by: {}", cause);
            }
        },
        Ok(content) => {
            println!("{}...",
                        content.chars()
                            .take(15)
                            .collect::<String>());
        }
    }
}

fn read_file() -> Result<String, Error> {
    let file_name = "Cargo.toml";
    let mut file = File::open(file_name)
                    .context("error opening the file")?;

    let mut content = String::new();
    file.read_to_string(&mut content)
        .context("error reading the file")?;

    Ok(content)
}
```

In this simple example, we get the first characters of the `Cargo.toml` file. As you can see, we are returning `std::io::Errors` converted into `failure::Errors` with the `?` operator. Then, we can iterate over the errors if they exist. If something goes wrong, this will be the output of the code. We have added some context for each of the potential errors, so that the output gets properly printed:

```
Error: error opening the file
Caused by: Permission denied (os error 13)
```

You can also create your error traits and derive the `Fail` trait, thanks to the `failure_derive` crate. I recommend checking the complete documentation and using it for all your new projects. It brings many advantages over doing it yourself and even using the predecessor `error-chain` crate.

Logging efficiently in Rust

Logging is one of the most important parts of many applications and it's good to know that Rust has us covered in this regard. The default go-to crate should be the `log` crate, which provides us with useful macros for logging. Then, you can use the backend you want for the loggers, such as the `env_logger` crate or the `log4rs` crate.

The `log` crate gives us some macros, mainly `trace!()`, `debug!()`, `info!()`, `warn!()`, and `error!()`, in ascending order of relevance, which we can use to log events that happen in our application. It provides some more boilerplate, but that is basically it, you will now have to configure how those macros behave. For that, you have the actual implementations.

If you want an easy to use, common logger, you should go for `env_logger`. It has a small footprint and can be configured with environment variables. If you need extra configuration for things such as multiple outputs, both console and files, and extra configuration, you should go for an alternative such as `log4rs`. Let's check a small `env_logger` example to see the power of this logging mechanism. You will need to add `log` and `env_logger` to your `Cargo.toml` file:

```
#[macro_use]
extern crate log;
extern crate env_logger;

fn main() {
    env_logger::init();

    trace!("Logging {} small thing(s)", 1);
```

```
        debug!("Some debug information:  {}",
               "the answer is 42");
        info!("This is an interesting information");
        error!("An error happened, do something!");
    }
```

If we run that using `cargo run`, we will see this output, since errors are shown by default:

```
ERROR 2018-01-17T18:23:45Z: test_crate: An error happened, do something!
```

But we can run it with a different `RUST_LOG` environment variable, such as `RUST_LOG=trace cargo run`. This should show the following:

```
      2018-01-17T18:27:12Z: test_crate: Logging 1 small thing(s)
DEBUG 2018-01-17T18:27:12Z: test_crate: Some debug information:  the answer is 42
 INFO 2018-01-17T18:27:12Z: test_crate: This is an interesting information
ERROR 2018-01-17T18:27:12Z: test_crate: An error happened, do something!
```

As you can see, colors denote the importance of the message. Note that running `cargo` with the `RUST_LOG` variable will show a lot of extra output, since cargo itself uses `env_logger`. I recommend you read the full documentation of this crate, since it enables you to change formatters, loggers, and much more besides the default behavior.

Creating command-line interfaces

Creating a command-line interface is not always easy. In C/C++, you need to start parsing arguments and then decide which flags are set and whether they comply with all the conditions. This is a non-issue in Rust thanks to **Command-Line Argument Parser (CLAP)**. The CLAP crate, enables us to create very complex command-line interfaces with just a bit of code.

Not only that; it will create the help menus for us and it will also be maintainable since it will be easy to add or remove parameters and flags. It will ensure that the input we receive is valid and it will even create command-line completion scripts for the most-used shells.

You can generate the complete CLI with macros, but I personally prefer to use simple Rust code. It has a few `helper` macros, though, to gather some information. Remember to add `clap` to your `Cargo.toml` file and let's see how we would create a simple command-line interface:

```
        #[macro_use]
        extern crate clap;
```

```
use clap::{App, Arg};

fn main() {
    let matches = App::new(crate_name!())
                    .version(crate_version!())
                    .about(crate_description!())
                    .author(crate_authors!())
                    .arg(
                        Arg::with_name("user")
                            .help("The user to say hello to")
                            .value_name("username")
                            .short("u")
                            .long("username")
                            .required(true)
                            .takes_value(true)
                    )
                    .get_matches();

    let user = matches.value_of("user")
            .expect("somehow the user did not give the username");

    println!("Hello, {}", user);
}
```

As you can see, we defined a CLI with the crate name, description, version, and authors, which will be taken from the `Cargo.toml` file at compile time so that we do not need to update it for every change. It then defines a required `user` argument, which takes a value and uses it to print the value. The `expect()` here is safe because `clap` makes sure that the argument is provided, since we asked it to with `required(true)`. If we simply execute `cargo run`, we will see the following error:

```
error: The following required arguments were not provided:
    --username <username>

USAGE:
    test_crate --username <username>

For more information try --help
```

It tells us that it needs the `username` parameter and points us to the `--help` flag, automatically added by `clap` along with the `-V` flag, to show the crate version information. If we run it with `cargo run -- --help`, we will see the `help` output. Note that any argument to cargo after a double dash will be passed as an argument to the executable. Let's check it:

```
test_crate 0.1.0
Razican <razican@protonmail.ch>


USAGE:
    test_crate --username <username>

FLAGS:
    -h, --help       Prints help information
    -V, --version    Prints version information

OPTIONS:
    -u, --username <username>      The user to say hello to
```

As we can see, it shows really well-formatted help text. If we want to actually see the result of passing a proper username, we can execute it with `cargo run -- -u {username}`:

```
[razican@laptop test_crate]$ cargo run -- -u Razican
    Finished dev [unoptimized + debuginfo] target(s) in 0.0 secs
     Running `target/debug/test_crate -u Razican`
Hello, Razican
```

Using Rust for web development

You might think that Rust is only meant to be used for complex system development, or that it should be used where security is the number one concern. Thinking of using it for web development might sound to you like huge overkill. We already have proven web-oriented languages that have worked until now, such as PHP or JavaScript, right?

This is far from true. Many projects use the web as their platform and for them, it's sometimes more important to be able to receive a lot of traffic without investing in expensive servers rather than using legacy technologies, especially in new products. This is where Rust comes in handy. Thanks to its speed and some really well thought out web-oriented frameworks, Rust performs even better than the legacy web programming languages.

Rust is even trying to replace some of the JavaScript on the client side of applications, since Rust can compile to WebAssembly, making it extremely powerful for heavy client-side web workloads. We will not learn how to compile for web clients in this book, but we will learn about some crates that allow you work on efficient web development with Rust.

Creating extremely efficient templates

We have seen that Rust is a really efficient language and as you have seen in the last two chapters, metaprogramming allows for the creation of even more efficient code. Rust has great templating language support, such as Handlebars and Tera. Rust's Handlebars implementation is much faster than the JavaScript implementation, while Tera is a template engine created for Rust based on Jinja2.

In both cases, you define a template file and then you use Rust to parse it. Even though this will be reasonable for most web development, in some cases, it might be slower than pure Rust alternatives. This is where the Maud crate comes in. We will see how it works and how it achieves orders of magnitude faster performance than its counterparts.

To use Maud, you will need nightly Rust, since it uses procedural macros. As we saw in previous chapters, if you are using `rustup` you can simply run `rustup override set nightly`. Then, you will need to add Maud to your `Cargo.toml` file in the `[dependencies]` section:

```
[dependencies]
maud = "0.17.2
```

Maud brings an `html!{}` procedural macro that enables you to write HTML in Rust. You will therefore need to import the necessary crate and macro in your `main.rs` or `lib.rs` file, as you will see in the following code. Remember to also add the procedural macro feature at the beginning of the crate:

```
#![feature(proc_macro)]

extern crate maud;
use maud::html;
```

You will now be able to use the `html!{}` macro in your `main()` function. This macro will return a `Markup` object, which you can then convert to a `String` or return to Rocket or Iron for your website implementation (you will need to use the relevant Maud features in that case). Let's see what a short template implementation looks like:

```
fn main() {
    use maud::PreEscaped;

    let user_name = "FooBar";
    let markup = html! {
        (PreEscaped("<!DOCTYPE html>"))
        html {
            head {
                title { "Test website" }
                meta charset="UTF-8";
            }
            body {
                header {
                    nav {
                        ul {
                            li { "Home" }
                            li { "Contact Us" }
                        }
                    }
                }
                main {
                    h1 { "Welcome to our test template!" }
                    p { "Hello, " (user_name) "!" }
                }
                footer {
                    p { "Copyright © 2017 - someone" }
                }
            }
        }
    };
    println!("{}", markup.into_string());
}
```

It seems like a complex template, but it contains just the basic information a new website should have. We first add a doctype, making sure it will not escape the content (that is what the `PreEscaped` is for) and then we start the HTML document with two parts: the `head` and the `body`. In the `head`, we add the required title and the `charset meta` element to tell the browser that we will be using UTF-8.

Then, the `body` contains the three usual sections, even though this can of course be modified. One `header`, one `main` section, and one `footer`. I added some example information in each of the sections and showed you how to add a dynamic variable in the `main` section inside a paragraph.

The interesting syntax here is that you can create elements with attributes, such as the `meta` element, even without content, by finishing it early with a semicolon. You can use any HTML tag and add variables. The generated code will be escaped, except if you ask for non-escaped data, and it will be minified so that it occupies the least space when being transmitted.

Inside the parentheses, you can call any function or variable that returns a type that implements the `Display` trait and you can even add any Rust code if you add braces around it, with the last statement returning a `Display` element. This works on attributes too.

This gets processed at compile time, so that at runtime it will only need to perform the minimum possible amount of work, making it extremely efficient. And not only that; the template will be typesafe thanks to Rust's compile-time guarantees, so you won't forget to close a tag or an attribute. There is a complete guide to the templating engine that can be found at `https://maud.lambda.xyz/`.

Connecting with a database

If we want to use SQL/relational databases in Rust, there is no other crate to think about than Diesel. If you need access to NoSQL databases such as Redis or MongoDB, you will also find proper crates, but since the most used databases are relational databases, we will check Diesel here.

Diesel makes working with MySQL/MariaDB, PostgreSQL, and SQLite very easy by providing a great ORM and typesafe query builder. It prevents all potential SQL injections at compile time, but is still extremely fast. In fact, it's usually faster than using prepared statements, due to the way it manages connections to databases. Without entering into technical details, we will check how this stable framework works.

The development of Diesel has been impressive and it's already working in stable Rust. It even has a stable 1.x version, so let's check how we can map a simple table. Diesel comes with a command-line interface program, which makes it much easier to use. To install it, run `cargo install diesel_cli`. Note that, by default, this will try to install it for PostgreSQL, MariaDB/MySQL, and SQLite.

For this short tutorial, you need to have SQLite 3 development files installed, but if you want to avoid installing all MariaDB/MySQL or PostgreSQL files, you should run the following command:

```
cargo install --no-default-features --features sqlite diesel_cli
```

Then, since we will be using SQLite for our short test, add a file named .env to the current directory, with the following content:

```
DATABASE_URL=test.sqlite
```

We can now run `diesel setup` and `diesel migration generate initial_schema`. This will create the `test.sqlite` SQLite database and a `migrations` folder, with the first empty initial schema migration. Let's add this to the initial schema `up.sql` file:

```
CREATE TABLE 'users' (
   'username' TEXT NOT NULL PRIMARY KEY,
   'password' TEXT NOT NULL,
   'email' TEXT UNIQUE
);
```

In its counterpart `down.sql` file, we will need to drop the created table:

```
DROP TABLE `users`;
```

Then, we can execute `diesel migration run` and check that everything went smoothly. We can execute `diesel migration redo` to check that the rollback and recreation worked properly. We can now start using the ORM. We will need to add diesel, `diesel_infer_schema`, and `dotenv` to our `Cargo.toml`. The `dotenv` crate will read the .env file to generate the environment variables. If you want to avoid using all the MariaDB/MySQL or PostgreSQL features, you will need to configure `diesel` for it:

```
[dependencies]
dotenv = "0.10.1"

[dependencies.diesel]
version = "1.1.1"
default-features = false
features = ["sqlite"]

[dependencies.diesel_infer_schema]
version = "1.1.0"
default-features = false
features = ["sqlite"]
```

Let's now create a structure that we will be able to use to retrieve data from the database. We will also need some boilerplate code to make everything work:

```
#[macro_use]
extern crate diesel;
#[macro_use]
extern crate diesel_infer_schema;
extern crate dotenv;

use diesel::prelude::*;
use diesel::sqlite::SqliteConnection;
use dotenv::dotenv;
use std::env;

#[derive(Debug, Queryable)]
struct User {
    username: String,
    password: String,
    email: Option<String>,
}

fn establish_connection() -> SqliteConnection {
 dotenv().ok();

 let database_url = env::var("DATABASE_URL")
 .expect("DATABASE_URL must be set");
 SqliteConnection::establish(&database_url)
 .expect(&format!("error connecting to {}", database_url))
}

mod schema {
 infer_schema!("dotenv:DATABASE_URL");
}
```

Here, the `establish_connection()` function will call `dotenv()` so that the variables in the `.env` file get to the environment, and then it uses that `DATABASE_URL` variable to establish the connection with the SQLite database and returns the handle.

The schema module will contain the schema of the database. The `infer_schema!()` macro will get the `DATABASE_URL` variable and connect to the database at compile time to generate the schema. Make sure you run all the migrations before compiling.

We can now develop a small `main()` function with the basics to list all of the users from the database:

```
fn main() {
    use schema::users::dsl::*;

    let connection = establish_connection();
    let all_users = users
        .load::<User>(&connection)
        .expect("error loading users");

    println!("{:?}", all_users);
}
```

 This will just load all of the users from the database into a list. Notice the `use` statement at the beginning of the function. This retrieves the required information from the schema for the `users` table so that we can then call `users.load()`.

As you can see in the guides at `diesel.rs`, you can also generate `Insertable` objects, which might not have some of the fields with default values, and you can perform complex queries by filtering the results in the same way you would write a `SELECT` statement.

Creating a complete web server

There are multiple web frameworks for Rust. Some of them work in stable Rust, such as Iron and Nickel Frameworks, and some don't, such as Rocket. We will talk about the latter since, even if it forces you to use the latest nightly branch, it's so much more powerful than the rest that it really makes no sense to use any of the others if you have the option to use Rust nightly.

Using Diesel with Rocket, apart from the funny wordplay joke, works seamlessly. You will probably be using the two of them together, but in this section we will learn how to create a small Rocket server without any further complexity. There are some boilerplate code implementations that add database, cache, OAuth, templating, response compression, JavaScript minification, and SASS minification to the website, such as my Rust web template (`https://github.com/Razican/Rust-web-template`) in GitHub if you need to start developing a real-life Rust web application.

Rocket trades that nightly instability, which will break your code more often than not, for simplicity and performance. Developing a Rocket application is really easy and the performance of the results is astonishing. It's even faster than using some other, seemingly simpler frameworks, and of course, it's much faster than most of the frameworks in other languages. So, how does it feel to develop a Rocket application?

We start by adding the latest `rocket` and `rocket_codegen` crates to our `Cargo.toml` file and adding a nightly override to our current directory by running `rustup override set nightly`. The `rocket` crate contains all the code to run the server, while the `rocket_codegen` crate is actually a compiler plugin that modifies the language to adapt it for web development. We can now write the default `Hello, world!` Rocket example:

```
#![feature(plugin)]
#![plugin(rocket_codegen)]

extern crate rocket;

#[get("/")]
fn index() -> &'static str {
    "Hello, world!"
}

fn main() {
    rocket::ignite().mount("/", routes![index]).launch();
}
```

In this example, we can see how we ask Rust to let us use plugins to then import the `rocket_codegen` plugin. This will enable us to use attributes such as `#[get]` or `#[post]` with request information that will generate boilerplate code when compiled, leaving our code fairly simple for our development. Also, note that this code has been checked with Rocket 0.3 and it might fail in a future version, since the library is not stable yet.

In this case, you can see that the `index()` function will respond to any GET request with a base URL. This can be modified to accept only certain URLs, or to get the path of something from the URL. You can also have overlapping routes with different priorities, so that if one is not taken for a request guard, the next will be tried.

And, talking about request guards, you can create objects that can be generated when processing a request that will only let the request process a given function if they are properly built. This means that you can, for example, create a `User` object that will get generated by checking the cookies in the request and comparing them in a Redis database, only allowing the execution of the function for logged-in users. This easily prevents many logic flaws.

The main() function ignites the Rocket and mounts the index route at /. This means that you can have multiple routes with the same path mounted at different route paths and they do not need to know about the whole path in the URL. In the end, it will launch the Rocket server and if you run it with cargo run, it will show the following:

```
   Configured for development.
      address:
      port:
      log:
      workers:
      secret key:
      limits:
      tls:
   Mounting '/':
      GET /
                                    http://localhost:8000
```

If you go to the URL, you will see the Hello, World! message. Rocket is highly configurable. It has a rocket_contrib crate which offers templates and further features, and you can create responders to add GZip compression to responses. You can also create your own error responders when an error occurs.

You can also configure the behavior of Rocket by using the Rocket.toml file and environment variables. As you can see in this last output, it is running in development mode, which adds some debugging information. You can configure different behaviors for staging and production modes and make them perform faster. Also, make sure that you compile the code in --release mode in production.

If you want to develop a web application in Rocket, make sure you check https://rocket.rs/ for further information. Future releases also look promising. Rocket will implement native CSRF and XSS prevention, which, in theory, should prevent all XSS and CSRF attacks at compile time. It will also make further customizations to the engine possible.

Summary

In this chapter, you learned about many crates that will make your life writing Rust code much easier. You learned how they can not only allow you to write less code, but that they can help you write faster code. We also saw how easy it is to use a crate from `https://crates.io/`, which gives us superpowers when using code written by others.

In the next chapter, you will learn how to develop your own macros, similar to the ones seen here, and you will also learn how to create your own procedural macros and plugins.

Creating Your Own Macros

9

In previous chapters, we saw how macros and metaprogramming, in general, can make your life much easier. We saw both, macros that reduce the required boilerplate code and macros that will speed up your final code. It's time for you to learn how to create your own macros.

In this chapter, you will learn how to create your own standard macros, how to create your own procedural macros and custom derives, and finally, how to use nightly features to create your own plugins. You will also see how the new declarative macros work.

The chapter is divided into three sections:

- **Macrosystem**: Understanding the `macro_rules!{}` macro
- **Procedural macros**: Learning how to create your own custom derives
- **Nightly metaprogramming**: Plugins and declarative macros

Creating your own standard macros

Since Rust 1.0, we have had a great macro system. Macros allow us to apply some code to multiple types or expressions, as they work by expanding themselves at compile time. This means that when you use a macro, you are effectively writing a lot of code before the actual compilation starts. This has two main benefits, first, the codebase can be easier to maintain by being smaller and reusing code, and second, since macros expand before starting the creation of object code, you can abstract at the syntactic level.

For example, you can have a function like this one:

```
fn add_one(input: u32) -> u32 {
    input + 1
}
```

This function restricts the input to u32 types and the return type to u32. We could add some more accepted types by using generics, which may accept &u32 if we use the Add trait. Macros allow us to create this kind of code for any element that can be written to the left of the + sign and it will be expanded differently for each type of element, creating different code for each case.

To create a macro, you will need to use a macro built in to the language, the macro_rules!{} macro. This macro receives the name of the new macro as a first parameter and a block with the macro code as a second element. The syntax can be a bit complex the first time you see it, but it can be learned quickly. Let's start with a macro that does just the same as the function we saw before:

```
macro_rules! add_one {
    ($input:expr) => {
        $input + 1
    }
}
```

You can now call that macro from your main() function by calling add_one!(integer);. Note that the macro needs to be defined before the first call, even if it's in the same file. It will work with any integer, which wasn't possible with functions.

Let's analyze how the syntax works. In the block after the name of the new macro (add_one), we can see two sections. In the first part, on the left of the =>, we see $input:expr inside parentheses. Then, to the right, we see a Rust block where we do the actual addition.

The left part works similarly (in some ways) to a pattern match. You can add any combination of characters and then some variables, all of them starting with a dollar sign ($) and showing the type of variable after a colon. In this case, the only variable is the $input variable and it's an expression. This means that you can insert any kind of expression there and it will be written in the code to the right, substituting the variable with the expression.

Macro variants

As you can see, it's not as complicated as you might think. As I wrote, you can have almost any pattern to the left of the `macro_rules!{}` side. Not only that, you can also have multiple patterns, as if it were a match statement, so that if one of them matches, it will be the one expanded. Let's see how this works by creating a macro which, depending on how we call it, will add one or two to the given integer:

```
macro_rules! add {
    {one to $input:expr} => ($input + 1);
    {two to $input:expr} => ($input + 2);
}

fn main() {
    println!("Add one: {}", add!(one to 25/5));
    println!("Add two: {}", add!(two to 25/5));
}
```

You can see a couple of clear changes to the macro. First, we swapped braces for parentheses and parentheses for braces in the macro. This is because in a macro, you can use interchangeable braces (`{` and `}`), square brackets (`[` and `]`), and parentheses (`(` and `)`). Not only that, you can use them when calling the macro. You have probably already used the `vec![]` macro and the `format!()` macro, and we saw the `lazy_static!{}` macro in the last chapter. We use brackets and parentheses here just for convention, but we could call the `vec!{}` or the `format![]` macros the same way, because we can use braces, brackets, and parentheses in any macro call.

The second change was to add some extra text to our left-hand side patterns. We now call our macro by writing the text `one to` or `two to`, so I also removed the `one` redundancy to the macro name and called it `add!()`. This means that we now call our macro with literal text. That is not valid Rust, but since we are using a macro, we modify the code we are writing before the compiler tries to understand actual Rust code and the generated code is valid. We could add any text that does not end the pattern (such as parentheses or braces) to the pattern.

The final change was to add a second possible pattern. We can now add one or two and the only difference will be that the right side of the macro definition must now end with a trailing semicolon for each pattern (the last one is optional) to separate each of the options.

A small detail that I also added in the example was when calling the macro in the `main()` function. As you can see, I could have added `one` or `two` to 5, but I wrote 25/5 for a reason. When compiling this code, this will be expanded to 25/5 + 1 (or 2, if you use the second variant). This will later be optimized at compile time, since it will know that 25/5 + 1 is 6, but the compiler will receive that expression, not the final result. The macro system will not calculate the result of the expression; it will simply copy in the resulting code whatever you give to it and then pass it to the next compiler phase.

You should be especially careful with this when a macro you are creating calls another macro. They will get expanded recursively, one inside the other, so the compiler will receive a bunch of final Rust code that will need to be optimized. Issues related to this were found in the CLAP crate that we saw in the last chapter, since the exponential expansions were adding a lot of bloat code to their executables. Once they found out that there were too many macro expansions inside the other macros and fixed it, they reduced the size of their binary contributions by more than 50%.

Macros allow for an extra layer of customization. You can repeat arguments more than once. This is common, for example, in the `vec![]` macro, where you create a new vector with information at compile time. You can write something like `vec![3, 4, 76, 87];`. How does the `vec![]` macro handle an unspecified number of arguments?

Complex macros

We can specify that we want multiple expressions in the left-hand side pattern of the macro definition by adding a * for *zero or more* matches or a + for *one or more* matches. Let's see how we can do that with a simplified `my_vec![]` macro:

```
macro_rules! my_vec {
    ($($x: expr),*) => {{
        let mut vector = Vec::new();
        $(vector.push($x);)*
        vector
    }}
}
```

Let's see what is happening here. First, we see that on the left side, we have two variables, denoted by the two $ signs. The first makes reference to the actual repetition. Each comma-separated expression will generate a $x variable. Then, on the right side, we use the various repetitions to push $x to the vector once for every expression we receive.

There is another new thing on the right-hand side. As you can see, the macro expansion starts and ends with a double brace instead of using only one. This is because, once the macro gets expanded, it will substitute the given expression for a new expression: the one that gets generated. Since what we want is to return the vector we are creating, we need a new scope where the last sentence will be the value of the scope once it gets executed. You will be able to see it more clearly in the next code snippet.

We can call this code with the `main()` function:

```
fn main() {
    let my_vector = my_vec![4, 8, 15, 16, 23, 42];
    println!("Vector test: {:?}", my_vector);
}
```

It will be expanded to this code:

```
fn main() {
    let my_vector = {
        let mut vector = Vec::new();
        vector.push(4);
        vector.push(8);
        vector.push(15);
        vector.push(16);
        vector.push(23);
        vector.push(42);
        vector
    };
    println!("Vector test: {:?}", my_vector);
}
```

As you can see, we need those extra braces to create the scope that will return the vector so that it gets assigned to the `my_vector` binding.

You can have multiple repetition patterns on the left expression and they will be repeated for every use, as needed on the right. There is a nice example illustrating this behavior in the first edition of the official Rust book, which I have adapted here:

```
macro_rules! add_to_vec {
    ($( $x:expr; [ $( $y:expr ),* ]);* ) => {
        &[ $($( $x + $y ),*),* ]
    }
}
```

In this example, the macro can receive one or more $x; [$y1, $y2,...] input. So, for each input, it will have one expression, then a semicolon, then a bracket with multiple sub-expressions separated by a comma, and finally, another bracket and a semicolon. But what does the macro do with this input? Let's check to the right-hand side of it.

As you can see, this will create multiple repetitions. We can see that it creates a slice (&[T]) of whatever we feed to it, so all the expressions we use must be of the same type. Then, it will start iterating over all $x variables, one per input group. So if we feed it only one input, it will iterate once for the expression to the left of the semicolon. Then, it will iterate once for every $y expression associated with the $x expression, add them to the + operator, and include the result in the slice.

If this was too complex to understand, let's look at an example. Let's suppose we call the macro with 65; [22, 34] as input. In this case, 65 will be $x, and 22, 24, and so on will be $y variables associated with 65. So, the result will be a slice like this: &[65+22, 65+34]. Or, if we calculate the results: &[87, 99].

If, on the other hand, we give two groups of variables by using 65; [22, 34]; 23; [56, 35] as input, in the first iteration, $x will be 65, while in the second one, it will be 23. The $y variables of 64 will be 22 and 34, as before, and the ones associated with 23 will be 56 and 35. This means that the final slice will be &[87, 99, 79, 58], where 87 and 99 work the same way as before and 79 and 58 are the extension of adding 23 to 56 and 23 to 35.

This gives you much more flexibility than the functions, but remember, all this will be expanded during compile time, which can make your compilation time much slower and the final codebase larger and slower still if the macro used duplicates too much code. In any case, there is more flexibility to it yet.

So far, all variables have been of the expr kind. We have used this by declaring $x:expr and $y:expr but, as you can imagine, there are other kinds of macro variables. The list follows:

- expr: Expressions that you can write after an = sign, such as 76+4 or if a==1 {"something"} else {"other thing"}.
- ident: An identifier or binding name, such as foo or bar.
- path: A qualified path. This will be a path that you could write in a use sentence, such as foo::bar::MyStruct or foo::bar::my_func.
- ty: A type, such as u64 or MyStruct. It can also be a path to the type.
- pat: A pattern that you can write at the left side of an = sign or in a match expression, such as Some(t) or (a, b, _).

- `stmt`: A full statement, such as a let binding like `let a = 43;`.
- `block`: A block element that can have multiple statements and a possible expression between braces, such as `{vec.push(33); vec.len()}`.
- `item`: What Rust calls *items*. For example, function or type declarations, complete modules, or trait definitions.
- `meta`: A meta element, which you can write inside of an attribute (`#[]`). For example, `cfg(feature = "foo")`.
- `tt`: Any token tree that will eventually get parsed by a macro pattern, which means almost anything. This is useful for creating recursive macros, for example.

As you can imagine, some of these kinds of macro variables overlap and some of them are just more specific than the others. The use will be verified on the right-hand side of the macro, in the expansion, since you might try to use a statement where an expression must be used, even though you might use an identifier too, for example.

There are some extra rules, too, as we can see in the Rust documentation (`https://doc.rust-lang.org/book/first-edition/macros.html#syntactic-requirements`). Statements and expressions can only be followed by `=>`, a comma, or a semicolon. Types and paths can only be followed by `=>`, the `as` or `where` keywords, or any commas, `=`, `|`, `;`, `:`, `>`, `[`, or `{`. And finally, patterns can only be followed by `=>`, the `if` or `in` keywords, or any commas, `=`, or `|`.

Let's put this in practice by implementing a small `Mul` trait for a currency type we can create. This is an adapted example of some work we did when creating the Fractal Credits digital currency. In this case, we will look to the implementation of the `Amount` type (`https://github.com/FractalGlobal/utils-rs/blob/49955ead9eef2d9373cc9386b90ac02b4d5745b4/src/amount.rs#L99-L102`), which represents a currency amount. Let's start with the basic type definition:

```
#[derive(Copy, Clone, PartialEq, Eq, PartialOrd, Ord)]
pub struct Amount {
    value: u64,
}
```

This amount will be divisible by up to three decimals, but it will always be an exact value. We should be able to add an `Amount` to the current `Amount`, or to subtract it. I will not explain these trivial implementations, but there is one implementation where macros can be of great help. We should be able to multiply the amount by any positive integer, so we should implement the `Mul` trait for `u8`, `u16`, `u32`, and `u64` types. Not only that, we should be able to implement the `Div` and the `Rem` traits, but I will leave those out, since they are a little bit more complex. You can check them in the implementation linked earlier.

The only thing the multiplication of an `Amount` with an integer should do is to multiply the value by the integer given. Let's see a simple implementation for `u8`:

```
use std::ops::Mul;

impl Mul<u8> for Amount {
    type Output = Self;

    fn mul(self, rhs: u8) -> Self::Output {
        Self { value: self.value * rhs as u64 }
    }
}

impl Mul<Amount> for u8 {
    type Output = Amount;

    fn mul(self, rhs: Amount) -> Self::Output {
        Self::Output { value: self as u64 * rhs.value }
    }
}
```

As you can see, I implemented it both ways so that you can put the `Amount` to the left and to the right of the multiplication. If we had to do this for all integers, it would be a big waste of time and code. And if we had to modify one of the implementations (especially for `Rem` functions), it would be troublesome to do it in multiple code points. Let's use macros to help us.

We can define a macro, `impl_mul_int!{}`, which will receive a list of integer types and then implement the `Mul` trait back and forward between all of them and the `Amount` type. Let's see:

```
macro_rules! impl_mul_int {
    ($($t:ty)*) => ($(
        impl Mul<$t> for Amount {
            type Output = Self;

            fn mul(self, rhs: $t) -> Self::Output {
                Self { value: self.value * rhs as u64 }
            }
        }

        impl Mul<Amount> for $t {
            type Output = Amount;

            fn mul(self, rhs: Amount) -> Self::Output {
                Self::Output { value: self as u64 * rhs.value }
```

```
            }
        }
    )*)
}

    impl_mul_int! { u8 u16 u32 u64 usize }
```

As you can see, we specifically ask for the given elements to be types and then we implement the trait for all of them. So, for any code that you want to implement for multiple types, you might as well try this approach, since it will save you from writing a lot of code and it will make it more maintainable.

Creating procedural macros

We have seen what standard macros can do for our crate. We can create complex compile-time code that can both reduce the verbosity of our code, making it more maintainable, and improve the performance of the final executable by performing operations at compile time instead of at runtime.

Nevertheless, standard macros can only do so much. With them, you can only modify some of the Rust grammar token processing, but you are still bound to what the `macro_rules!{}` macro can understand. This is where procedural macros, also known as macros 1.1 or custom derives, come into play.

With procedural macros, you can create libraries that will be called by the compiler when deriving their name in some structure or enumeration. You can effectively create a custom trait, `derive`.

Implementing a simple trait

Let's see how this can be done by implementing a simple trait for a structure or enumeration. The trait we will be implementing is the following:

```
trait TypeName {
    fn type_name() -> &'static str;
}
```

This `trait` should return the name of the current structure or enumeration as a string. Implementing that by hand is really easy, but it doesn't make sense to implement it manually, one by one, for our types. The best thing to do is to derive it with a procedural macro. Let's see how we can do that.

First, we will need to create a library crate. As per convention, it should have the parent crate's name and then the `-derive` suffix. In this case, we do not have a name for the crate, but let's call the library `type-name-derive`:

```
cargo new type-name-derive
```

This should create a new folder next to the `src/` folder, named `type-name-derive`. We can now add it to the `Cargo.toml` file:

```
[dependencies]
type-name-derive = { path = "./type-name-derive" }
```

In the `main.rs` file of our crate, we will need to add the crate and use its macros:

```
#[macro_use]
extern crate type_name_derive;

trait TypeName {
    fn type_name() -> &'static str;
}
```

Let's now start with the actual derivation development. We will need to use two crates—syn and quote. We will add them to the `Cargo.toml` file inside the `type-name-derive` directory:

```
[dependencies]
syn = "0.12.10"
quote = "0.4.2"
```

The `syn` crate gives us some useful types and functions to work with the source tree and token streams of Rust. We need this because all our macro will see is a bunch of information about the source code of our structure or enumeration. We will need to parse it and get information from it. The `syn` crate is a Nom parser that will transform that Rust source code into something we can easily use.

The `quote` crate gives us the `quote!{}` macro, which we will use to implement the source code of our implementation directly. It basically allows us to write almost *normal* Rust code instead of compiler tokens to implement the trait.

There is other extra information we will need to include in the `Cargo.toml` file. We need to inform cargo and the Rust compiler that this crate is a procedural macro crate. For that, we will need to add this to the file:

```
[lib]
proc-macro = true
```

Then, we need to start with the initial schema of the `./type-name-derive/src/lib.rs` file:

```
extern crate proc_macro;
extern crate syn;
#[macro_use]
extern crate quote;

use proc_macro::TokenStream;

#[proc_macro_derive(TypeName)]
pub fn type_name(input: TokenStream) -> TokenStream {
    // some code
}
```

As you can see, we first imported the required definitions. The `proc_macro` crate is built in the compiler and gives us the `TokenStream` type. This type represents a stream of Rust tokens (characters in your source files). We then import the `syn` and `quote` crates. As we saw earlier, we will need to use the `quote!{}` macro from the quote crate, so we import the macros too.

The syntax for implementing a custom derive is really simple. We need to define a function with a `proc_macro_derive` attribute of the value of the trait we want to derive. The function will take ownership of a token stream and return another (or the same) token stream so that the compiler can later process the new generated Rust code.

To implement the trait, I prefer to divide the token parsing and the actual trait implementation into two functions. For that, let's first write the code inside our `type_name()` function:

```
// Parse the input tokens into a syntax tree
let input = syn::parse(input).unwrap();

// Build the output
let expanded = impl_type_name(&input);

// Hand the output tokens back to the compiler
expanded.into()
```

The token stream first gets converted into a `DeriveInput` structure. This structure contains the properly parsed data from the input token stream; deserialized into the information of the type here, we will add the `#[derive]` attribute. In a production environment, those `unwrap()` functions should probably be changed for `expect()`, so that we can add some text if things go wrong.

Later, we use that information to call the `impl_type_name()` function, which we haven't yet defined. That function will take that information about the structure or enumeration and will return a series of tokens. Since we will use the quote crate to create those tokens, they will need to be converted into Rust compiler token streams later and returned to the compiler.

Let's now implement the `impl_type_name()` function:

```
fn impl_type_name(ast: &syn::DeriveInput) -> quote::Tokens {
    let name = &ast.ident;
    quote! {
        impl TypeName for #name {
            fn type_name() -> &'static str {
                stringify!(#name)
            }
        }
    }
}
```

As you can see, this implementation is really simple. We get the name of the structure or enumeration from the **advanced source tree** (**AST**), and then use it inside the `quote!{}` macro, where we implement the `TypeName` macro for the structure or enumeration with that name. The `stringify!()` macro is a native Rust macro that gets a token and returns a compile time string representation of it. In this case, the `name`.

Let's see if this works by adding some code in the `main()` function of our parent crate and adding a couple of types that will derive our implementation:

```
#[derive(TypeName)]
struct Alice;

#[derive(TypeName)]
enum Bob {}

fn main() {
    println!("Alice's name is {}", Alice::type_name());
    println!("Bob's name is {}", Bob::type_name());
}
```

If you execute `cargo run`, you will see that the output is the following, as one would expect:

```
Alice's name is Alice
Bob's name is Bob
```

Implementing complex derivations

The `syn` and `quote` crates allow for really complex derivations. And, not only that, we do not necessarily need to derive a trait; we can implement any kind of code for the given structure or enumeration. This means that we can derive builder patterns, as we saw in the previous chapter, which will actually create a new structure or `Getters` and `Setters` for our structure.

That is what we are going to do for our next example. We will create structures and give them some methods to `get` and `set` the fields of the structure. In Rust, convention says that `Getters` should have the name of the field, without any prefix or a suffix such as `get`. So, for a field named `foo`, the `Getter` should be `foo()`. For mutable `Getters`, the function should have the `_mut` suffix, so in this case it would be `foo_mut()`. Setters should have the name of the field preceded by a `set_` prefix. So for a field named `bar`, it should be `set_bar()`.

Let's start with the creation of this new `getset-derive` procedural macro crate. As before, remember to set the `proc_macro` variable in the `[lib]` section of the `Cargo.toml` file to true and to add the `syn` and `quote` crates as dependencies.

Implementing getters

We will add two derives, `Getters` and `Setters`. We will start with the first one by creating the required boilerplate:

```
extern crate proc_macro;
extern crate syn;
#[macro_use]
extern crate quote;

use proc_macro::TokenStream;

#[proc_macro_derive(Getters)]
pub fn derive_getters(input: TokenStream) -> TokenStream {
    // Parse the input tokens into a syntax tree
    let input = syn::parse(input).unwrap();

    // Build the output
    let expanded = impl_getters(&input);

    // Hand the output tokens back to the compiler
    expanded.into()
}
```

```
fn impl_getters(ast: &syn::DeriveInput) -> quote::Tokens {
    let name = &ast.ident;
    unimplemented!()
}
```

We will not only need the name of the structure, we will also need any further generics added to the structure and `where` clauses. We didn't bother with these in our previous example, but we should add them in this more complex one. Gladly, the `syn` crate gives us all we need.

Let's write the next piece of code in the `impl_getters()` function:

```
fn impl_getters(ast: &syn::DeriveInput) -> quote::Tokens {
    use syn::{Data, Fields};

    let name = &ast.ident;
    let (impl_generics, ty_generics, where_clause) =
                            ast.generics.split_for_impl();

    match ast.data {
        Data::Struct(ref structure) => {
            if let Fields::Named(ref fields) = structure.fields {
                let getters: Vec<_> =
                                fields.named.iter()
                                    .map(generate_getter)
                                    .collect();

                quote! {
                    impl #impl_generics #name #ty_generics
                        #where_clause {
                        #(#getters)*
                    }
                }
            } else {
                panic!("you cannot implement getters for unit \
                        or tuple structs");
            }
        },
        Data::Union(ref _union) => {
            unimplemented!("sorry, getters are not implemented \
                            for unions yet");
        }
        Data::Enum(ref _enum) => {
            panic!("you cannot derive getters for enumerations");
        }
    }
}
```

```
fn generate_getter(field: &syn::Field) -> quote::Tokens {
    unimplemented!("getters not yet implemented")
}
```

We have a lot going on here. First, as you can see, we get the generics from the
`ast.generics` field and we use them later in the `quote!` macro. We then check which type
of data we have. We cannot implement getters or setters for enumerations, unit structs, or
structures with no named fields, such as `Foo(T)`, so we panic in those cases. Even though
it's still not possible to derive anything for unions yet, we can specifically filter the options
with the `syn` crate, so we just add that for potential future changes in the language.

In the case of a structure with named fields, we get a list of the fields and, for each of them,
we implement the getter. For that, we map them to the `generate_getter()` function,
defined at the bottom but still unimplemented.

Once we have the list of getters, we call the quote `!{}` macro to generate the tokens. As you
can see, we add the generics for the `impl` block so that if we had any in the structure, such
as `Bar<T, F, G>`, they would be added to the implementation.

To add all the getters from a vector, we use the `#(#var)*` syntax and the same as with the
`macro_rules!{}` macro, it will add one after the other. We can use this syntax with any
type implementing the `IntoIterator` trait, in this case, `Vec<quote::Tokens>`.

So, now we have to actually implement one getter. We have the `generate_getter()`
function which receives a `syn::Field`, so we have all the information we need. The
function will return `quote::Tokens`, so we will need to use the `quote!{}` macro inside.
You can probably implement it yourself if you have been following, by checking the `syn`
crate documentation at `docs.rs`. Let's see how it looks fully implemented:

```
fn generate_getter(field: &syn::Field) -> quote::Tokens {
    let name = field.ident
                    .expect("named fields must have a name");
    let ty = &field.ty;

    quote! {
        fn #name(&self) -> &#ty {
            &self.#name
        }
    }
}
```

As you can see, this is really simple. We get the identifier or name of the attribute, which should exist given that we are only implementing it for structures for named fields, and then get the type of the field. We then create the getter and return a reference to the internal data.

We could improve this further by adding exceptions for types that have their borrowed counterparts, such as `String` or `PathBuf`, returning `&str` and `Path` respectively, but I don't think it's worth it.

We could also add the documentation of the field to the generated getter. For that, we would use the `field.attrs` variable and get the contents of the attribute named `doc`, which is the one that includes the documentation text. Nevertheless, it's not so easy, because the name of the attribute is stored as a path and we would need to convert it to a string. But I invite you to try it with the `syn` crate documentation.

Implementing setters

The second part of this exercise will be to implement setters for our structure. Usually this is done by creating a `set_{field}()` function for each field. Moreover, it's common practice to use generics for it so that they can be used with many different types. For example, for a `String` field, it would be great if we didn't need to always use an actual `String` type and we could use a `&str`, a `Cow<_, str>`, or a `Box<str>`.

We only need to declare the input as `Into<String>`. This makes things a little bit more complex, but our API will look much better. To implement the new setters, it would only mean changing a little bit of what we saw earlier and most of the code would be duplicated.

To avoid that, we will use the strategy pattern so that we simply change the `generate_getter()` function to the `generate_setter()`, one for each field. I also moved the field retrieving a new function. Let's see how it looks:

```
use syn::{DeriveInput, Fields, Field, Data};
use syn::punctuated::Punctuated;
use syn::token::Comma;

fn get_fields(ast: &DeriveInput) -> &Punctuated<Field, Comma> {
    match ast.data {
        Data::Struct(ref structure) => {
            if let Fields::Named(ref fields) = structure.fields {
                &fields.named
            } else {
                panic!("you cannot implement setters or getters \
                    for unit or tuple structs");
```

```
                }
            },
            Data::Union(ref _union) => {
                unimplemented!("sorry, setters and getters are not \
                                implemented for unions yet");
            }
            Data::Enum(ref _enum) => {
                panic!("you cannot derive setters or getters for \
                        enumerations");
            }
        }
    }
}
```

Much better, right? It returns an iterator over the fields, which is what we need for our functions. We now create the method implementation function, which will receive a function as an argument, and will then be used for each field:

```
fn impl_methods<F>(ast: &DeriveInput, strategy: F) -> Tokens
where F: FnMut(&Field) -> Tokens {
    let methods: Vec<_> = get_fields(ast).iter()
                                          .map(strategy)
                                          .collect();

    let name = &ast.ident;
    let (impl_generics, ty_generics, where_clause) =
                        ast.generics.split_for_impl();

    quote! {
        impl #impl_generics #name #ty_generics #where_clause {
            #(#methods)*
        }
    }
}
```

As you can see, apart from small naming changes to make the meaning of bindings clearer, the only big change was to add a FnMut in the where signature of the function, which will be the getter or setter implementer. Therefore, to call this new function, we will need to change the derive_getters() method and add the new derive_setters() function:

```
#[proc_macro_derive(Getters)]
pub fn derive_getters(input: TokenStream) -> TokenStream {
    // Parse the input tokens into a syntax tree
    let input = syn::parse(input).unwrap();

    // Build the output
    let expanded = impl_methods(&input, generate_getter);

    // Hand the output tokens back to the compiler
```

```
            expanded.into()
    }

    #[proc_macro_derive(Setters)]
    pub fn derive_setters(input: TokenStream) -> TokenStream {
        // Parse the input tokens into a syntax tree
        let input = syn::parse(input).unwrap();

        // Build the output
        let expanded = impl_methods(&input, generate_setter);

        // Hand the output tokens back to the compiler
        expanded.into()
    }
```

As you can see, both methods are exactly the same, except that, when calling the
`impl_methods()` function, they use a different strategy. The first one will generate getters
and the second one setters. Finally, let's see what the `generate_setters()` function will
look like:

```
    use syn::Ident;

    fn generate_setter(field: &Field) -> Tokens {
        let name = field.ident
                    .expect("named fields must have a name");
        let fn_name = Ident::from(format!("set_{}", name));
        let ty = &field.ty;

        quote! {
            fn #fn_name<T>(&mut self, value: T) where T: Into<#ty> {
                self.#name = value.into();
            }
        }
    }
```

The code is similar in most aspects to the `generate_getter()` function, but it has some
differences. First, the function name is not the same as the `name`, since it needs the `set_`
prefix. For that, we create a string with the field name after it and we create an identifier
with that name.

We then construct the setter by using the new function name, using a mutable `self` and
adding a new input variable to the function, the value. Since we want this value to be
generic, we use the `T` type that we define later in the where clause as being a type that can
be transformed into our field type (`Into<#ty>`). We finally assign the converted value to
our field.

Let's see how this getter and setter setup works by creating a short example in the `main.rs` file of our parent crate. We add the procedural macro dependency to the `Cargo.toml` file and we define a structure:

```
#[macro_use]
extern crate getset_derive;

#[derive(Debug, Getters, Setters)]
struct Alice {
    x: String,
    y: u32,
}
```

Nothing special about it; except the `Getters` and `Setters` derive. As you see, we don't need to derive an actual trait. Now, we add a simple `main()` function to test the code:

```
fn main() {
    let mut alice = Alice {
        x: "this is a name".to_owned(),
        y: 34
    };
    println!("Alice: {{ x: {}, y: {} }}",
            alice.x(),
            alice.y());

    alice.set_x("testing str");
    alice.set_y(15u8);
    println!("{:?}", alice);
}
```

We create a new `Alice` structure and set the two fields in it. When printing the structure, we can see that the `Alice::x()` and `Alice::y()` getters can be used directly. Note that the double braces are for escaping.

Then, since we have a mutable variable, we use the setters to change the values of the `x` and `y` fields. As you can see, we don't have to provide a `String` or a `u32`; we can provide any type that can be converted directly to those without failing. Finally, since we implemented the `Debug` trait for `Alice`, we can print its contents without using the getters. The result after executing `cargo run` should be the following:

```
Alice: { x: this is a name, y: 34 }
Alice { x: "testing str", y: 15 }
```

Procedural macros or custom derives allow for really complex code generation, and you can even further customize the user experience. As we saw in the previous chapter, with the `serde` crate we could use the `#[serde]` attribute. You can add custom attributes to your derive crate by defining them in the `#[proc_macro_derive]` attribute, like this:

```
#[proc_macro_derive(Setters, attributes(generic))]
```

You can then use them by checking the attributes of the structure/enumeration or its fields via the `attrs` fields in `Field`, `DeriveInput`, `Variant`, or `FieldValue` structures. You could, for example, let the developer decide whether they wanted generics in the setters or to fine-tune the attributes that should be generic.

Extra information can be found in the official documentation at `https://doc.rust-lang.org/book/first-edition/procedural-macros.html#custom-attributes`.

Metaprogramming in nightly Rust

Until now, we have stayed in stable Rust, since it allows forward compatibility. There are some nightly features, though, that can help us improve our control over the code we generate. Nevertheless, all of them are experimental and they might change or even get removed before being stabilized.

Therefore, you should take into account that using nightly features will probably break your code in the future and it will take more effort to maintain it to be compatible with new Rust versions. Nevertheless, we will have a quick look at two new features that are coming to Rust.

Understanding compiler plugins

The Rust nightly compiler accepts loading extensions, called **plugins**. They effectively change the way the compiler behaves, so they can modify the language itself. A plugin is a crate, similar to the procedural macro crate we created previously.

The difference between a procedural or standard macro and a plugin is that, while the first two modify the Rust code they are given, a plugin is able to perform extra computations that can greatly improve the performance of your crate.

Since these plugins get loaded inside the compiler, they will have access to a lot of information that standard macros don't have. Moreover, this requires using the `rustc` compiler and the `libsyntax` library as external crates, which means that you will be loading a lot of the compiler code when compiling the plugin.

Therefore, do not add your plugin as an external crate to your binaries as it will create a huge executable with a lot of compiler code. To use a plugin without adding it as a library, you will need the nightly compiler and you will have to add `#![feature(plugin)]` and `#![plugin({plugin_name})]` attributes to your crate.

When developing a new plugin, you will need to create the crate with some extra information in the `Cargo.toml` file, as we did with the procedural macro:

```
[lib]
plugin = true
```

Then, in the `lib.rs` file, you will need to import the required libraries and define the plugin registrar. The bare minimum for the plugin to work would be the following:

```
#![crate_type="dylib"]
#![feature(plugin_registrar, rustc_private)]

extern crate syntax;
extern crate syntax_pos;
extern crate rustc;
extern crate rustc_plugin;

use rustc_plugin::Registry;

#[plugin_registrar]
pub fn plugin_registrar(reg: &mut Registry) {
    unimplemented!()
}
```

Even though, in this example, the `rustc`, `syntax`, and `syntax_pos` crates are not being used, it's almost certain you will need them when developing the plugin, since they have the required types for you to change any behaviour. The `Registry` object lets you register multiple types of new language items, such as macros or syntax extensions. For each of them, you will need to define a function to receive the compiler tokens and modify them to produce the desired output.

The `#![crate_type = "dylib"]` attribute tells the compiler to create a dynamic library with the crate, instead of the normal static one. This enables the library to be loaded by the compiler. The `plugin_registrar` nightly feature lets us create the actual plugin registrar function and the `rustc_private` feature allows us to use the private Rust compiler types so that we can use the compiler internals.

At the time of writing, the only online documentation for these crates is the one hosted by Manish Goregaokar, but that should change soon. On his website, you can find the API documentation for `rustc_plugin` (`https://manishearth.github.io/rust-internals-docs/rustc_plugin/index.html`), for `rustc` (`https://manishearth.github.io/rust-internals-docs/rustc/index.html`), for `syntax` (`https://manishearth.github.io/rust-internals-docs/syntax/index.html`), and for `syntax_pox` (`https://manishearth.github.io/rust-internals-docs/syntax_pos/index.html`). I invite you to read the API of those crates and to create small plugins for the compiler. Nevertheless, remember that the syntax will probably change, which makes it more difficult to maintain.

Declarative macros

The next thing that is coming to Rust are declarative macros, macros 2.0, or macros by example. It's true that some call standard macros declarative macros too, since they are based on the same principle. But I wanted to make this difference known so that we learn about some improvements that these new macros will bring to the language.

These new macros introduce the `macro` keyword, which will work similarly to the `macro_rules!{}` macro, but using a syntax more close to the function syntax than to the current syntax. Not only that, it will also add modularization to macros so that you can have two macros with the same name in the same crate, as long as they are in different modules. This extra modularization will make integration between crates much easier.

Sadly, there is still no syntax proposition for these macros, and the current nightly implementation is not much more than a placeholder for what is yet to come. I invite you to keep yourself up to date on the standardization of these new macros and even to define a future syntax for them by contributing to the community.

Summary

In this chapter, you have learned how to create your own macros. First, we saw the standard macros and created some that could help you develop more quickly and create more efficient code. Then, you learned about procedural macros and how to derive your own code for your structures and enumeration. Finally, you found out about two features that might be coming to stable Rust in the future, which can currently be used in nightly Rust—plugins and declarative macros.

In the two remaining chapters, we will talk about concurrency in Rust. As you will see, once our single-threaded code is fast enough, the next step toward faster execution is to compute it in parallel.

.

10
Multithreading

So far, we have seen how to make our code faster and faster by optimizing various aspects of how we code, but there is still one point left to optimize: making our code work in parallel. In this chapter, you will learn how **fearless concurrency** works in Rust by using threads to process your data.

During this chapter, you will learn the following:

- `Send` and `Sync` traits—how does Rust achieve memory safety?
- Basic threading in Rust—creating and managing threads
- Moving data between threads
- Crates to make multithreading easier and faster

Concurrency in Rust

For a long time, it has not made sense to perform all tasks sequentially in a computer. Of course, sometimes you need to perform some tasks before others, but in most real-world applications, you will want to run some tasks in parallel.

You might, for example, want to respond to HTTP requests. If you do one after the other, the overall server will be slow. Especially when you get many requests per second and some of them take time to complete. You probably want to start responding to others before you finish with the current one.

Furthermore, we now have multiple processors in almost any computer or server, even in most mobile phones. This means that not only can we process other tasks in parallel while our main task is idle, we can really use one processor for each task by using threads. This is a feature that we must use to our advantage when developing high-performance applications.

The main issue with concurrency is that it's hard. We are not used to thinking in parallel, and as programmers we make mistakes. We only have to check some of the security vulnerabilities or bugs in our most-used systems, developed by the greatest programmers, to see that it's difficult to make it right.

Sometimes, we try to change a variable without remembering that another task might be reading it, or even changing it at the same time. Imagine a request counter in the HTTP example. If we separate the load between two processors, and each processor receives a request, the shared counter should go up by two, right?

Each thread wants to add 1 to the counter. For that, they load the current counter in the CPU, they add one to it and then save it again in the RAM. This takes some time, especially loading it from RAM, which means that if they both load the counter at the same time, they will both have the current counter in the CPU.

If both add one to the counter and save it back, the value in the RAM will only add one request, instead of two, because both processors will save the new +1 value in the RAM. This is what we call a data race. There are some tools that avoid this behavior, such as atomic variables, semaphores, and mutexes, but we sometimes forget to use them.

One of the best-known features in Rust is the fearless concurrency. This means that as long as we use safe Rust, we shouldn't be able to create a data race. This solves our issue but, how do they do it?

Understanding the Send and Sync traits

The secret ingredients for this to work are the `Send` and `Sync` traits. They are traits known to the compiler, so it will check whether they are the types we use want to use to implement them and act accordingly. You cannot implement `Send` or `Sync` for your types directly. The compiler will know whether your types are `Send` or `Sync` by checking whether the contained fields are `Sync` or `Send`, in the case of structures or enumerations with fields.

Let's now understand how they work. First of all, you should note that neither Send nor Sync traits add methods to a given type. This means that, once compiled, they will not occupy any memory or add any extra overhead to your binary. They will only be checked at compile time to make sure that multithreading is safe. You cannot directly implement Send or Sync for your types unless you are using an unsafe block, so the compiler will do it for you where appropriate.

The Send trait

A structure implementing the Send trait is safe to be moved between threads. This means that you can safely transfer ownership of a Send type between threads. The standard library implements Send for the types that can actually be moved across thread boundaries, and the compiler will automatically implement it for your types if they can also be moved between threads. If a type is only composed of Send types, it will be a Send type.

Most types in the standard library implement the Send trait. You can safely move ownership of a u32 to another thread, for example. This means that the previous thread will not be able to use it again and that the new thread will be in charge of dropping it once it gets out of scope.

There are some exceptions, though. Raw pointers cannot be safely moved to another thread, since they have no safety guards. You can copy a raw pointer multiple times, and it could happen that one gets to one thread and the other stays in the current one. If both try to manipulate the same memory at the same time, it will create undefined behavior.

The other exception is the reference-counted pointer or Rc type. This type can easily and efficiently create shared pointers to a given memory location. It will be safe since the type itself has some memory guarantees to make sure that if a mutable borrow exists, no other borrows can be made, and that if one or more non-mutable borrows exists, no mutable borrow can be made. The information pointed by the pointer will be dropped at the same time the last reference gets out of scope.

This works by having a counter that adds 1 each time a reference gets created by calling the clone() method and that subtracts 1 once a reference gets dropped. You might have already realized the issue that will arise when sharing it between threads: if two threads drop a reference at the same time, the reference count might only subtract 1. This means that when the last reference gets dropped, the counter won't be zero, and it will not drop the Rc, creating a memory leak.

Since Rust cannot allow memory leaks, the Rc type is not Send. There is an equivalent shared pointer that can be shared between threads, the atomically reference-counted pointer or Arc. This type makes sure that each addition or subtraction to the reference count gets performed atomically, so that if a new thread wants to add or subtract one reference, it will need to wait for the other threads to finish updating that counter. This makes it thread-safe, but it will be slower than an Rc due to the checks that need to be performed. So, you should use Rc if you don't need to send a reference to another thread.

The Sync trait

The Sync trait, on the other hand, represents a type that can be shared between threads. This refers to actually sharing the variable without transferring its ownership to the new thread.

As with the Send trait, raw pointers and Rc are not Sync, but there is another family of types that implement not Send but not Sync. A Cell can be safely sent between threads, but it cannot be shared. Let's review how a Cell works.

A cell that can be found in the std::cell module is a container that will have some inner data. This data will be another type. Cells are used for interior mutability, but what is that? Interior mutability is the option to change the contents of a variable without it being mutable. This might sound counter-intuitive, especially in Rust, but it's possible.

The two safe types of cells are Cell and RefCell. The first ones implement interior mutability by moving values in and out of the Cell. This means that you will be able to insert a new value in the cell or get the current cell value if it's a Copy type, but you won't be able to use its mutable methods if you are using a complex type, such as a vector or a HashMap. It's useful for small types such as integers, for example. An Rc will use a Cell to store a count of the references so that you can call the clone() method on a non-mutable Rc and still update the count of references. Let's see an example:

```
use std::cell::Cell;

fn main() {
    let my_cell = Cell::new(0);
    println!("Initial cell value: {}", my_cell.get());

    my_cell.set(my_cell.get() + 1);
    println!("Final cell value: {}", my_cell.get());
}
```

Note that the `my_cell` variable is not mutable, but the program still compiles and the output is the following:

```
Initial cell value: 0
Final cell value: 1
```

A `RefCell` does a similar thing, but it can be used with any kind of type, and you can get mutable references to the value inside if there are no other references to it. This internally uses unsafe code, of course, since Rust does not allow this. For this to work, it has a flag that lets the `RefCell` know whether it's currently borrowed or not. If it's borrowed for read, more read-only borrows can be generated with the `borrow()` method, but no mutable borrow can be done. If it's mutably borrowed with the `borrow_mut()` method, you will not be able to borrow it mutably or non-mutably.

These two methods will check the current borrow status at runtime, not at compile time, which is standard for Rust rules, and panic if the current state is not correct. They have non-panicking alternatives named `try_borrow()` and `try_borrow_mut()`. Since all the checks are done at runtime, they will be slower than the usual Rust rules, but they allow for this interior mutability. Let's see an example:

```rust
use std::cell::RefCell;
use std::collections::HashMap;

fn main() {
    let hm = HashMap::new();
    let my_cell = RefCell::new(hm);
    println!("Initial cell value: {:?}", my_cell.borrow());

    my_cell.borrow_mut().insert("test_key", "test_value");
    println!("Final cell value: {:?}", my_cell.borrow());
}
```

Once again, note that the `my_cell` variable is not mutable, and yet this code compiles and we get a mutable borrow to it, which allows us to insert a new key/value pair into the hash map. The output, as expected, is the following:

```
Initial cell value: {}
Final cell value: {"test_key": "test_value"}
```

On the other hand, since the borrow flag is not thread safe, the whole `RefCell` structure will not be `Sync`. You can safely send the complete ownership of the cell to a new thread, but you cannot have shared references to it. If you want to better understand how `Rc`, Cells, and RefCells work, we talked about them in `Chapter 3`, *Memory Management in Rust*.

There are thread-safe alternatives that allow interior mutability, called Mutexes. A `Mutex` stores the guard in an actual system `Mutex`, which synchronizes the threads before accessing the data. This makes it `Sync` but also slower. We will see how they work in this chapter.

Other types of concurrency in Rust

There are other ways of achieving parallel computing in Rust and in many other languages. In this chapter, we will talk about multithreading, where each thread has access to shared memory and creates its own stacks so that it can work independently. Ideally, you should have about the same number of threads working at the same time as the number of virtual CPUs in your PC/server.

This is usually twice the number of CPU cores, thanks to hyperthreading, where one core can run two threads at the same time by using its own hardware scheduler to decide which parts of each thread run at a given point in time.

The main issue with threads is that if you don't put a limit and run too many of them, maybe because some of them are idle and your CPU should be able to run the others, you will consume a lot of RAM. This is because of all the stacks that need to be created per thread. It is not uncommon for some web servers to create one thread per request. This will make things much slower when the load is high, since it will require a lot of RAM.

Another approach to concurrency is asynchronous programming. Rust has great tools for this kind of use and we will see them in the next chapter. The best improvement that asynchronous programming brings is the possibility for one thread to run multiple I/O requests while not blocking the actual thread.

Not only that, if the thread goes idle, it will not need to sleep for some time and then it will poll for new requests. The underlying operating system will wake the thread up when there is new information for it. This approach will, therefore, use the minimum possible resources for I/O operations.

But what about programs that do not need I/O? In those cases, things can be executed in parallel further than using threads. Most processors nowadays allow vectorization. Vectorization uses some special CPU instructions and registers where you can enter more than one variable and perform the same operation in all of them at the same time. This is extremely useful for high-performance computing, where you need to apply a certain algorithm multiple times to different datasets. With this approach, you can perform multiple additions, subtractions, multiplications, and divisions at the same time.

The special instructions used for vectorization are called the **SIMD** family, from **Single Instruction Multiple Data**. You can use them by running the assembly directly with the `asm!{}` macro in nightly Rust, and the compiler will try to automatically vectorize your code, even though this is not usually as good as professionals can achieve manually. There are multiple proposals to stabilize SIMD intrinsics in 2018. This way, you will be able to use this instruction with some abstraction from assembly. There is some effort going on in the `faster` crate (`https://crates.io/crates/faster`).

Understanding multithreading

Now that we understand the different approaches for concurrency in Rust, we can start with the most basic one: creating threads. If you have previously used languages such as Java or C++, you will probably be familiar with the `new Thread()` syntax in the former or the `std::thread` in the latter. In both cases, you will need to specify some code that the new thread will run, and some extra information the thread will have. In both cases, you can start threads and wait for them to finish.

Creating threads

In Rust, things are similar to the C++ approach, where we have the `std::thread` module with the `spawn()` function. This function will receive a closure or a pointer to a function and execute it. It will return a handle to the thread, and we will be able to manage it from outside. Let's see how this works:

```
use std::thread;

fn main() {
    println!("Before the thread!");

    let handle = thread::spawn(|| {
        println!("Inside the thread!");
    });
```

```
    println!("After thread spawn!");

    handle.join().expect("the thread panicked");
    println!("After everything!");
}
```

This will output something similar to this:

```
Before the thread!
After thread spawn!
Inside the thread!
After everything!
```

The **Inside the thread!** and **After thread spawn!** messages could be ordered in any way, in theory, even though in this simple example it is easy to see that spawning the thread will take more time than printing in the screen buffer.

Nevertheless, this example shows some valuable information on how to work with threads. First, when the **Before the thread!** message gets printed, there is only one thread in execution: the main thread, running the main() function.

Then, we spawn a new thread with the std::thread::spawn() function, and we pass a simple closure to it. This closure will just print the **Inside the thread!** message in the console. This happens at the same time as the printing of the **After thread spawn!** message. In fact, in some programming languages, you might see that the characters of both messages get mixed and the final message is just a lot of incomprehensible characters.

Rust avoids this by only accessing the standard output file descriptor with a Mutex. The println!() macro will lock stdout while it writes the message, and if a new message wants to be written, it will have to wait until the first write finishes.

This has both advantages and disadvantages. As a clear advantage, the printed messages are clearly readable, since one of the threads (the main thread or the second thread) will always arrive before the other. On the other hand, it means that while the second thread is waiting for the first one to finish printing on the screen, it will be blocked and won't be able to do any computation.

You will need to make sure that you take that into account, and don't print frequently from many threads while performing computations. In fact, since Rust is a thread-safe language, it will happen with any shared resource, so you will need to be careful to avoid overhead.

You might think that this is a bad approach for performance, since it will make things slower, but actually, it's the only possible approach if the integrity of the data needs to be preserved. In other languages, you will need to implement the solution yourself, or use existing solutions explicitly to avoid memory corruption.

Before the end of the example code, we can see that we call the `join()` method in the thread handle. This will make the current thread wait for the other one to finish. You might note that I added a call to the `expect()` method after it. This is because the `join()` method returns a `Result` because it might have panicked before finishing.

Panicking in Rust

Let's first understand what a thread panic is. You might already know that you can cause a panic by calling the `unwrap()` or `expect()` methods in an `Option` or `Result`, or even by calling directly to `panic!()`. There are multiple ways of panicking: the `unimplemented!()` macro panics, letting the user know that the feature is not implemented, the `assert!()` macro family will panic if the conditions are not satisfied, and indexing a slice out of bounds will also panic, but, what is a panic?

When talking about a single-threaded application, you might think that a panic is like exiting the program with an error, similar to the `exit()` function in C/C++. What might sound new to you is that a panic is something that happens at the thread level. If the main thread panics, the whole program exits, but if a non-main thread panics, you can recover from it.

But, is a panic really a simple program end? Actually, it's much more than that. In C/C++, when you exit a program, the memory just gets handed back to the kernel and then it just ends. Rust, on the other hand, due to its memory safety guarantees, makes sure that it calls all the destructors in the current stack. This means that all the variables will be dropped gracefully.

This is what is called **stack unwinding**, but it's not the only option. As we saw in the first chapter, where we explained how to configure the behavior in the `Cargo.toml` file, you can also opt to abort panics, which will mimic the standard C/C++ behavior.

The main advantage of the unwinding panic is, of course, that you can perform cleaning operations if things go bad. You can, for example, close files, write last minute logs, and update some databases just by implementing the `Drop` trait in your structures.

The main disadvantage, though, as we already mentioned in Chapter 1, *Common Performance Pitfalls,* is that each time we call the unwrap() or expect() methods, for example, a new branch appears. Either things go wrong and the thread panics or things go as they should. If they panic, the compiler needs to add the whole code for the stack unwinding, which makes executables noticeably bigger.

Now that you know how panics work, let's look at how we can recover from them:

```
use std::thread;

fn main() {
    println!("Before the thread!");

    let handle = thread::Builder::new()
        .name("bad thread".to_owned())
        .spawn(|| {
            panic!("Panicking inside the thread!");
        })
        .expect("could not create the thread");
    println!("After thread spawn!");

    if handle.join().is_err() {
        println!("Something bad happened :(");
    }
    println!("After everything!");
}
```

As you can see, I added some more boilerplate code. I added a name to the thread, for example, which is a good practice so that we know what each thread is called if something goes wrong. I changed the console print inside the second thread for an explicit panic, and then I checked if things were wrong when joining the thread. What is important here is that you should never just call expect() or unwrap() when joining a thread, since it could make your whole program fail.

For this example, the output should be similar to the following:

```
Before the thread!
After thread spawn!
thread 'bad thread' panicked at 'Panicking inside the thread!', src/main.rs:9:12
note: Run with `RUST_BACKTRACE=1` for a backtrace.
Something bad happened :(
After everything!
```

There is an extra tip when working with panicking threads. If you have a structure that implements the Drop trait, the drop() method will be called when panicking or when going out of scope.

You can find out whether the current thread is panicking by calling the
`std::thread::panicking()` function. Let's see how it works:

```
use std::thread;

struct MyStruct {
    name: String,
}

impl Drop for MyStruct {
    fn drop(&mut self) {
        if thread::panicking() {
            println!("The thread is panicking with the {} struct!",
self.name);
        } else {
            println!("The {} struct is out of scope :(", self.name);
        }
    }
}

fn main() {
    let my_struct = MyStruct {
        name: "whole program".to_owned(),
    };

    {
        let scoped_struct = MyStruct {
            name: "scoped".to_owned(),
        };
    }

    let handle = thread::Builder::new()
        .name("bad thread".to_owned())
        .spawn(|| {
            let thread_struct = MyStruct {
                name: "thread".to_owned(),
            };
            panic!("Panicking inside the thread!");
        })
        .expect("could not create the thread");
    println!("After thread spawn!");

    if handle.join().is_err() {
        println!("Something bad happened :(");
    }
    println!("After everything!");
}
```

Let's first see what this code does. It adds a new `MyStruct` structure, which has a name in it and that implements the Drop trait. Then, it creates one instance of the structure with the `whole program` name. This structure will be dropped at the end of the `main()` function.

Then, in an artificial scope, it adds a scoped instance of the structure that will be dropped just at the end of that inner scope. Finally, inside the thread, it creates a new structure that should be dropped at the end of the thread, which will be unwound.

The Drop implementation of the `MyStruct` structure uses the `std::thread::panicking()` function to check whether it's being dropped while panicking or simply because it went out of scope. Here we have the output of this example:

```
The scoped struct is out of scope :(
After thread spawn!
thread 'bad thread' panicked at 'Panicking inside the thread!', src/main.rs:34:12
note: Run with `RUST_BACKTRACE=1` for a backtrace.
The thread is panicking with the thread struct!
Something bad happened :(
After everything!
The whole program struct is out of scope :(
```

As we can see, the first message is the drop of the inner scope binding. Then, the new thread spawns, it panics, and the binding inside the thread is dropped while unwinding the stack. Finally, after the last message in the `main()` function, the first binding we created gets dropped.

Moving data between threads

We saw with the `Send` and `Sync` traits that the first one allows for a variable to be sent between threads, but how does that work? Can we just use a variable created in the main thread inside our secondary thread? Let's try it:

```rust
use std::thread;

fn main() {
    let my_vec = vec![10, 33, 54];

    let handle = thread::Builder::new()
        .name("my thread".to_owned())
        .spawn(|| {
            println!("This is my vector: {:?}", my_vec);
        })
        .expect("could not create the thread");
```

```
    if handle.join().is_err() {
        println!("Something bad happened :(");
    }
}
```

What we did was create a vector outside the thread and then use it from inside. But it seems it does not work. Let's see what the compiler tells us:

```
error[E0373]: closure may outlive the current function, but it borrows `my_vec`, which is owned by the current function
 --> src/main.rs:8:16
  |
8 |          .spawn(|| {
  |                 ^^ may outlive borrowed value `my_vec`
9 |              println!("This is my vector: {:?}", my_vec);
  |                                                   ------ `my_vec` is borrowed here
help: to force the closure to take ownership of `my_vec` (and any other referenced variables), use the `move` keyword
  |
8 |          .spawn(move || {
  |                 ^^^^^^^
error: aborting due to previous error

error: Could not compile `test_crate`.
```

That's interesting. The compiler noticed that the `my_vec` binding would be dropped at the end of the `main()` function, and that the inner thread could live longer. This is not the case in our example, since we `join()` both threads before the end of the `main()` function, but it could happen in a scenario where a thread is creating more threads and then ending itself. This would make the reference inside the thread invalid, and Rust does not allow that.

The move keyword

Nevertheless, it gives a great explanation of something we can do. We have two options: share the binding between the threads or send it to the second one. Since we won't use it in the main thread, we can add the `move` keyword before the closure and send the vector to the new thread, since it's `Send`. Let's see how we can make it work:

```
use std::thread;

fn main() {
    let my_vec = vec![10, 33, 54];

    let handle = thread::Builder::new()
        .name("my thread".to_owned())
        .spawn(move || {
            println!("This is my vector: {:?}", my_vec);
        })
        .expect("could not create the thread");
```

```
        if handle.join().is_err() {
            println!("Something bad happened :(");
        }
    }
```

This now compiles and shows the list of numbers in the console, perfect! But, what if we want to be able to see it in the main thread, too? Trying to print the vector after the spawning of the second thread won't work, since the variable has been moved to the new thread, and we already saw that if we don't move the vector we cannot use it inside the thread. What can we do?

Sharing data between threads

There is one special reference-counted pointer that can be shared between threads that we already mentioned: std::sync::Arc. The main difference from the Rc is that the Arc counts the references with an atomic counter. This means that the kernel will make sure that all updates to the reference count will happen one by one, making it thread-safe. Let's see it with an example:

```
use std::thread;
use std::sync::Arc;

fn main() {
    let my_vec = vec![10, 33, 54];
    let pointer = Arc::new(my_vec);

    let t_pointer = pointer.clone();
    let handle = thread::Builder::new()
        .name("my thread".to_owned())
        .spawn(move || {
            println!("Vector in second thread: {:?}", t_pointer);
        })
        .expect("could not create the thread");

    println!("Vector in main thread: {:?}", pointer);

    if handle.join().is_err() {
        println!("Something bad happened :(");
    }
}
```

As you can see, the vector is used both inside the second thread and in the main thread. You might be wondering what `clone()` means in the pointer. Are we cloning the vector? Well, that would be the easy solution, right? The real deal is that we are just getting a new reference to the vector. That's because the `Clone` trait is not a normal clone in the `Arc`. It will return a new `Arc`, yes, but it will also increase the reference count. And since both instances of `Arc` will have the same pointers to the reference counter and the vector, we will be effectively sharing the vector.

How is it possible to simply debug the vector pointer inside the `Arc`? This is an interesting trick. `Arc<T>` implements `Deref<T>`, which means that it will automatically dereference to the vector it's pointing to when calling the debug. Interestingly enough, there are two traits that allow that automatic dereference: `Deref` and `DerefMut`. As you might guess, the former gives you an immutable borrow of the contained value, while the latter gives you a mutable borrow.

`Arc` only implements `Deref`, not `DerefMut`, so we are not able to mutate what we have inside of it. But wait, we have cells that can mutate while being immutable, right? Well, there is an issue with them. The behavior we have seen from the `Arc`, of being able to be shared among threads, is only thanks to implementing the `Sync` trait, and it will only implement it if the inner value implements `Sync` and `Send`. Cells can be sent between threads, they implement `Send`, but they do not implement `Sync`. `Vec`, on the other hand, implements whatever the inside values implement, so in this case, it was both `Send` and `Sync`.

So, is that it? Can't we mutate anything inside an `Arc`? As you might have guessed, that's not the case. If what we want to share between threads is an integer or a Boolean, we can use any of the `std::sync::atomic` integers and Booleans, even though some are not stable yet. They implement `Sync` and they have interior mutability with their `load()` and `store()` methods. You will only need to specify the memory ordering of the operation. Let's see how that works:

```
use std::thread;
use std::sync::Arc;
use std::sync::atomic::{AtomicUsize, Ordering};

fn main() {
    let my_val = AtomicUsize::new(0);
    let pointer = Arc::new(my_val);

    let t_pointer = pointer.clone();
    let handle = thread::Builder::new()
        .name("my thread".to_owned())
        .spawn(move || {
```

```
            for _ in 0..250_000 {
                let cur_value = t_pointer.load(Ordering::Relaxed);
                let sum = cur_value + 1;
                t_pointer.store(sum, Ordering::Relaxed);
            }
        })
        .expect("could not create the thread");

    for _ in 0..250_000 {
        let cur_value = pointer.load(Ordering::Relaxed);
        let sum = cur_value + 1;
        pointer.store(sum, Ordering::Relaxed);
    }

    if handle.join().is_err() {
        println!("Something bad happened :(");
    }

    let a_int = Arc::try_unwrap(pointer).unwrap();
    println!("Final number: {}", a_int.into_inner());
}
```

If you run this program multiple times, you will see that the final number will be different each time, and none of them will be 500,000 (it could happen, but it's almost impossible). What we have is similar to a data race:

```
[razican@laptop test_crate]$ ./target/debug/test_crate
Final number: 278960
[razican@laptop test_crate]$ ./target/debug/test_crate
Final number: 273890
[razican@laptop test_crate]$ ./target/debug/test_crate
Final number: 299785
[razican@laptop test_crate]$ ./target/debug/test_crate
Final number: 270108
[razican@laptop test_crate]$ ./target/debug/test_crate
Final number: 286985
[razican@laptop test_crate]$ ./target/debug/test_crate
Final number: 281446
[razican@laptop test_crate]$ ./target/debug/test_crate
Final number: 268530
```

But wait, can't Rust prevent all data races? Well, this is not exactly a data race. When we save the integer, we don't check whether it has changed, so we are overriding whatever was written there. We are not using the advantages Rust gives us. It will make sure that the state of the variable is consistent, but it won't prevent logic errors.

The issue is that when we store it back, that value has already changed. To avoid it, atomics have the great `fetch_add()` function and its friends `fetch_sub()`, `fetch_and()`, `fetch_or()`, and `fetch_xor()`. They will perform the complete operation atomically. They also have the great `compare_and_swap()` and `compare_exchange()` functions, which can be used to create locks. Let's see how that would work:

```
use std::thread;
use std::sync::Arc;
use std::sync::atomic::{AtomicUsize, Ordering};

fn main() {
    let my_val = AtomicUsize::new(0);
    let pointer = Arc::new(my_val);

    let t_pointer = pointer.clone();
    let handle = thread::Builder::new()
        .name("my thread".to_owned())
        .spawn(move || {
            for _ in 0..250_000 {
                t_pointer.fetch_add(1, Ordering::Relaxed);
            }
        })
        .expect("could not create the thread");

    for _ in 0..250_000 {
        pointer.fetch_add(1, Ordering::Relaxed);
    }

    if handle.join().is_err() {
        println!("Something bad happened :(");
    }

    let a_int = Arc::try_unwrap(pointer).unwrap();
    println!("Final number: {}", a_int.into_inner());
}
```

As you can see now, the result is 500,000 every time you run it. If you want to perform more complex operations, you will need a lock. You can do that with an `AtomicBool`, for example, where you can wait for it to be `false`, then swap it with `true` and then perform operations. You would need to make sure that all your threads only change values when the lock is set to `true` by them, by using some memory ordering. Let's see an example:

```
use std::thread;
use std::sync::Arc;
use std::sync::atomic::{AtomicBool, AtomicUsize, Ordering};
```

```
fn main() {
    let my_val = AtomicUsize::new(0);
    let pointer = Arc::new(my_val);
    let lock = Arc::new(AtomicBool::new(false));

    let t_pointer = pointer.clone();
    let t_lock = lock.clone();
    let handle = thread::Builder::new()
        .name("my thread".to_owned())
        .spawn(move || {
            for _ in 0..250_000 {
                while t_lock.compare_and_swap(
                        false, true, Ordering::Relaxed) {}
                let cur_value = t_pointer.load(Ordering::Relaxed);
                let sum = cur_value + 1;
                t_pointer.store(sum, Ordering::Relaxed);
                t_lock.store(false, Ordering::Relaxed);
            }
        })
        .expect("could not create the thread");

    for _ in 0..250_000 {
        while lock.compare_and_swap(
            false, true, Ordering::Relaxed) {}
        let cur_value = pointer.load(Ordering::Relaxed);
        let sum = cur_value + 1;
        pointer.store(sum, Ordering::Relaxed);
        lock.store(false, Ordering::Relaxed);
    }

    if handle.join().is_err() {
        println!("Something bad happened :(");
    }

    let a_int = Arc::try_unwrap(pointer).unwrap();
    println!("Final number: {}", a_int.into_inner());
}
```

If you run it, you will see that it works perfectly. But this only works because in both threads we only change the value between the lock acquisition and the lock release. In fact, this is so safe that we could avoid using an atomic integer altogether, even though Rust won't allow us to do so in safe code.

Now that we have seen how to mutate integers shared between threads, you might be wondering if something similar can be done with other types of bindings. As you can probably guess, it can. You will need to use `std::sync::Mutex`, and it will be much more expensive in performance terms than using atomic operations, so use them with caution. Let's see how they work:

```rust
use std::thread;
use std::sync::{Arc, Mutex};

fn main() {
    let my_vec = Arc::new(Mutex::new(Vec::new()));

    let t_vec = my_vec.clone();
    let handle = thread::Builder::new()
        .name("my thread".to_owned())
        .spawn(move || {
            for i in 0..50 {
                t_vec.lock().unwrap().push(i);
            }
        })
        .expect("could not create the thread");

    for i in 0..50 {
        my_vec.lock().unwrap().push(i);
    }

    if handle.join().is_err() {
        println!("Something bad happened :(");
    }

    let vec_mutex = Arc::try_unwrap(my_vec).unwrap();
    let f_vec = vec_mutex.into_inner().unwrap();
    println!("Final vector: {:?}", f_vec);
}
```

It will output something similar to this:

```
Final vector: [0, 1, 2, 3, 4, 5, 6, 7, 8, 9, 10, 11, 12, 13, 14, 15, 16, 17, 18, 19, 20, 21, 22, 23, 24, 25, 26, 27, 28, 29, 30, 31, 32, 33, 34, 35, 36, 37, 38, 39, 40, 41, 42, 43, 44, 45, 46, 47, 48, 49, 0, 1, 2, 3, 4, 5, 6, 7, 8, 9, 10, 11, 12, 13, 14, 15, 16, 17, 18, 19, 20, 21, 22, 23, 24, 25, 26, 27, 28, 29, 30, 31, 32, 33, 34, 35, 36, 37, 38, 39, 40, 41, 42, 43, 44, 45, 46, 47, 48, 49]
```

If you analyze the output closely, you will see that it will first add all numbers from **0** to **49** and then do the same again. If both threads were running in parallel, shouldn't all numbers be randomly distributed? Maybe two **1**s first, then two **2**s, and so on?

The main issue with sharing information between threads is that when the Mutex locks, it requires synchronization from both threads. This is perfectly fine and safe, but it takes a lot of time to switch from one thread to another to write in the vector. This is why the kernel scheduler allows for one of the threads to work for some time before locking the Mutex. If it was locking and unlocking the Mutex for each iteration, it would take ages to finish.

This means that if your loops were more than 50 iterations, maybe something like 1 million per loop, you would see that after some time, one of the threads would stop to give priority to the second one. In small numbers of iterations, though, you will see that one runs after the other.

 A Mutex gets locked when you call lock() and gets unlocked when it goes out of scope. In this case, since there is no binding to it, it will go out of scope after calling push(i), so we could add more computation after it and it would be done without requiring synchronization between threads. Sometimes, it might even be useful to create artificial scopes to unlock the Mutex as soon as possible if our work involves more than one line and we need a binding.

There is an extra issue we have to take into account when working with Mutexes: thread panicking. If your thread panics while the Mutex is locked, the lock() function in another thread will return a Result::Err(_), so if we call unwrap() every time we lock() our Mutex, we can get into big trouble, since all threads would panic. This is called Mutex poisoning and there is a way to avoid it.

When a Mutex is poisoned because a thread panicked while having it locked, the error result of calling the lock() method will return the poisoning error. We can recover from it by calling the into_inner() method. Let's see an example of how this would work:

```
use std::thread;
use std::sync::{Arc, Mutex};
use std::time::Duration;

fn main() {
    let my_vec = Arc::new(Mutex::new(Vec::new()));

    let t_vec = my_vec.clone();
    let handle = thread::Builder::new()
        .name("my thread".to_owned())
```

```
        .spawn(move || {
            for i in 0..10 {
                let mut vec = t_vec.lock().unwrap();
                vec.push(i);
                panic!("Panicking the secondary thread");
            }
        })
        .expect("could not create the thread");

    thread::sleep(Duration::from_secs(1));

    for i in 0..10 {
        let mut vec = match my_vec.lock() {
            Ok(g) => g,
            Err(e) => {
                println!("The secondary thread panicked, recovering...");
                e.into_inner()
            }
        };
        vec.push(i);
    }

    if handle.join().is_err() {
        println!("Something bad happened :(");
    }

    let vec_mutex = Arc::try_unwrap(my_vec).unwrap();
    let f_vec = match vec_mutex.into_inner() {
        Ok(g) => g,
        Err(e) => {
            println!("The secondary thread panicked, recovering...");
            e.into_inner()
        }
    };
    println!("Final vector: {:?}", f_vec);
}
```

As you can see in the code, the second thread will panic after inserting the first number in the vector. I added a small 1-second sleep in the main thread to make sure that the secondary thread would execute before the main one. If you run it, you will get something similar to this:

```
thread 'my thread' panicked at 'Panicking the secondary thread', src/main.rs:15:17
note: Run with `RUST_BACKTRACE=1` for a backtrace.
The secondary thread panicked, recovering…
The secondary thread panicked, recovering…
The secondary thread panicked, recovering…
The secondary thread panicked, recovering…
The secondary thread panicked, recovering…
The secondary thread panicked, recovering…
The secondary thread panicked, recovering…
The secondary thread panicked, recovering…
The secondary thread panicked, recovering…
The secondary thread panicked, recovering…
Something bad happened :(
The secondary thread panicked, recovering…
Final vector: [0, 0, 1, 2, 3, 4, 5, 6, 7, 8, 9]
```

As you can see, once a `Mutex` has been poisoned, it will stay poisoned for all of its life. You should therefore try to avoid any behavior that could lead to a panic once you get the lock in a `Mutex`. In any case, you can still use it and as you can see, the final vector will contain values from both threads; only the 0 from the secondary thread, until the panic, and then the rest from the main thread. Make sure not to `unwrap()` a `Mutex` in a critical application, as it will make all your threads panic if you do it in all your threads after the first panic.

Channels between threads

There is an extra way of sending information between two or more threads. They are called channels, or more specifically, multi-producer, single-consumer FIFO communication primitives.

Let's first analyze what that means. Since they are multi-producer channels, you can send the data to the receiver from multiple threads at the same time. In the same way, since they are single-consumers, only one receiver will receive data from all the associated senders in the channel. Finally, FIFO comes from **first input, first output**, which means that the messages in the channel will be ordered by their creation timestamp, and you will only be able to read the second `message` after reading the first one in the receiver.

These channels are located in the `std::sync::mpsc` module, and they are really useful for logging or telemetry, for example. One thread can manage the I/O interface with the communication or logging mechanism, while the others can send this thread the information they want to log or communicate. An approach using these channels is being studied for OpenStratos, for a stratospheric balloon-control software being written in Rust.

A channel consists of a `Sender` and a `Receiver`. `Sender` implements `Clone`, so that cloning the sender, multiple threads can send information to the associated receiver. There are two types of senders: `Sender` and `SyncSender`. The former will just send the message to the receiver without checking anything extra, while the latter will send the message only when the receiver's buffer has enough space. It will block the current thread until the message is sent.

Channels are created using the `channel()` and `sync_channel()` functions in the `std::sync::mpsc` module. They will return a tuple with a `Sender` or `SyncSender`, respectively, as the first element and a `Receiver` as the second one. Since `Sender` and `Receiver` implement `Send`, they can safely be sent to another thread with the `move` keyword. In the case of a synchronous channel, the `sync_channel()` will require a `usize` to set the buffer size. The `Sender` will block if the buffer is full. On the other hand, asynchronous channels work as if they had an infinite buffer, they will always accept sending new data.

Each channel can only send or receive one particular type of data, so if a channel is configured to send `u32`, only one `u32` per message can be sent. You can configure it to send your own types, though, such as a custom `Frame` type with all the information you might want to send. Let's see how a channel works:

```
use std::thread;
use std::sync::mpsc::*;
use std::time::Duration;

fn main() {
    let (sender, receiver) = channel();

    let handles: Vec<_> = (1..6)
        .map(|i| {
            let t_sender = sender.clone();
            thread::Builder::new()
                .name(format!("sender-{}", i))
                .spawn(move || {
                    t_sender.send(
                        format!("Hello from sender {}!", i)
                    ).unwrap();
                })
```

```
                 .expect("could not create the thread")
        })
        .collect();

    while let Ok(message) = receiver.recv_timeout(Duration::from_secs(1)) {
        println!("{}", message);
    }
    for handle in handles {
        handle.join().unwrap();
    }
    println!("Finished");
}
```

As you can see in the code, five threads get created with an iterator, and their handles are collected in a vector. These threads will have a name containing the thread number, and will send the `Hello from sender {}!` message to the receiver. For each thread, the sender gets cloned so that the clone can be moved to the thread closure.

Then, a `while` loop will check with a 1-second timeout for the messages. It should be enough, since messages will be sent as soon as the threads start. In the case that no message gets received for one second (or all the senders get out of scope), the `while` loop will stop printing the messages and the threads will be joined. Finally, a completion message will be printed.

If you run this example, you will see an output similar to this one:

```
Hello from sender 2!
Hello from sender 1!
Hello from sender 3!
Hello from sender 5!
Hello from sender 4!
Finished
```

As you can see, the threads are not executed in any particular order. They will send the message to the receiver, and the receiver will read them in the received order. Since this example is asynchronous, we don't need to wait for the receiver to empty the buffer to send new messages, so it's really lightweight. In fact, we could join the threads before reading any messages from the receiver.

Multithreading crates

Until now, we have only been using the standard library to manipulate threads, but thanks to the great *crates.io* ecosystem, we can make use of more approaches that will improve our development speed as well as the performance of our code.

Non-blocking data structures

One of the issues we saw earlier was that if we wanted to share something more complex than an integer or a Boolean between threads and if we wanted to mutate it, we needed to use a `Mutex`. This is not entirely true, since one crate, Crossbeam, allows us to use great data structures that do not require locking a `Mutex`. They are therefore much faster and more efficient.

Often, when we want to share information between threads, it's usually a list of tasks that we want to work on cooperatively. Other times, we want to create information in multiple threads and add it to a list of information. It's therefore not so usual for multiple threads to be working with exactly the same variables, since as we have seen, that requires synchronization and it will be slow.

This is where Crossbeam shows all its potential. Crossbeam gives us some multithreaded queues and stacks, where we can insert data and consume data from different threads. We can, in fact, have some threads doing an initial processing of the data and others performing a second phase of the processing. Let's see how we can use these features. First, add `crossbeam` to the dependencies of the crate in the `Cargo.toml` file. Then, we start with a simple example:

```
extern crate crossbeam;

use std::thread;
use std::sync::Arc;

use crossbeam::sync::MsQueue;

fn main() {
    let queue = Arc::new(MsQueue::new());

    let handles: Vec<_> = (1..6)
        .map(|_| {
            let t_queue = queue.clone();
            thread::spawn(move || {
                for _ in 0..1_000_000 {
                    t_queue.push(10);
```

```
            }
        })
    })
    .collect();

for handle in handles {
    handle.join().unwrap();
}

let final_queue = Arc::try_unwrap(queue).unwrap();
let mut sum = 0;
while let Some(i) = final_queue.try_pop() {
    sum += i;
}

println!("Final sum: {}", sum);
}
```

Let's first understand what this example does. It will iterate 1,000,000 times in 5 different threads, and each time it will push a 10 to a queue. Queues are FIFO lists, first input, first output. This means that the first number entered will be the first one to `pop()` and the last one will be the last to do so. In this case, all of them are a 10, so it doesn't matter.

Once the threads finish populating the queue, we iterate over it and we add all the numbers. A simple computation should make you able to guess that if everything goes perfectly, the final number should be 50,000,000. If you run it, that will be the result, and that's not all. If you run it by executing `cargo run --release`, it will run blazingly fast. On my computer, it took about one second to complete. If you want, try to implement this code with the standard library `Mutex` and vector, and you will see that the performance difference is amazing.

As you can see, we still needed to use an `Arc` to control the multiple references to the queue. This is needed because the queue itself cannot be duplicated and shared, it has no reference count.

Crossbeam not only gives us FIFO queues. We also have LIFO stacks. LIFO comes from last input, first output, and it means that the last element you inserted in the stack will be the first one to `pop()`. Let's see the difference with a couple of threads:

```
extern crate crossbeam;

use std::thread;
use std::sync::Arc;
use std::time::Duration;
```

```
use crossbeam::sync::{MsQueue, TreiberStack};

fn main() {
    let queue = Arc::new(MsQueue::new());
    let stack = Arc::new(TreiberStack::new());

    let in_queue = queue.clone();
    let in_stack = stack.clone();
    let in_handle = thread::spawn(move || {
        for i in 0..5 {
            in_queue.push(i);
            in_stack.push(i);
            println!("Pushed :D");
            thread::sleep(Duration::from_millis(50));
        }
    });

    let mut final_queue = Vec::new();
    let mut final_stack = Vec::new();

    let mut last_q_failed = 0;
    let mut last_s_failed = 0;

    loop {
        // Get the queue
        match queue.try_pop() {
            Some(i) => {
                final_queue.push(i);
                last_q_failed = 0;
                println!("Something in the queue! :)");
            }
            None => {
                println!("Nothing in the queue :(");
                last_q_failed += 1;
            }
        }

        // Get the stack
        match stack.try_pop() {
            Some(i) => {
                final_stack.push(i);
                last_s_failed = 0;
                println!("Something in the stack! :)");
            }
            None => {
                println!("Nothing in the stack :(");
                last_s_failed += 1;
            }
```

```
        }

        // Check if we finished
        if last_q_failed > 1 && last_s_failed > 1 {
            break;
        } else if last_q_failed > 0 || last_s_failed > 0 {
            thread::sleep(Duration::from_millis(100));
        }
    }

    in_handle.join().unwrap();

    println!("Queue: {:?}", final_queue);
    println!("Stack: {:?}", final_stack);
}
```

As you can see in the code, we have two shared variables: a queue and a stack. The secondary thread will push new values to each of them, in the same order, from 0 to 4. Then, the main thread will try to get them back. It will loop indefinitely and use the try_pop() method. The pop() method can be used, but it will block the thread if the queue or the stack is empty. This will happen in any case once all values get popped, since no new values are being added, so the try_pop() method will help not to block the main thread and end gracefully.

The way it checks whether all the values were popped is by counting how many times it failed to pop a new value. Every time it fails, it will wait for 100 milliseconds, while the push thread only waits for 50 milliseconds between pushes. This means that if it tries to pop new values two times and there are no new values, the pusher thread has already finished.

It will add values as they are popped to two vectors and then print the result. In the meantime, it will print messages about pushing and popping new values. You will understand this better by seeing the output:

```
Nothing in the queue :(
Nothing in the stack :(
Pushed :D
Pushed :D
Something in the queue! :)
Something in the stack! :)
Pushed :D
Something in the queue! :)
Something in the stack! :)
Something in the queue! :)
Something in the stack! :)
Nothing in the queue :(
Nothing in the stack :(
Pushed :D
Something in the queue! :)
Something in the stack! :)
Pushed :D
Something in the queue! :)
Something in the stack! :)
Nothing in the queue :(
Nothing in the stack :(
Nothing in the queue :(
Nothing in the stack :(
Queue: [0, 1, 2, 3, 4]
Stack: [1, 2, 0, 3, 4]
```

Note that the output can be different in your case, since threads don't need to be executed in any particular order.

In this example output, as you can see, it first tries to get something from the queue and the stack but there is nothing there, so it sleeps. The second thread then starts pushing things, two numbers actually. After this, the queue and the stack will be `[0, 1]`. Then, it pops the first item from each of them. From the queue, it will pop the `0` and from the stack it will pop the `1` (the last one), leaving the queue as `[1]` and the stack as `[0]`.

It will go back to sleep and the secondary thread will insert a `2` in each variable, leaving the queue as `[1, 2]` and the stack as `[0, 2]`. Then, the main thread will pop two elements from each of them. From the queue, it will pop the `1` and the `2`, while from the stack it will pop the `2` and then the `0`, leaving both empty.

The main thread then goes to sleep, and for the next two tries, the secondary thread will push one element and the main thread will pop it, twice.

It might seem a little bit complex, but the idea is that these queues and stacks can be used efficiently between threads without requiring a `Mutex`, and they accept any `Send` type. This means that they are great for complex computations, and even for multi-staged complex computations.

The Crossbeam crate also has some helpers to deal with epochs and even some variants of the mentioned types. For multithreading, Crossbeam also adds a great utility: scoped threads.

Scoped threads

In all our examples, we have used standard library threads. As we have discussed, these threads have their own stack, so if we want to use variables that we created in the main thread we will need to *send* them to the thread. This means that we will need to use things such as `Arc` to share non-mutable data. Not only that, having their own stack means that they will also consume more memory and eventually make the system slower if they use too much.

Crossbeam gives us some special threads that allow sharing stacks between them. They are called scoped threads. Using them is pretty simple and the crate documentation explains them perfectly; you will just need to create a `Scope` by calling `crossbeam::scope()`. You will need to pass a closure that receives the Scope. You can then call `spawn()` in that scope the same way you would do it in `std::thread`, but with one difference, you can share immutable variables among threads if they were created inside the scope or moved to it.

This means that for the queues or stacks we just talked about, or for atomic data, you can simply call their methods without requiring an `Arc`! This will improve the performance even further. Let's see how it works with a simple example:

```
extern crate crossbeam;

fn main() {
    let all_nums: Vec<_> = (0..1_000_u64).into_iter().collect();
    let mut results = Vec::new();

    crossbeam::scope(|scope| {
        for num in &all_nums {
            results.push(scope.spawn(move || num * num + num * 5 + 250));
        }
    });
```

```
        let final_result: u64 = results.into_iter().map(|res|
    res.join()).sum();
        println!("Final result: {}", final_result);
    }
```

Let's see what this code does. It will first just create a vector with all the numbers from 0 to 1000. Then, for each of them, in a `crossbeam` scope, it will run one scoped thread per number and perform a supposedly complex computation. This is just an example, since it will just return a result of a simple second-order function.

Interestingly enough, though, the `scope.spawn()` method allows returning a result of any type, which is great in our case. The code will add each result to a vector. This won't directly add the resulting number, since it will be executed in parallel. It will add a result guard, which we will be able to check outside the scope.

Then, after all the threads run and return the results, the scope will end. We can now check all the results, which are guaranteed to be ready for us. For each of them, we just need to call `join()` and we will get the result. Then, we sum it up to check that they are actual results from the computation.

This `join()` method can also be called inside the scope and get the results, but it will mean that if you do it inside the `for` loop, for example, you will block the loop until the result is generated, which is not efficient. The best thing is to at least run all the computations first and then start checking the results. If you want to perform more computations after them, you might find it useful to run the new computation in another loop or iterator inside the `crossbeam` scope.

But, how does `crossbeam` allow you to use the variables outside the scope freely? Won't there be data races? Here is where the magic happens. The scope will join all the inner threads before exiting, which means that no further code will be executed in the main thread until all the scoped threads finish. This means that we can use the variables of the main thread, also called **parent stack**, due to the main thread being the parent of the scope in this case without any issue.

We can actually check what is happening by using the `println!()` macro. If we remember from previous examples, printing to the console after spawning some threads would usually run even before the spawned threads, due to the time it takes to set them up. In this case, since we have `crossbeam` preventing it, we won't see it. Let's check the example:

```
extern crate crossbeam;

fn main() {
    let all_nums: Vec<_> = (0..10).into_iter().collect();
```

```
crossbeam::scope(|scope| {
    for num in all_nums {
        scope.spawn(move || {
            println!("Next number is {}", num);
        });
    }
});

println!("Main thread continues :)");
}
```

If you run this code, you will see something similar to the following output:

```
Next number is 1
Next number is 0
Next number is 2
Next number is 3
Next number is 6
Next number is 4
Next number is 5
Next number is 7
Next number is 8
Next number is 9
Main thread continues :)
```

As you can see, scoped threads will run without any particular order. In this case, it will first run the 1, then the 0, then the 2, and so on. Your output will probably be different. The interesting thing, though, is that the main thread won't continue executing until all the threads have finished. Therefore, reading and modifying variables in the main thread is perfectly safe.

There are two main performance advantages with this approach; Arc will require a call to malloc() to allocate memory in the heap, which will take time if it's a big structure and the memory is a bit full. Interestingly enough, that data is already in our stack, so if possible, we should try to avoid duplicating it in the heap. Moreover, the Arc will have a reference counter, as we saw. And it will even be an atomic reference counter, which means that every time we clone the reference, we will need to atomically increment the count. This takes time, even more than incrementing simple integers.

Most of the time, we might be waiting for some expensive computations to run, and it would be great if they just gave all the results when finished. We can still add some more chained computations, using scoped threads, that will only be executed after the first ones finish, so we should use scoped threads more often than normal threads, if possible.

Thread pooling

So far, we have seen multiple ways of creating new threads and sharing information between them. Nevertheless, as we saw at the beginning of the chapter, the ideal number of threads we should spawn to do all the work should be around the number of virtual processors in the system. This means we should not spawn one thread for each chunk of work. Nevertheless, controlling what work each thread does can be complex, since you have to make sure that all threads have work to do at any given point in time.

Here is where thread pooling comes in handy. The `Threadpool` crate will enable you to iterate over all your work and for each of your small chunks, you can call something similar to a `thread::spawn()`. The interesting thing is that each task will be assigned to an idle thread, and no new thread will be created for each task. The number of threads is configurable and you can get the number of CPUs with other crates. Not only that, if one of the threads panics, it will automatically add a new one to the pool.

To see an example, first, let's add `threadpool` and `num_cpus` as dependencies in our `Cargo.toml` file. Then, let's see an example code:

```
extern crate num_cpus;
extern crate threadpool;

use std::sync::atomic::{AtomicUsize, Ordering};
use std::sync::Arc;

use threadpool::ThreadPool;

fn main() {
    let pool = ThreadPool::with_name("my worker".to_owned(),
num_cpus::get());
    println!("Pool threads: {}", pool.max_count());

    let result = Arc::new(AtomicUsize::new(0));

    for i in 0..1_0000_000 {
        let t_result = result.clone();
        pool.execute(move || {
            t_result.fetch_add(i, Ordering::Relaxed);
```

```
        });
    }

    pool.join();

    let final_res = Arc::try_unwrap(result).unwrap().into_inner();
    println!("Final result: {}", final_res);
}
```

This code will create a thread pool of threads with the number of logical CPUs in your computer. Then, it will add a number from 0 to 1,000,000 to an atomic `usize`, just to test parallel processing. Each addition will be performed by one thread. Doing this with one thread per operation (1,000,000 threads) would be really inefficient. In this case, though, it will use the appropriate number of threads, and the execution will be really fast. There is another crate that gives thread pools an even more interesting parallel processing feature: Rayon.

Parallel iterators

If you can see the big picture in these code examples, you'll have realized that most of the parallel work has a long loop, giving work to different threads. It happened with simple threads and it happens even more with scoped threads and thread pools. It's usually the case in real life, too. You might have a bunch of data to process, and you can probably separate that processing into chunks, iterate over them, and hand them over to various threads to do the work for you.

The main issue with that approach is that if you need to use multiple stages to process a given piece of data, you might end up with lots of boilerplate code that can make it difficult to maintain. Not only that, you might find yourself not using parallel processing sometimes due to the hassle of having to write all that code.

Luckily, Rayon has multiple data parallelism primitives around iterators that you can use to parallelize any iterative computation. You can almost forget about the `Iterator` trait and use Rayon's `ParallelIterator` alternative, which is as easy to use as the standard library trait!

Rayon uses a parallel iteration technique called **work stealing**. For each iteration of the parallel iterator, the new value or values get added to a queue of pending work. Then, when a thread finishes its work, it checks whether there is any pending work to do and if there is, it starts processing it. This, in most languages, is a clear source of data races, but thanks to Rust, this is no longer an issue, and your algorithms can run extremely fast and in parallel.

Let's look at how to use it for an example similar to those we have seen in this chapter. First, add `rayon` to your `Cargo.toml` file and then let's start with the code:

```
extern crate rayon;

use rayon::prelude::*;

fn main() {
    let result = (0..1_000_000_u64)
        .into_par_iter()
        .map(|e| e * 2)
        .sum::<u64>();

    println!("Result: {}", result);
}
```

As you can see, this works just as you would write it in a sequential iterator, yet, it's running in parallel. Of course, running this example sequentially will be faster than running it in parallel thanks to compiler optimizations, but when you need to process data from files, for example, or perform very complex mathematical computations, parallelizing the input can give great performance gains.

Rayon implements these parallel iteration traits to all standard library iterators and ranges. Not only that, it can also work with standard library collections, such as `HashMap` and `Vec`. In most cases, if you are using the `iter()` or `into_iter()` methods from the standard library in your code, you can simply use `par_iter()` or `into_par_iter()` in those calls and your code should now be parallel and work perfectly.

But, beware, sometimes parallelizing something doesn't automatically improve its performance. Take into account that if you need to update some shared information between the threads, they will need to synchronize somehow, and you will lose performance. Therefore, multithreading is only great if workloads are completely independent and you can execute one without any dependency on the rest.

Summary

In this chapter, we saw how our sequential algorithms can easily gain performance by running in parallel. This parallelism can be obtained in multiple ways, and in this chapter, we learned about multithreading. We saw how multithreading is really safe in Rust, and how we can take advantage of the crate ecosystem to improve our performance even more.

We learned about some performance enhancements we can develop for our multithreaded code, and how to use all the available tools to our advantage. You can now develop a high-performance concurrent application in Rust using multiple threads.

In the next chapter, we will look at asynchronous programming. The primitives we will look at enable us to write concurrent programs that won't lock our threads if we are waiting for some computation, without even requiring us to spawn new threads!

11
Asynchronous Programming

Until now, the only way we have seen to achieve concurrency in Rust is to create multiple threads, one way or another, to share the work. Nevertheless, those threads sometimes need to stop and look for something, such as a file or a network response. In those cases, the whole thread will be blocked and it will need to wait for the response.

This means that if we want to achieve a low latency for things such as an HTTP server, one way to do it is by spawning one thread per request, so that each request can be served as quickly as possible even if others block.

As we have seen, spawning hundreds of threads is not scalable, since each thread will have its own memory and will consume resources even if it's blocked. In this chapter, you will learn a new way of doing things by using asynchronous programming.

In this chapter, you will learn about the following:

- Asynchronous primitives with `mio`
- Using `futures`
- The new `async/await` syntax and generators
- Asynchronous I/O with `tokio` and `websockets`

Introduction to asynchronous programming

If you want to achieve high performance in computing, you will need to run tasks concurrently. Whether you are running complex computations that take days, such as machine learning training, or you are running a web server that needs to respond to thousands of requests per second, you will need to do more than one thing at the same time.

Thankfully, as we have already seen, our processors and operating systems are prepared for concurrency, and in fact, multithreading is a great way to achieve it. The main issue is that as we saw in the previous chapter, we should not be using more threads than logical CPUs in our computer.

We can, of course, but some threads will be waiting for others to execute, and the kernel will be orchestrating how much time each thread gets in the CPU. This will consume even more resources and make the overall process slower. It can sometimes be useful, though, to have more threads than the number of cores. Maybe some of them only wake up once every few seconds to do small tasks, or we know that most of them will block due to some I/O operation.

When a thread blocks, the execution stops. No further instruction will run in the CPU until it gets unblocked. This can happen when we read a file, for example. Until the reading ends, no further instruction will be executed. This of course, depends on how we read the file.

But in the latter case, instead of creating more threads we can do better—asynchronous programming. When programming asynchronously, we let the code continue being executed while we are still waiting for a certain result. That will avoid blocking the thread and let you use less threads for the same task, while still being concurrent. You can also use asynchronous programming for tasks not related to I/O, but if they are CPU bound (their bottleneck is the CPU), you won't get speed improvements, since the CPU will always be running at its best. To learn how asynchronous I/O works in Rust, let's first dive into how the CPU handles I/O.

Understanding I/O in the CPU

The `std::io` module in Rust handles all input/output operations. These operations can vary from keyboard/mouse input to reading a file, or from using TCP/IP sockets to command-line utilities (`stdio/stderr`). But how does it work internally?

Instead of understanding how the Rust standard library does it, we will dig some levels deeper to understand how it works at CPU level. We will later go back to see how the kernel provides this functionality to Rust. This will be based mostly in the x86_64 platform and Linux kernel, but other platforms handle these things similarly.

There are two main types of I/O architecture: channel-based I/O and memory-mapped I/O. Channel-based I/O is really niche and is not used in modern PCs or most servers. In CPU architectures such as x86/x86_64 (most modern day Intel and AMD CPUs), memory-mapped I/O is used. But what does it mean?

As you should know by now, the CPU gets all the required information for its work from the RAM memory. As we saw in previous chapters, this information will later be cached in the CPU cache, and it won't be used until it gets to the CPU registers, but this is not so relevant for now. So, if the CPU wants to get information about what key was pressed on the keyboard, or what TCP frames the website you are visiting is sending, it needs to either have some extra hardware channel to those input/output interfaces, or those interfaces have to change something in the RAM.

The first option is the channel-based I/O. CPUs that use channel-based I/O have dedicated channels and hardware for I/O operations. This usually increases the price of the CPUs a lot. On the other hand, in memory-mapped I/O the second option gets used—the memory gets somehow modified when an I/O operation happens.

Here, we have to pause a little bit to understand this better. Even though we may think that all our memory is in our RAM sticks, it's not exactly like that. Memory is divided into virtual and physical memory. Each program has one virtual memory address available for each addressable byte with the size of a CPU word. This means that a 32-bit CPU will have 2^{32} virtual memory addresses available for each of its programs and a 64-bit CPU will have 2^{64} addresses. This would mean having 4 GiB of RAM in the case of 32-bit computers and 16 EiB of RAM in the case of a 64-bit CPU. **EiBs** are **exbibytes**, or 1,014 **PiB** (**pebibytes**). Each PiB is 1024 **GiB** (**gibibytes**). Remember that gibibytes are the two-power version of **gigabytes** (**GB**). And all of this is true for each of the processes in the CPU.

There are some issues with this. First, if we have two processes, we would need double the amount of memory, right? But the kernel can only address that amount of memory (it's a process itself). So we need **translation tables** (**TLBs**), that tell each process where their memory is. But even though we may have 4 GiB of RAM for 32-bit CPUs, we don't have 16 EiB of RAM anywhere. Not only that, 32-bit CPUs have existed long before we were able to create PCs with 4 GiB of RAM. How can a process address more RAM than what we have installed?

The solution is simple—we call that address space the virtual memory space, and the real RAM the physical memory space. If a process requires more memory than the available physical memory, two things can happen—either our kernel can move some memory addresses out of RAM into the disk and allocate some more RAM for this process, or it will receive an out-of-memory error. The first option is called page swapping, and it's really common in Unix systems, where you sometimes even decide how much space in the disk you want to provide for that.

Moving information from the RAM to the disk will slow things down a lot, since the disk itself is really slow compared to the RAM (even modern day SSDs are much slower than RAM). Nevertheless, here we find that there is some I/O happening to swap that memory information to the disk, right? How does that happen?

Well, we said that the virtual memory space was specific for each process, and we said that the kernel was another process. This means that the kernel also has the whole memory space available for it to use. This is where memory-mapped I/O comes in. The CPU will decide to map new devices to some addresses. This means that the kernel will be able to read information about the I/O interface just by reading some concrete positions in its virtual address space.

In this regard, there are some variants as to how to read that information. Two main ways exist—port-mapped I/O and direct memory access or DMA. Port-mapped I/O is used, of course, for TCP/IP, serial, and other kinds of peripheral communication. It will have some certain addresses allocated to it. These addresses will be a buffer, which means that as the input comes, it will write one by one the next memory address. Once it gets to the end, it will start from the beginning again, so the kernel has to be fast enough to read the information before it gets rewritten. It can also block the port, stopping the communication.

In the case of DMA, the memory space of the device will be directly mapped in the virtual memory. This enables accessing that memory as if it were part of the virtual address space of the current PC. Which approach is used depends on the task and the device we want to communicate with. You may now be wondering how the kernel handles all this for your programs.

Getting the kernel to control the I/O

When a new TCP/IP connection gets established, or when a new key is pressed on the keyboard, the kernel must know about it so that it can act accordingly. There are two ways of doing this—the kernel could be looking to those ports or memory addresses once and again to look for changes, which would make the CPU work for nothing most of the time, or the kernel could be notified by a CPU interrupt.

As you can imagine, most kernels decide to go for the second option. They are idle, letting other processes use the CPU until there's a change in some I/O port or address. This makes the CPU interrupt at a hardware level, and gives control to the kernel. The kernel will check what happened and decide accordingly. If there is some process waiting for that interrupt, it will wake that process and let it know that there is some new information for it.

It may be, though, that the process waiting for the information is already awake. This happens in asynchronous programming. The process will keep on performing some computations while it's still waiting for the I/O transaction. In this case, the process will have registered some callback function in the kernel, so that the kernel knows what to call once the I/O operation is ready.

This means that while the I/O operation was being performed, the process was doing useful things, instead of being blocked and waiting for the kernel to return the result of the I/O operation. This enables you to use the CPU almost all the time, without pausing the execution, making your code perform better.

Asynchronous programming from the programmer's perspective

Until now, we have seen how I/O works from a hardware and software perspective. We mentioned that it is possible to have our process working while waiting for the I/O, but how do we do it?

The kernel has some things to help us with this. In the case of Linux, it has the `epoll()` system call, which lets the kernel know that our code wants to receive some information from an I/O interface, but that it doesn't need to lock itself until the information is available. The kernel will know what callback to run when the information is ready, and meanwhile, our program can do a lot of computations.

This is very useful, for example, if we are processing some data and we know that in the future we will need some information from a file. We can ask the kernel to get the information from the file while we continue the computation, and as soon as we need the information from the file, we won't need to wait for the file reading operation—the information will just be there. This reduces the disk read latency a lot, since it will be almost as fast as reading from the RAM instead of the disk.

We can use this approach for TCP/IP connections, serial connections, and, in general, anything that requires I/O access. This `epoll()` system call comes directly from the Linux C API, but in Rust we have great wrappers that make all of this much easier without overhead. Let's check them out.

Understanding futures

If we use the `std::io::Read` and `std::io::Write` traits in our code, we will be able to easily read and write data from I/O interfaces, but every time we do it, the thread doing the call will block until the data is received. Luckily, the great crate ecosystem Rust has brings us great opportunities to improve this situation.

In many programming languages, you can find the concept of *not yet available data*. In JavaScript, for example, they are called promises, and in Rust, we call them futures. A future represents any data that will be available at some point in the future but may not be available yet. You can check whether a future has a value at any time, and get it if it does. If not, you can either perform some computation in the meantime or block the current thread until the value gets there.

Rust futures not only give us this feature, but they even give us tons of helpful APIs that we can use to improve the readability and reduce the amount of code written. The `futures` crate does all this with *zero-cost* abstractions. This means that it will not require extra allocations and the code will be as close as possible to the best assembly code you could write to make all this possible.

Futures not only work for I/O; they can be used with any kind of computation or data. We will be using the 0.2.x version of the futures crate in these examples. At the time of writing, that version is still in the alpha development phase, but it's expected to be released really soon. Let's see an example of how futures work. We will first need to add the futures crate as a dependency in the `Cargo.toml` file, and then we can start writing some code in the `main.rs` file of our project:

```
extern crate futures;

use futures::prelude::*;
use futures::future::{self, FutureResult};
use futures::executor::block_on;

fn main() {
    let final_result = some_complex_computation().map(|res| (res - 10) /
7);

    println!("Doing some other things while our result gets generated");

    match block_on(final_result) {
        Ok(res) => println!("The result is {}", res),
        Err(e) => println!("Error: {}", e),
    }
}

fn some_complex_computation() -> FutureResult<u32, String> {
    use std::thread;
    use std::time::Duration;

    thread::sleep(Duration::from_secs(5));

    future::ok(150)
}
```

In this example, we have a simulated complex computation that takes around 5 seconds. This computation returns a `Future`, and we can therefore use useful methods to modify the result once it gets generated. These methods come from the `FutureExt` trait.

Then, the `block_on()` function will wait until the given future is no longer pending. You may think that this is exactly the same as when we were working with threads, but the interesting thing is that we are only using one thread here. The future will be computed once the main thread has some spare time, or when we call the `block_on()` function.

This, of course, does not make much sense for computationally intense applications, since we will in any case have to do the computation in the main thread, but it makes a lot of sense for I/O access. We can think of a `Future` as the asynchronous version of a `Result`.

As you can see in the `FutureExt` trait documentation at `https://docs.rs/futures/0.2.0-alpha/futures/trait.FutureExt.html`, we have tons of combinators to use. In this case, we used the `map()` method, but we can also use other methods such as `and_then()`, `map_err()`, `or_else()`, or even joins between futures. All these methods will run asynchronously one after the other. Once you call the `block_on()` function, you will get the `Result` of the final future.

Future combinators

And now that we mentioned joins, it is actually possible to have two co-dependent futures. Maybe we have information from two files, we generate one future reading from each file, and then we want to combine the information from them. We don't need to block the thread for that; we can use the `join()` method, and the logic behind it will make sure that once the closure we write gets called, both futures will have received the final value.

This is really useful when creating concurrency dependency graphs. If you have many small computations that you want to parallelise, you can create a closure or a function for each of the parts, and then use `join()` and other methods, such as `and_then()`, to decide which computations need to run some of them in parallel while still receiving all the required data for each step. The `join()` method comes in five variants depending on how many futures you need for your next computation.

But simple futures is not the only thing this crate gives us. We can also use the `Stream` trait, which works similarly to the `Iterator` trait, but asynchronously. This is extremely useful for inputs that come one by one and are not just a one-time value. This happens with TCP, serial, or any connection that uses byte streams, for example.

With this trait, and especially with the `StreamExt` trait, we have almost the same API as with iterators, and we can create a complete iterator that can, for example, retrieve HTTP data from a TCP connection byte by byte and asynchronously. This has many applications in web servers, and we have already seen crates in the community migrating to asynchronous APIs.

The crate also offers an asynchronous version of the Write trait. With the Sink and the SinkExt traits you can send data to any output object. This could be a file, a connection, or even some kind of streaming computation. Sink and Stream work great together, since the send_all() method in the SinkExt trait lets you send a whole Stream to the Sink. You could, for example, asynchronously read a file byte by byte, do some computation for each of them or in chunks, and then write the result in another file just by using these combinators.

Let's see an example. We will be using the futures-timer crate, and unfortunately it's not yet available for futures 0.2.0. So, let's update our Cargo.toml file with the following [dependencies] section:

```
[dependencies]
futures = "0.1"
futures-timer = "0.1"
```

Then, let's write the following code in our main.rs file:

```
extern crate futures;
extern crate futures_timer;

use std::time::Duration;

use futures::prelude::*;
use futures_timer::Interval;
use futures::future::ok;

fn main() {
    Interval::new(Duration::from_secs(1))
        .take(5)
        .for_each(|_| {
            println!("New interval");
            ok(())
        })
        .wait()
        .unwrap();
}
```

If you execute cargo run for this example, it will generate five new lines with the New interval text, one every second. The Interval just returns a () every time the configured interval times out. We then only take the first five and run the closure inside the for_each loop. As you can see, the Stream and StreamExt traits works almost the same way as the Iterator trait.

Asynchronous I/O in Rust

When it comes to I/O operations, there is a go-to crate. It's called `tokio`, and it handles asynchronous input and output operations seamlessly. This crate is based in MIO. MIO, from Metal IO, is a base crate that provides a really low-level interface to asynchronous programming. It generates an event queue, and you can use a loop to gather all the events one by one, asynchronously.

As we saw earlier, these events can be anything from *a TCP message was received* to *the file you requested is partially ready*. There are tutorials to create small TCP servers in MIO, for example, but the idea of MIO is not using the crate directly, but using a facade. The most known and useful facade is the `tokio` crate. This crate, by itself, only gives you some small primitives, but it opens the doors to many asynchronous interfaces. You have, for example, `tokio-serial`, `tokio-jsonrpc`, `tokio-http2`, `tokio-imap`, and many, many more.

Not only that, you have also utilities such as `tokio-retry` that will automatically retry the I/O operation if an error happens. Tokio is really easy to use, it has an extremely low footprint, and it enables you to create incredibly fast services with its asynchronous operations. As you probably have already noticed, it is mostly centred around communication. This is due to all the helpers and capabilities it provides for these cases. The core crate also has file reading capabilities, so you should be covered for any I/O-bound operation, as we will see.

We will see first how to develop a small TCP echo server using Tokio. You can find similar tutorials on the Tokio website (`https://tokio.rs/`), and it is worthwhile to follow all of them. Let's therefore start by adding `tokio` as a dependency to the `Cargo.toml` file. Then, we will use the `TcpListener` from the `tokio` crate to create a small server. This structure binds a TCP socket listener to a given address, and it will asynchronously execute a given function for each of the incoming connections. In that function, we will asynchronously read any potential data that we could find in the socket and return it, doing an `echo`. Let's see what it looks like:

```
extern crate tokio;

use tokio::prelude::*;
use tokio::net::TcpListener;
use tokio::io;

fn main() {
    let address = "127.0.0.1:8000".parse().unwrap();
    let listener = TcpListener::bind(&address).unwrap();

    let server = listener
```

```
    .incoming()
    .map_err(|e| eprintln!("Error accepting connection: {:?}", e))
    .for_each(|socket| {
        let (reader, writer) = socket.split();
        let copied = io::copy(reader, writer);

        let handler = copied
            .map(|(count, _reader, _writer)| println!("{} bytes
              received", count))
            .map_err(|e| eprintln!("Error: {:?}", e));

        tokio::spawn(handler)
    });

tokio::run(server);
}
```

Let's analyze the code. The listener creates an asynchronous stream of incoming connections with the incoming() method. For each of them, we check whether it was an error and print a message accordingly, and then, for the correct ones, we get the socket and get a writer and a reader by using the split() method. Then, Tokio gives us a Copy future that gets created with the tokio::io::copy() function. This future represents data that gets copied from a reader to a writer asynchronously.

We could have written that future ourselves by using the AsyncRead and AsyncWrite traits, but it's great to see that Tokio already has that example future. Since the behavior we want is to return back whatever the connection was sending, this will work perfectly. We then add some extra code that will be executed after the reader returns **End of File** or **EOF** (when the connection gets closed). It will just print the number of bytes that were copied, and it will handle any potential errors that may appear.

Then, in order for the future to perform its task, something needs to execute it. This is where Tokio executors come in—we call tokio::spawn(), which will execute the future in the default executor. What we just created is a stream of things to do when a connection comes, but we now need to actually run the code. For that, Tokio has the tokio::run() function, which starts the whole Tokio runtime process and starts accepting connections.

The main future we created, the stream of incoming connections, will be executed at that point and will block the main thread. Since the server is always waiting for new connections, it will just block indefinitely. Still, this does not mean that the execution of the futures is synchronous. The thread will go idle without consuming CPU, and when a connection comes, the thread will be awakened and the future executed. In the future itself, while sending the received data back, it will not block the execution if there is no more data. This enables the running of many connections in only one thread. In a production environment, you will probably want to have similar behavior in multiple threads, so that each thread can handle multiple connections.

It's now time to test it. You can start the server by running `cargo run` and you can connect to it with a TCP tool such as Telnet. In the case of Telnet, it buffers the sent data line by line, so you will need to send a whole line to receive the echo back. There is another area where Tokio is especially useful—parsing frames. If you want to create your own communication protocol, for example, you may want to get chunks of those TCP bytes as frames, and then convert them to your type of data.

Creating Tokio codecs

In Tokio, we have the concept of a codec. A codec is a type that divides a slice of bytes into frames. Each frame will contain certain information parsed from the stream of bytes. In our case, we will read the input of the TCP connection and divide it into chunks each time we find the `a` letter. A production-ready codec will probably be more complex, but this example will give us a good enough base to implement our own codecs. We will need to implement two traits from the `tokio-io` crate, so we will need to add it to the `[dependencies]` section of our `Cargo.toml` file and import it with `extern crate tokio_io;`. We will need to do the same with the `bytes` crate. Now, let's start writing the code:

```
extern crate bytes;
extern crate tokio;
extern crate tokio_io;

use std::io;

use tokio_io::codec::{Decoder, Encoder};
use bytes::BytesMut;

#[derive(Debug, Default)]
struct ADividerCodec {
    next_index: usize,
}
```

```
impl Decoder for ADividerCodec {
    type Item = String;
    type Error = io::Error;

    fn decode(&mut self, buf: &mut BytesMut)
    -> Result<Option<Self::Item>, Self::Error> {
        if let Some(new_offset) =
            buf[self.next_index..].iter().position(|b| *b == b'a') {
            let new_index = new_offset + self.next_index;
            let res = buf.split_to(new_index + 1);
            let res = &res[..res.len() - 1];
            let res: Vec<_> = res.into_iter()
                .cloned()
                .filter(|b| *b != b'\r' && *b != b'\n')
                .collect();
            let res = String::from_utf8(res).map_err(|_| {
                io::Error::new(
                    io::ErrorKind::InvalidData,
                    "Unable to decode input as UTF8"
                )
            })?;
            self.next_index = 0;
            Ok(Some(res))
        } else {
            self.next_index = buf.len();
            Ok(None)
        }
    }

    fn decode_eof(&mut self, buf: &mut BytesMut)
    -> Result<Option<String>, io::Error> {
        Ok(match self.decode(buf)? {
            Some(frame) => Some(frame),
            None => {
                // No terminating 'a' - return remaining data, if any
                if buf.is_empty() {
                    None
                } else {
                    let res = buf.take();
                    let res: Vec<_> = res.into_iter()
                        .filter(|b| *b != b'\r' && *b != b'\n')
                        .collect();
                    let res = String::from_utf8(res).map_err(|_| {
                        io::Error::new(
                            io::ErrorKind::InvalidData,
                            "Unable to decode input as UTF8"
                        )
                    })?;
```

```
                        self.next_index = 0;
                        Some(res)
                    }
                }
            })
        }
    }
```

This is a lot of code; let's analyse it carefully. We created a structure, named `ADividerCodec`, and we implemented the `Decode` trait for it. This code has two methods. The first and most important one is the `decode()` method. It receives a buffer containing data coming from the connection and it needs to return either some data or none. In this case, it will try to find the position of the `a` letter, in lower case. If it finds it, it will return all the bytes that were read until then. It also removes new lines, just to make the printing more clear.

It creates a string with those bytes, so it will fail if we send non-UTF-8 bytes. Once we take bytes from the front of the buffer, the next index should point to the first element in the buffer. If there was no `a` in the buffer, it will just update the index to the last element that was read, and just return `None`, since there isn't a full frame ready. The `decode_eof()` method will do a similar thing when the connection gets closed. We use strings as the output of the codec, but you can use any structure or enumeration to represent your data or commands, for example.

We also need to implement the `Encode` trait so that we can use the `framed()` method from Tokio. This just represents how the data would be encoded in a new byte array if we wanted to use bytes again. We will just get the bytes of the strings and append an `a` to it. We will lose new line information, though. Let's see what it looks like:

```
impl Encoder for ADividerCodec {
    type Item = String;
    type Error = io::Error;

    fn encode(&mut self, chunk: Self::Item, buf: &mut BytesMut)
    -> Result<(), io::Error> {
        use bytes::BufMut;

        buf.reserve(chunk.len() + 1);
        buf.put(chunk);
        buf.put_u8(b'a');
        Ok(())
    }
}
```

To see how it works, let's implement a simple `main()` function and use Telnet to send some text with a letters in it:

```
use tokio::prelude::*;
use tokio::net::TcpListener;

fn main() {
    let address = "127.0.0.1:8000".parse().unwrap();
    let listener = TcpListener::bind(&address).unwrap();

    let server = listener
        .incoming()
        .map_err(|e| eprintln!("Error accepting connection: {:?}", e))
        .for_each(|socket| {
            tokio::spawn(
                socket
                    .framed(ADividerCodec::default())
                    .for_each(|chunk| {
                        println!("{}", chunk);
                        Ok(())
                    })
                    .map_err(|e| eprintln!("Error: {:?}", e)),
            )
        });

    println!("Running Tokio server...");
    tokio::run(server);
}
```

We could send this text, for example:

```
[razican@laptop test_crate]$ telnet 127.0.0.1 8000
Trying 127.0.0.1...
Connected to 127.0.0.1.
Escape character is '^]'.
This is a test, We are just checking that everything gets split "a" by "a".
Testing also a new line, to see what happens.
```

The output in the server will be similar to this:

```
Running Tokio server...
This is
 test, We
re just checking th
t everything gets split "
" by "
".Testing
lso
 new line, to see wh
t h
```

Note that I didn't close the connection, so the last part of the last sentence was still in the buffer.

WebSockets in Rust

If you work in web development, you know that WebSockets are one of the most useful protocols to speed up communication with the client. Using them allows your server to send information to the client without the latter requesting it, therefore avoiding one extra request. Rust has a great crate that allows the implementation of WebSockets, named websocket.

We will analyze a small, asynchronous WebSocket echo server example to see how it works. We will need to add websocket, futures, and tokio-core to the [dependencies] section of our Cargo.toml file. The following example has been retrieved and adapted from the asynchronous server example in the websocket crate. It uses the Tokio reactor core, which means that it requires a core object and its handle. The WebSocket requires this behavior since it's not a simple I/O operation, which means that it requires some wrappers, such as connection upgrades to WebSockets. Let's see how it works:

```rust
extern crate futures;
extern crate tokio_core;
extern crate websocket;

use websocket::message::OwnedMessage;
use websocket::server::InvalidConnection;
use websocket::async::Server;

use tokio_core::reactor::Core;
use futures::{Future, Sink, Stream};
```

```
fn main() {
    let mut core = Core::new().unwrap();
    let handle = core.handle();
    let server = Server::bind("127.0.0.1:2794", &handle).unwrap();

    let task = server
        .incoming()
        .map_err(|InvalidConnection { error, .. }| error)
        .for_each(|(upgrade, addr)| {
            println!("Got a connection from: {}", addr);

            if !upgrade.protocols().iter().any(|s| s == "rust-websocket") {
                handle.spawn(
                    upgrade
                        .reject()
                        .map_err(|e| println!("Error: '{:?}'", e))
                        .map(|_| {}),
                );
                return Ok(());
            }

            let fut = upgrade
                .use_protocol("rust-websocket")
                .accept()
                .and_then(|(client, _)| {
                    let (sink, stream) = client.split();

                    stream
                        .take_while(|m| Ok(!m.is_close()))
                        .filter_map(|m| match m {
                            OwnedMessage::Ping(p) => {
                                Some(OwnedMessage::Pong(p))
                            }
                            OwnedMessage::Pong(_) => None,
                            _ => Some(m),
                        })
                        .forward(sink)
                        .and_then(|(_, sink)| {
                            sink.send(OwnedMessage::Close(None))
                        })
                });

            handle.spawn(
                fut.map_err(|e| {
                    println!("Error: {:?}", e)
                }).map(|_| {}));
            Ok(())
        });
```

```
        core.run(task).unwrap();
    }
```

Most of the code, as you can see, is really similar to the code used in the previous examples. The first change that we see is that for each connection, before actually accepting the connection, it will check if the socket can be upgraded to the `rust-websocket` protocol. Then, it will upgrade the connection protocol to that protocol and accept the connection. For each connection, it will receive a handle to the client and some headers. All this is done asynchronously, of course.

We discard the headers, and we divide the client into a sink and a stream. A sink is the asynchronous equivalent to a synchronous writer, in `futures` terminology. It starts taking bytes from the stream until it closes, and, for each of them, it replies with the same message. It will then call the `forward()` method, which consumes all the messages in the stream, and then it sends a connection closed message. The future we just created is then spawned using the handle we took from the core. This means that, for each connection, this whole future will be run. The Tokio core then runs the whole server task.

If you get the example client implementation from the crate's Git repository (`https://github.com/cyderize/rust-websocket/blob/master/examples/async-client.rs`), you will be able to see how the server replies to whatever the client sends. Once you understand this code, you will be able to create any WebSocket server you need.

Understanding the new Generators

A new feature is coming to Rust in 2018—asynchronous generators. Generators are functions that can yield elements before returning from the function and resume executing later. This is great for the loops that we have seen in this chapter. With generators, we could directly replace many of the callbacks with the new `async`/`await` syntax.

This is still an unstable feature that can only be used in nightly, so it may be that the code you write becomes obsolete before stabilization. Let's see a simple example of a generator:

```
#![feature(generators, generator_trait)]

use std::ops::{Generator, GeneratorState};

fn main() {
    let mut generator = || {
        for i in 0..10 {
            yield i;
        }
```

```
            return "Finished!";
    };

    loop {
        match generator.resume() {
            GeneratorState::Yielded(num) => println!("Yielded {}", num),
            GeneratorState::Complete(text) => {
                println!("{}", text);
                break;
            }
        }
    }
}
```

You will need to execute `rustup override add nightly` to run the example. If you run it, you will see this output:

```
Yielded 0
Yielded 1
Yielded 2
Yielded 3
Yielded 4
Yielded 5
Yielded 6
Yielded 7
Yielded 8
Yielded 9
Finished!
```

The interesting thing here is that the generator function can perform any computation, and you can resume the computation once a partial result gets yielded, without needing buffers. You can test this by doing the following—instead of yielding something from the generator, just use it to print in the console. Let's see an example:

```
#![feature(generators, generator_trait)]

use std::ops::Generator;

fn main() {
    let mut generator = || {
        println!("Before yield");
        yield;
        println!("After yield");
    };

    println!("Starting generator...");
```

```
    generator.resume();
    println!("Generator started");
    generator.resume();
    println!("Generator finished");
}
```

If you run this example, you will see the following output:

```
Starting generator...
Before yield
Generator started
After yield
Generator finished
```

As you can see, the function pauses its execution when it gets to a `yield` statement. If there is any data in that yield statement, the caller will be able to retrieve it. Once the generator is resumed, the rest of the function gets executed, until a `yield` or a `return` statement.

This, of course, is of great advantage for the `futures` we saw earlier. This is why the `futures-await` crate was created. This crate uses generators to make the implementation of asynchronous futures much easier. Let's rewrite the TCP echo server we created before using this crate. We will need to add the `0.2.0` version of the `futures-await` to the `[dependencies]` section of our `Cargo.toml` file and then start using a bunch of nightly features. Let's see some example code:

```rust
#![feature(proc_macro, conservative_impl_trait, generators)]

extern crate futures_await as futures;

use futures::prelude::*;
use futures::executor::block_on;

#[async]
fn retrieve_data_1() -> Result<i32, i32> {
    Ok(1)
}

#[async]
fn retrieve_data_2() -> Result<i32, i32> {
    Ok(2)
}

#[async_move]
fn add_data() -> Result<i32, i32> {
    Ok(await!(retrieve_data_1())? + await!(retrieve_data_2())?)
```

```
    }

fn main() {
    println!("Result: {:?}", block_on(add_data()));
}
```

This example will have two asynchronous functions that could, for example, be retrieving information from the network. They get called by the `add_data()` function, which will wait for them to return before adding them up and returning a result. If you run it, you will see that the result is `Ok(3)`. The line importing the `futures_await` crate as `futures` makes sense because the `futures-await` crate is just a small wrapper around the futures crate, and all the usual structures, functions, and traits are available.

The whole generators and `async`/`await` syntax is still being heavily worked on, but the Rust 2018 roadmap says it should be stabilized before the end of the year.

Summary

In this last chapter of the book, you learned to use asynchronous programming to avoid creating too many threads. You can now use just the right amount of threads and still run the workload in parallel and efficiently in networking applications. To be able to do that, you first learned about the futures crate, which give us the minimum primitives to use when working with asynchronous programming in Rust. You then learned how the MIO-based Tokio works, and created your first servers.

Before understanding external crates, you learned about WebSockets and grasped the Tokio core reactor syntax. Finally, you learned about the new generators syntax and how the `futures` crate is being adapted to make use of this new syntax. Make sure to stay up to date about the news on when this great compiler feature will be stabilized.

Now that the book came to an end, we can see that high performance can be achieved in Rust in multiple and complimentary ways. We can first start by improving our sequential code as we saw in the first chapters. These improvements come from various techniques, starting from a proper compiler configuration and ending in small tips and tricks with the code. As we saw, some tools will help us in this labour.

We can then use metaprogramming to improve both the maintainability of the code and the performance, by reducing the amount of work the software has to do at runtime. We saw that new ways of metaprogramming are arriving this year to Rust.

Finally, the last step to make things faster is to run tasks concurrently, as we saw in the last two chapters. Depending on the requirements of our project, we will use multithreading or/and asynchronous programming.

You should now be able to improve the performance of your Rust applications and even to start learning deeper concepts of high performance programming. It has been a pleasure to guide you through these topics in the Rust programming language, and I hope you enjoyed the read.

Other Books You May Enjoy

If you enjoyed this book, you may be interested in these other books by Packt:

Rust Cookbook
Vigneshwer Dhinakaran

ISBN: 978-1-78588-025-4

- Understand system programming language problems and see how Rust provides unique solutions
- Get to know the core concepts of Rust to develop fast and safe applications
- Explore the possibility of integrating Rust units into existing applications to make them more efficient
- Achieve better parallelism, security, and performance
- Explore ways to package your Rust application and ship it for deployment in a production environment
- Discover how to build web applications and services using Rust to provide high-performance to the end user

Network Programming with Rust
Abhishek Chanda

ISBN: 978-1-78862-489-3

- Appreciate why networking is important in implementing distributed systems
- Write a non-asynchronous echo server over TCP that talks to a client over a network
- Parse JSON and binary data using parser combinators such as nom
- Write an HTTP client that talks to the server using reqwest
- Modify an existing Rust HTTTP server and add SSL to it
- Master asynchronous programming support in Rust
- Use external packages in a Rust project

Leave a review - let other readers know what you think

Please share your thoughts on this book with others by leaving a review on the site that you bought it from. If you purchased the book from Amazon, please leave us an honest review on this book's Amazon page. This is vital so that other potential readers can see and use your unbiased opinion to make purchasing decisions, we can understand what our customers think about our products, and our authors can see your feedback on the title that they have worked with Packt to create. It will only take a few minutes of your time, but is valuable to other potential customers, our authors, and Packt. Thank you!

Index

Made in the USA
Middletown, DE
15 February 2019